Women and
Globalization
in the Arab Middle East

Women and Globalization in the Arab Middle East

Gender, Economy, and Society

edited by
Eleanor Abdella Doumato
Marsha Pripstein Posusney

LYNNE
RIENNER
PUBLISHERS

BOULDER
LONDON

Published in the United States of America in 2003 by
Lynne Rienner Publishers, Inc.
1800 30th Street, Boulder, Colorado 80301
www.rienner.com

and in the United Kingdom by
Lynne Rienner Publishers, Inc.
3 Henrietta Street, Covent Garden, London WC2E 8LU

Library of Congress Cataloging-in-Publication Data
Women and globalization in the Arab Middle East : gender, economy, and society/
edited by Eleanor Abdella Doumato and Marsha Pripstein Posusney.
    p. cm.
  Includes bibliographical references and index.
  ISBN 1-58826-110-7 (alk. paper)—ISBN 1-58826-134-4 (pb. : alk. paper)
  1. Women in development—Middle East.   2. Women in development—Arab
countries.   3. Women—Middle East—Economic conditions.   4. Women—Arab
countries—Economic conditions.   5. Women—Middle East—Social conditions.
6. Women—Arab countries—Social conditions.   7. Globalization—Economic aspects.
8. Globalization—Social aspects.   I. Doumato, Eleanor Abdella.   II. Posusney,
Marsha Pripstein.

  HQ1240.5.M628   W67   2002
  305.42'0956—dc21

                                                        2002073941

British Cataloguing in Publication Data
A Cataloguing in Publication record for this book
is available from the British Library.

Printed and bound in the United States of America

The paper used in this publication meets the requirements
of the American National Standard for Permanence of
Paper for Printed Library Materials Z39.48-1984.

  5   4   3   2   1

Contents

**Part 1   Women in Reforming Middle Eastern Economies:
            Employment, Production, and Reproduction**

Part 2   Case Studies

Tables and Figures

Tables

Figures

Acknowledgments

This book has its roots in a conference, "Women and Structural Adjustment in the Middle East: Gender, Jobs, and Activism," which was held at Brown University in spring 1997. In the years since that event, our understanding of these issues has developed, while the social and economic processes we are focusing on in the region continue to unfold. The manuscript was close to completion just before the tragic events of September 11, 2001; in the aftermath, we have added a new chapter on Saudi Arabia and an epilogue.

We are grateful to the Watson Institute for International Studies (WIIS) at Brown University, under the directorship of Thomas J. Biersteker, for its sponsorship of the original conference and for its support of the development of this manuscript. Fred Fullerton of WIIS provided invaluable assistance in editing and manuscript preparation. We would also like to thank Cleo Lindgren at Bryant College for providing clerical support. Bridget Julian and Karen Williams at Lynne Rienner Publishers have been superb editors and a pleasure to work with.

Marsha Pripstein Posusney
Eleanor Abdella Doumato

Introduction:
The Mixed Blessing of Globalization

In a science classroom at the women's campus of King Sa'ud University in Riyadh, students listen attentively to their professor's lecture, except that the professor is not present in the same room. Instead, he is speaking to them and even answering their questions through closed-circuit television. Not too long ago, women could only study subjects taught by women instructors in classrooms located on the all-women campus, and this was to comply with the kingdom's policy of sex segregation in schools and all public places. Technology has changed all that. An educational system that once completely excluded girls has been infused with petrodollars and transformed in little more than a generation into an extensive network of public schools, colleges, and universities with the best technology and facilities money can buy. For women, the results are particularly dramatic. New communications technologies not only allow women to study subjects previously unavailable to them, but are also changing society, making it possible for women to pursue advanced degrees in medicine, law, chemistry, the humanities, and the social sciences.

At the same time, however, for the vast majority of college-educated women, Saudi Arabia remains a land of unemployment, and the reason lies largely in the very technologies and development programs that brought women into the education system in the first place. Since the mid-1970s, women have been graduating from humanities faculties in greater numbers than men, with higher honors and in fewer years, and consequently many are prepared both psychologically and intellectually to enter the workforce. These women, however, find themselves victims of their own success. The Saudi

1

economy cannot begin to absorb such large numbers of graduates as workers, whether men or women. Moreover, society at large continues to place a high value on sex segregation, which limits women's employment options to healthcare, education, and other areas of work in which men and women—at least theoretically—can be separated from each other.

The global oil market plays a role in underwriting sex segregation, albeit indirectly. By subsidizing duplicate educational facilities and hi-tech classrooms, along with duplicate shopping malls, sex-separate offices and women's sections of ministries, drivers for the family car, and servants to act as intermediaries for women, oil money validates Saudi Arabia's parochial interpretation of Islamic values of modesty, pronouncing women's segregation workable in a modernizing economy when in fact it is not. At the same time, the penetration of Western culture resulting from Saudis traveling abroad, the influx of foreigners into the kingdom, the introduction of Western education models, satellite television, and the Internet, fuels a defensive reinforcing of religious conservatism pegged to the segregation and maternal role of women, which appeals to men and women alike. One result of this conservatism, especially on the part of those who feel threatened by change, is an appeal to the state to enforce rules of sex segregation, and the state is ready to oblige by placing logistical obstacles in the path to employment, such as banning women's driving or riding alone in a car with a hired driver.

Everywhere in the Middle East, as in Saudi Arabia, the global spread of free-market capitalism has been accompanied by sophisticated communications technology, advances in education, lifestyle changes, and the hegemonic cultural, political, and economic penetration of the West. The specific effects of globalization differ from place to place as local economic, political, and social factors influence the speed by which countries are linked to the global marketplace and the nature of that linkage. But as the Saudi example illustrates, the same process of globalization that facilitates development can also lead to ambiguous, and sometimes contradictory, outcomes, and these outcomes may be different for women as opposed to men. As women's lives are affected, their needs and responses in turn become an important variable influencing the pace and form globalization takes within the region's different countries. In the Saudi case, Western cultural penetration brings about new opportunities but also a conservative reaction, which produces feminist responses, which redefine tradition while also reinforcing it. Elsewhere the dynamic may be different, but it is equally dialectical.

This book seeks to capture this dialectic by presenting gendered analyses of the economic impact of globalization in the Arab Middle East, including its political, social, and cultural entailments.[1] To do this we have brought together methodologies from political economy, anthropology, and history. We begin with regional economic studies, followed by country-specific cases that focus on the political, social, and cultural entailments that accompany global economic integration. As the authors of these collected chapters show, economic integration and its entailments touch women's lives: in their access to employment, their capacity to engage in community activism, and the shape of gender ideologies that affect every aspect of their lives.

Globalization: Economy, Culture, and Politics

The term *globalization* is commonly used to refer to economic processes associated with the near-universal triumph of the capitalist model of development after the collapse of the Soviet Union. In this sense it refers to the increasing international integration of markets for goods, services, and capital itself, and the surrender by countries of control over growing segments of their national economies as they adopt policies to facilitate this integration.[2] We accept this definition, but at the same time we recognize that the impact of the global economy cannot be adequately assessed apart from the political and cultural phenomenon that global capitalist penetration entails. Trade in consumer goods, for example, is dominated by exports from advanced industrial countries, and the very products being transferred carry reflections of the cultures in which they were produced, while the marketing necessary to stimulate demand for these products may act as a conduit for these cultures. In an international economy dominated by advanced industrial powers, especially the United States, the expansion of global trade intrinsically entails the spread of a culture that is decidedly American, from the ubiquitous establishment of McDonald's restaurants, to genetically altered foods, the music of MTV, Hollywood films, Apache helicopters, "Baywatch," and the English language.[3] This phenomenon is reinforced by the accompanying explosion of information and entertainment technologies, their growing availability throughout the world, and until quite recently, their domination by Western corporations. While local news media have historically reflected the interests and viewpoints of their audiences, regional news networks, such as Al Jazeera, now challenge the hegemony of such global news networks as CNN with their capacity to monopolize the distribution of information in regional markets, deciding what is newsworthy and creating news as they report it.

promoting ideology as condition of economic relations not good or bad

Global economic dominance has also provided Western powers with a lever to promote a liberal Western political agenda: under U.S. and European auspices, albeit very selectively, institutions of democracy and civil society are being tied to preferential economic relations and fostered across the globe through local quasi- and nongovernmental organizations, international agencies, and private interest groups. Besides placing the debate over a common standard of human rights on the international agenda, the promotion of these institutions has resonated strongly with indigenous democracy movements.

At the same time, new communications technologies that defy government attempts at censorship are promoting political activism by bringing news and information to regions where access has previously been tightly controlled, allowing people to communicate with each other in ways never before possible and creating higher expectations for individual participation in the political process. With the arrival of satellite television and Internet access, people in the region are gaining the information necessary to think critically about their governments and a new medium through which they can express discontent. As a result, seemingly fixed ideas about culture and political legitimacy are being transformed into arenas of contestation.

Champions of globalization anticipate positive consequences worldwide, bringing growth and prosperity to all the developing countries that embrace it, along with freedom and "democratic peace" (Friedman, 1999, echoing Fukayama). However, as the explosive protest demonstrations against the World Trade Organization's 2000 meeting in Genoa revealed, in spite of impressive changes, globalization has not brought benefits to everyone. Economic liberalization brings increased vulnerability to the vagaries of the world market, and can also subject local economies to the internal politics of more powerful countries and to the demands of supranational political organizations, international companies, and monetary institutions.

At the same time, rising aspirations to participate in the political process often cannot be fulfilled, and there is invariably some degree of backlash from those who feel culturally alienated and resentful of the Western intrusion, who feel their political position threatened, or who feel themselves dislocated socially. Worldwide we find attempts to reinforce religious identities, authenticate culture, confirm established economic and political alliances, and exclude ethnic minorities, and these are everywhere byproducts of the same forces bringing about global integration (Barber, 1996).

Everywhere in the world, globalization appears as a many-faceted process having both positive and negative consequences for the lives of ordinary citizens. In the Middle East, as elsewhere, globalization has far-reaching implications not only for the economy, but also for politics and culture, and these implications may be experienced differently by women as opposed to men.

Globalization and Women in the Middle East: Gender, Jobs, and Activism

Because of its impact on a country's economy, politics, and culture, globalization is a process crucially interrelated with the evolving role of women in Middle Eastern societies, with implications for their opportunities to work and organize, and for shifts in societal attitudes toward gender. The economic aspects of globalization's effect on women must be understood in the context of the state-centered economic strategies prevalent in the region through most of the latter half of the twentieth century. As Chapter 1 illustrates, during the 1960s and 1970s most countries in the region witnessed a considerable expansion in the economic role of the state. State-led efforts to promote literacy prompted a decline in child labor and the expansion of female labor force participation. The rapidly expanding government sector, with its guarantees of job security and social protection, became the employment of choice, especially for women. But fuller integration into the global economy has required the undoing of these etatist policies in favor of market-oriented strategies of development. Structural adjustment programs have meant the elimination of food subsidies and price controls, the free-floating of currencies, the removal of barriers to foreign trade and investment, cutbacks in government employment, and privatization of state-owned enterprises.

Advocates of economic liberalization believe these reforms will bring growth and prosperity to reforming countries. Women in particular have been expected to benefit from the development of export-oriented industries, which in other regions favor female employment. In addition, the shrinking of the state has led to an expansion of informal-sector activities in the spheres of commerce, production, and services. Women have traditionally played an extensive role in informal market activities, and their participation has come to be promoted by multilateral lending agencies and development experts as an engine of growth. However, because the public sector has been the most hospitable to women in most Middle Eastern countries, as well as the most generous in terms of maternity and childcare benefits, the shrinking of government employment threatens to reduce job opportunities for women and at the same time make the combining of work with child-rearing more difficult. Moreover, if structural adjustments cause family incomes to decline and social safety nets to be weakened, the challenges of managing a household, traditionally a woman's responsibility, increase, especially for poorer and unemployed women.

These changing economic circumstances have an impact on women's organizational activity. Women's voluntary associations that meet for economic, social, religious, and educational purposes have a well-established historical presence in every country in the region. In recent years, however, in some places, locally formed nongovernmental organizations have increased in number, stepping in to support women and the family where the state no longer guarantees employment or has failed to provide social services. Examples include Islamic charitable societies that provide daycare for working mothers, and food and income subsidies for families in need, especially in Egypt, Algeria, and Palestine. In more affluent areas, such as Kuwait, Islamic organizations of different religious orientations operate services for women that are similar to those offered by the Young Women's Christian Association, including lectures on women's health issues, exercise facilities, cultural programs, and occasions for sociability. Sometimes these charitable societies also serve as conduits for religiously conservative agendas that appeal to women, because they incorporate a discourse of women's empowerment while affirming deeply held traditions and religious values.

Women's groups with a secular agenda have also proliferated as a grassroots mechanism for self-help when war and political crises have separated families from their means of livelihood and torn communities apart, particularly in Lebanon and Palestine. In addition, international development aid (funneled through institutions such as the United Nations, the World Bank, and U.S. Agency for International Development) has funded a myriad of development-oriented organizations and projects specifically for women, such as the UN Development Fund for Women (UNIFEM) and Women in Development (WID), which offer opportunities for women to establish research and development projects that in turn employ women on the local level or support women's entrepreneurship. International funding for women's organizational projects has not been an unmixed blessing, however, as these projects sometimes benefit only an educated elite (Carapico, 2000) and lead to more disparities in wealth, more unemployment, and fewer social services (Kandiyoti, 1995).

Women's organizational activities have also been encouraged as a result of international support for a common standard of human rights, especially in the post–Gulf War era, and a new international push to recognize women as individuals entitled to these rights—as opposed to having rights defined by religious or family values. The post–Gulf War era has seen a proliferation of local groups that seek to improve women's legal protections through courts, legislatures, research, and public education. These include groups funded both privately and through a variety of international agencies, such as the Jordanian Women's Union and the Center for Egyptian Women Legal Assistance, the Female Genital Mutilation (FMG) Task Force, and the Canadian-based Sisterhood is Global, which (with funds provided by U.S. government agencies) operates ongoing, rights-oriented education projects in Middle Eastern countries.

Throughout the region, however, all organizational activity, whether for men or women, is affected by a lack of democracy, and in most countries the downsizing of state social services and the rise in public consciousness about democracy and human rights has been accompanied by heightened security measures that make organized group activity difficult or impossible. In many countries organizations cannot function without a permit from the government, and then only within government-imposed budget constraints (Mughni, 2000). In a few places, such as Saudi Arabia, any unauthorized gathering is considered subversive and its participants are liable to prosecution, as occurred in 1990 when women demonstrated for the right to drive a car. In addition, an organization may acquire government approval but be subject to arbitrary closure, such as occurred in Egypt in 2000 with the closing of the Ibn Khaldun Center and the incarceration of its director and staff.

The Cultural Context: Changing Gender Ideologies

Underlying the changes in job opportunities and activist organizing are gender ideologies, socially ascribed attributes assigned to sex difference that shape public opinion and drive social policies regarding women. These ideologies, far from being fixed in nature or religion, are influenced by changing economic and social conditions and subject to manipulation for political ends. Gender ideologies have undergone dramatic shifts since the secularizing postcolonial era of the 1960s and 1970s, when development programs were aggressively adopted along with Western dress, languages, education, and models of relationships between the sexes. Not everyone was comfortable with these changes. Especially discomforting to some was the intrusion of the Western entertainment media, with its films, television programs, and advertisements that portray women as sexually defined and sexually promiscuous, leading many to view Western societies as degenerate and disrespectful of women. More important, these ubiquitous images, appearing at a time in which women were succeeding in higher education and in the workforce in ever greater numbers, also raised concerns that emulating Western women would threaten the economic, social, and legal privileges enjoyed by men. By the 1980s, with the ruralization of the cities, the model of the Iranian Islamic revolution, and the failure of governments to satisfy their people's heightened expectations for democratic liberalism and a better standard of living, significant sectors in all Middle Eastern societies became increasingly conservative, and the "Islamist" phenomenon became part of the political landscape.

One theme in Islamist agendas across the region has been the idealization of women as wives and mothers who stay at home, care for their families, and raise a new generation of good Muslim children. While in most countries Islamism operated in opposition to established governments, the Islamists' portrayal of the ideal woman as homemaker was warmly supported by those governments wishing to appease socially conservative constituencies. The controls and limitations placed on women have been especially encouraged by regimes that rely on communal or family alliances for support, as these alliances are often patriarchal and tend to represent the very groups that equate male control over women with moral and religious values.[4] From an economic perspective, the icon of "domesticated womanhood" has had a further appeal to women as well as to governments dealing with unemployment problems: for women, the model of domesticated womanhood helps to transform the sting of lost employment into dedication to the noble calling of family; for government, discouraging women in the workforce helps to open up job opportunities for men. At the same time, the continual rise in the numbers of women being educated and the rise in their level of achievement has itself fueled conservative reactions that authoritarian governments have willingly exploited.

This model is neither constant nor ubiquitous, as the political manipulation of Islam has also been harnessed to bring women into the job market. In Sudan, for example, as Chapter 8 shows, the Islamist ideal woman was transformed into militia girl and breadwinner, and in Gulf War Saudi Arabia, gender ideologies were manipulated to encourage service to the nation so that the model became—however briefly—woman as civil defense operative. Like worldwide nationalist ideologies that have been deployed to welcome women as workers in times of labor shortages, fighters in times of war, and partisans in times of revolution, Islamist ideologies that encourage activism on the part of women fade away or assume a domestic agenda when the cause is achieved or the perceived threat resolved.

More important in the evolution of gender ideologies is the development of Islamic feminism, a discursive, forward-looking movement generated by women to rationalize their activism and employment outside the home—not as a product of changing economic opportunities or emulation of Western cultural models, but as the product of a true, indigenous Islamic heritage (Badran, 2002). Aggressively employed by the newly educated elite, the discourse of Islamic feminism insists that women are entitled to the kind of religious education that was previously the prerogative of men (Cooke, 2001; Yamani, 1996). The goal is to empower women to reinterpret sacred text to their own advantage by, for example, resurrecting women from the Islamic past to serve as models for reinterpreting and expanding Islamic margins for women's behavior. In addition, Islamic feminists have turned the male Islamists' emphasis on

Islamic dress into a vehicle to legitimate their presence in public service, in employment, and in educational arenas where access had previously been denied or circumscribed. In Iran, for example, the imposition of dress codes in the wake of the revolution accompanied an increase in women's employment (Moghadem, 2000). In Kuwait, at the same time that Islamist members of the National Assembly were trying to segregate the sexes at the university, women students were adopting conservative dress as a political statement, insisting on their right to choice. In Egypt, the wave of religious conservatism, far from excluding women, heralded women's entrance for the first time into the mosques for prayer and study, while everywhere the Islamist revival sparked a commitment to charitable giving, self-help through women's activist organizations, and renewed demands for reformation of family law.

Despite these demands, family law has remained particularly resistant to feminist attempts at reform. In every country in the region except Turkey, Muslim family law remains in force, and even though attempts at reform have occurred in various places, and interpretation and application of Muslim family law differs somewhat from country to country and also among social classes, in general these laws render women less able to make independent decisions affecting their personal and economic lives. Hence women stand in a weaker position than men when it comes to divorce, which a man may initiate at will while a woman must show cause; a man may take additional wives with or without the current wife's approval, and bring a new wife into the family home; child custody laws generally give priority to the father over the mother after the child is weaned, or later in childhood, severely curtailing women's bargaining power when it comes to seeking divorce or tolerating an additional wife. In some countries a woman's father or brother can execute a marriage on behalf of a daughter or sister without her knowledge, even though this practice is contrary to Islamic law, and a woman inherits less than male heirs equally distant from the deceased, although the fact that a woman is entitled to inherit, can be a *waqf* (pious foundation) beneficiary, and is not legally obligated to contribute to the household income allows some to amass considerable wealth. Unlike a male citizen, a woman's nationality may not be automatically passed to her spouse and children should she marry someone from another country, which hinders access to state economic benefits allocated only to citizens.

At the outset of the twenty-first century, Islamism as a political movement to control public policy is increasingly being challenged. This is happening not only because leadership in these movements has been widely suppressed, but also because of the failure of Islamist governments such as those of Iran, Sudan, and Pakistan to achieve social justice, along with the violence associated with the Islamist movement in Algeria and the bizarre repression of women by Afghanistan's now-deposed Taliban, which barred girls from attending school, forbade women to work, and made wearing the tentlike burqa mandatory. Despite disenchantment with the movement's promised goals, however, even in the most liberal environments such as Tunisia and Lebanon, women still have to contend with some version of conservative gender ideology. Furthermore, in the name of Islam, some states in the region continue to enforce sex segregation in schools and in other public facilities, which results in inequalities in educational and work opportunities, and in access to community resources. In fact, a paradigm for the dilemma of Middle Eastern women today may well be the case of a female Saudi biochemist who, in the year 2000, just prior to winning a promotion to an administrative position overseeing 200 mostly male employees at the laboratory of the National Guard Hospital in Riyadh, was arrested in a restaurant by religious police and held in confinement overnight. Her misdeed: dining in a restaurant with a female colleague and her colleague's fiancé, a man to whom the biochemist was not related.

Recognition of such cultural and political constraints is a necessary—even critical—component of understanding the impact of globalization on women in the Middle East. It should not be surprising that in the Middle East there is a significant disparity between men and women in terms of their level of education, income, and labor force participation rates, since everywhere in the world the rates are higher for men. What is surprising, and what confirms the importance of factoring culture and politics into economic analyses, is that the disparity between men and women is significantly greater in the Middle East than in the rest of the developing world.

Outline of the Book

Following this chapter, the book is divided into two parts. Part 1 provides general overviews of the economics and demographics of the region, and provides specific analyses of the trends in women's labor force participation and fertility behavior. Part 2 presents case studies of six countries in the region. These studies vary in the emphasis they place on economic, social, or cultural developments, but together provide a coherent and fascinating picture of the dynamics of gender and globalization across the Middle East.

Part 1

Part 1 looks broadly at economic and demographic trends in the Middle East and North Africa (MENA). Its purpose is to provide a general framework for the specific country and case studies that follow. At the same time, these chapters enable us to provide at least perfunctory information on some of the countries that we were unable to cover in greater depth in the volume.

Authors Karen Pfeifer and Marsha Posusney begin by showing in Chapter 1 how the countries of the region can be grouped into different categories according to various economic indicators. These measures, including the role of oil in the economy, the domestic market size, average per capita income, and balance of payments situation, each carry different implications for the economic challenges faced by Middle Eastern countries as they link more extensively into the international marketplace. Pfeifer and Posusney then trace in more detail the implementation of state-centered development strategies in the region, and the economic impact of these policies. They show how countries with little or no oil resources, as well as those combining oil wealth with large populations, suffered worsening balance of payments problems in the 1980s, which prompted the implementation of reform programs. Looking at countries considered by the International Monetary Fund to have achieved developmental success (Egypt, Tunisia, Morocco, and Jordan), the authors explore the effects of these economic liberalization measures, showing how standard stabilization and structural adjustment packages have produced macroeconomic stability, but also stagnant or increasing poverty levels, widening gaps in income, and a loss of job benefits and employment security for public-sector workers.

The oil-rich countries with smaller populations have been unconstrained by foreign debt and have therefore been able to implement market-oriented reforms more slowly. Nevertheless, these countries have been quite vulnerable to external shocks. Saudi Arabia in particular saw an average per capita drop in gross domestic product of more than 50 percent from the early 1980s to the mid-1990s, a consequence of the oil price crash combined with burgeoning population growth. During the oil boom years, these countries became dependent on cheap foreign labor to perform menial tasks, while native citizens were given "soft" civil service positions. A central component of efforts to reduce government spending has therefore been campaigns, in each country, to indigenize the workforce by weaning the population from dependence on public-sector employment.

In Chapter 2, World Bank economists Zafiris Tzannatos and Iqbal Kaur examine a variety of social and economic indicators regarding women in MENA, and compare these to indicators for other developing regions of the world. Their chapter focuses on those countries of the region that are active borrowers from the Bank—Algeria, Egypt, Iran, Jordan, Lebanon, Morocco, Tunisia, and Yemen—for which the best data are available. Turning first to social indicators, the authors observe that the MENA countries are in the middle range among developing regions when it comes to female life expectancy at birth and female illiteracy. However, the MENA countries lag behind other regions in maternal mortality.

Employment statistics indicate that women's employment rates in MENA are the lowest in the world, although female labor force participation in MENA is increasing faster than in other region. The greatest increase in female employment appears to be occurring in the informal sector, with preliminary data suggesting that it is primarily less educated and younger women who have recently migrated from rural to urban areas who are being absorbed into this sector. By industry, agriculture remains the largest employer of women. By contrast, female employment in services is on the increase; in the manufacturing sector the proportion of women remains low and does not show much change over time.

Statistics also show that working women in MENA are heavily concentrated in lower-level white-collar jobs, and underrepresented in managerial and professional positions, and the MENA region compares unfavorably with other developing areas in this regard. Overall, MENA registers the highest degree of gender segregation in employment, and this segregation appears to be on the upswing in MENA, whereas it is declining in other developing regions. Tzannatos and Kaur present some preliminary evidence that religion may be a factor in this gap. Refraining from drawing remedial conclusions from their data, the authors suggest that better data overall, as well as more concrete studies of conditions in particular countries, are needed before effective policy recommendations can be developed.

In Chapter 3, Jennifer Olmsted addresses changing fertility patterns in the region, and the way structural adjustment programs (SAPs), which are closely linked to the trend toward globalization, may contribute to these changes. Challenging the usual policy approach to fertility, which focuses on family planning and other direct fertility policies, Olmsted argues for a holistic, feminist approach that addresses the impact of economic incentives and cultural constraints, as well as the effect of macroeconomic policies related to structural adjustment.

Population growth rates in the region are among the world's highest. As supporting their burgeoning populations has strained fiscal budgets, some governments have made reducing fertility rates a priority. At the same time, SAPs may have an uncertain impact on fertility rates. Numerous feminist scholars have argued that SAPs lead to increased hardship for women. SAPs often include cuts in government spending, in particular in the areas of public-sector employment, education, and social services, such as antipoverty programs. Each of these cuts in spending may have a particularly adverse impact on women, which in turn may impact fertility outcomes. For instance, cuts in education programs may reduce girls' access to education. Since education and fertility are generally negatively correlated, reductions in educational achievements may again put upward pressure on fertility.

Women's fertility decisions may also be impacted by changes in their access to labor markets. In the MENA region women prefer working in the public sector, and public-sector jobs have been cut due to structural adjustment. Since female labor force participation is generally associated with a reduction in childbearing, declining public-sector job opportunities for women could also reduce incentives to reduce fertility. On the other hand, increased economic hardship may push more women into the informal labor market. The net impact of this shift is difficult to gauge. On the one hand, women may have fewer children, as they juggle paid labor and reproductive responsibilities. On the other hand, women may increasingly view children as the only remaining social safety net during an era of structural adjustment and globalization.

Finally, Olmsted notes that the rise of Islamism in the region is in part a reaction against SAPs and globalization. Muslim fundamentalists often advocate for a return to stricter gender roles and for women's primary role as reproducers. This too could have an adverse impact on fertility in the region. Olmsted concludes by pointing out that while it is generally the case that fertility has been declining in the region (in some cases quite rapidly), some countries have had far more success than others, and continued progress toward this goal is not ensured.

Part 2

Taken together, the chapters in Part 1 demonstrate the similarities and variations across the region in economic endowments, development strategies, and their combined outcome in individual countries. The case studies in Part 2 elaborate on how these differences play themselves out in the unfolding of gender dynamics in different countries as globalization progresses.

In Chapters 4 and 5, economists Heba Nassar and Ragui Assaad, respectively, study the effects of structural adjustment on female employment in Egypt. Egypt warrants extra attention here for several reasons. First, because it is the most populous Arab country, greater numbers of women are affected by developments there than in the smaller countries of the area. Second, Egypt has historically played the role of an economic trendsetter in the region.[5] Finally, and partially at the urging of international financial institutions, there has been a burgeoning of studies of economic development issues, including women's employment, in Egypt in the last decade, making possible the presentation of both significant quantities of statistical data as well as policy debates. The latter are reflected in these two chapters.

Heba Nassar begins her analysis by showing how standard economic theories of labor-market behavior take no account of gender, resulting in an underestimation of females' contributions to economic activity. She shows how in Egypt, changing definitions of work, influenced by greater attentiveness to gender, have resulted in dramatic upward reassessments of female labor force participation. A significant degree of occupational segmentation by gender continues to exist. Because a high proportion of employed women, especially educated women, work in sectors targeted for employment cutbacks, women are especially vulnerable to the effects of economic reform and structural adjustment programs (ERSAPs). Women also tend to be concentrated in clerical positions for which supply exceeds demand, and so when laid off they have more difficult finding alternative jobs. Women are thus threatened with prolonged unemployment even as the other components of Egypt's ERSAPs are raising the cost of living, prompting more women to seek work.

Loss of employment in the public sector also may mean loss of benefits such as social insurance, guaranteed maternity leave, and easier access to childcare, while the long and inflexible hours required in the private sector means that women who are laid off from government jobs may be able to manage only part-time work, without any social protections, in the informal sector. Nassar concludes with a number of recommendations for easing the negative effects of ERSAPs on women in Egypt and elsewhere. These include extending childcare to the formal private sector, affirmative action programs to guarantee minimum employment quotas for women in both sectors, job training to encourage female entry into nontraditional areas, and increased access to credit to promote female self-employment.

Ragui Assaad notes that among developing countries, those in the MENA region stand out in terms of their low female participation in wage labor, their relatively high unemployment rates, the extent to which the employment of educated women is dependent on the public sector, and their relatively poor record of promoting labor-intensive, export-oriented industries. Consistent with comparative international experience, those MENA countries that have had more success in developing export industries, namely Tunisia and Morocco, also have higher proportions of women in manufacturing occupations than those that are less successful, namely Egypt, Algeria, Jordan, and Syria. Thus in these latter countries, greater attention to one cornerstone of structural adjustment—export promotion—can help to alleviate female unemployment, albeit with jobs that are low-wage and may be unstable.

In Egypt, the government's guaranteed employment scheme instituted in the 1960s, along with the expansion of technical secondary education, encouraged many females to seek vocational secondary school certificates for white-collar employment. But as the wait for government and public-sector appointments has steadily lengthened since the 1980s, the returns to this education have fallen. The private sector has placed little value on these degrees, resulting in low wages and high female unemployment for this category of education. In addition, for women with such skills, self-employment does not appear to be an option. Thus, in contrast to Nassar, Assaad does not see subsidized credit and technical assistance to new businesses as measures likely to make a significant dent in female unemployment. Instead, he advocates overhauling the secondary education system to teach skills more in line with the needs of private-sector employers.

Finally, Assaad suggests that the low rates of female employment in the private sector are due to a widespread perception on the part of employers that the nonwage costs of hiring female workers are large—due to high turnover, absenteeism, unwillingness to work long hours, and costly female-specific legal protections. While such perceptions may be based in part on entrenched stereotypes, they militate against employers hiring women so long as male labor is plentiful. Ways must therefore be found to shift some of the costs of women's reproductive role away from private-sector employers and women workers to society as a whole. Publicly supported childcare and maternity benefits that are provided through the social insurance system are two recommended ways to achieve this, but can only be implemented gradually because of the strain they will place on the fiscal budget.

Chapters 4 and 5 thus confirm that the process of globalization does have distinct economic consequences for female employment. In the Egyptian case, structural adjustment, at least in the short run, appears to be having a negative impact as privatization reduces the opportunities for women in the public sector, while the private sector has not yet proven capable of absorbing sufficient numbers of female job seekers. The consequences of this can only be revealed over time, even as various hoped-for remedies are introduced.

Against the backdrop of similar economic changes, the remaining case studies show how globalization's impact on women is dialectally related to women's activism and the gender ideologies that shape public opinion and drive social policies regarding women. A proliferation of women's activist organizations is revealed, but so too is the manipulation of gender by the state, and by male-dominated political movements, in order to harness the energies of women in the service of some broader interest, such as family, economy, or Islam.

Organizations of civil society such as commercial, religious, self-help, and other common-interest groups are thought by some scholars to underpin movements toward democracy and contribute to the process of economic and political liberalization. Because of their traditional role as caregivers, women are expected to be more supportive of regimes that demonstrate respect for human rights. Some suggest that women's organizations are less likely to be co-opted by the state, because they are seen as less of a threat by authoritarian regimes. Using Jordan as a case study, Laurie Brand shows in Chapter 6 that these suppositions may or may not be the case in actuality. The deciding factors in what role women will play in a liberalization process, she shows, are first the extent of women's organizing before the opening toward liberalization, and second, the nature of organizational activity in relation to the state.

Brand shows that women's groups in Jordan have been just as constrained by preexisting practices and social structures as are men's, and that women's groups express no particular inclination or ability to spearhead civility of practice. In fact, women's activist agenda has been monopolized by agencies close to the ruling powers that choose to keep changes for women within society's religious and cultural traditions in order to appeal not only to religious conservatives but also to its more secular camps. The success of these closely held women's organizations in holding down reformist movements has been helped not only by the weakness of a tradition of civil society, but also by the "the enthusiasm of the international donor community to fund anything that calls itself an NGO," as Brand notes, even when tied intimately to the agenda of the state.

The state has similarly constrained women's activism in Tunisia, as Emma Murphy shows in Chapter 7, even though its manipulation of gender has assumed a more liberal veneer. Tunisian women in the 1990s found themselves on the front line in the debate between the regime and the Islamists. Partly in response to an Islamist challenge, the Ben Ali regime became increasingly repressive; women related to members of the Islamist movement and those who wear the hijab (veil) have become particular targets of discrimination. Using another tactic, the state hopes to deflate the Islamist appeal by incorporating women into the regime and accommodating their interests.

The growing popularity of Islamist movements threatens to undermine the liberal and egalitarian state policies that some Tunisian women have come to enjoy. Tunisia's first president, Habib Bourbuiba, had promulgated a code of personal status aimed at rebuilding family relationships on the basis of the legal equality of the sexes. He also set standards for women's health and reproductive rights in the country's constitution and labor laws, and ratified international conventions concerning women's rights. Although these laws were meant to structurally alter the power relationships between men and women, Murphy shows that they could not change the fundamental attitudes in society that undergird gender inequalities. Many areas of gender disparity in fact remained, such as levels of employment, income, and access to education. Moreover, economic liberalization has eroded the income-earning potential of both men and women, so that economic reforms that put men under threat of losing employment have brought about a social reaction making female employment less acceptable while reinforcing the cultural ideal of the male as breadwinner. Meanwhile, because the fortunes of women have been tied to the benevolence of the regime, women are vulnerable to the withdrawal of government support in the face of competing interests. And because power is monopolized by the regime at the expense of civil institutions, women have been unable to develop the mechanisms for independent, feminist political struggle.

The rise of Islamism also provides the backdrop to changing gender dynamics in Sudan. Sondra Hale shows in Chapter 8 how economic restructuring there coincided with the invention of an "authentic" Sudanese citizen as "modern Muslim," and the ways in which women have been central to this construction. A poor economy, combined with internal warfare, has thrown women into new or reinvented roles encouraged by the state, whereby women, like men, have been forced to leave school to join the military struggle. Women are placed, however, in the paramilitary National Service, fulfilling jobs that are extensions of their domestic roles, such as nursing and preparing food for the soldiers. At the same time, changes in class structures, forced male outmigration, and the imperatives of international capital and its agencies have forced women to assume greater responsibility for the family economy, including reduced reliance on imports. On top of this increased economic burden, new state ideologies bestow on women the added responsibility of reproducing a new generation of devout and "authentic" Muslims.

The assumption of this dual burden to "tend the nation" has

come about just as education has given rise to women's search to justify their emancipation in "original" Islam, and to rationalize female subordination as a product not of Islam, but of Arab patriarchy, from which they can disassociate themselves. In this interpretation, which Hale labels as "liberal feminist," each of the shifts in identity construction from mother to Muslim to militia woman to National Service volunteer can be viewed as being compatible with Islam, and therefore more easily internalized and accepted by women themselves. Focusing on this connection between gender and the definition of citizenship according to economic imperatives, Hale shows how the success of the Islamic Republic is partly the result of the successful mobilization of public consciousness within the northern population about citizenship in an Islamic nation.

In Kuwait, as Mary Ann Tétreault shows in Chapter 9, structural adjustment produced a contest between potential winners and losers over diminishing resources. With the decline of oil revenues in the 1990s, the burden of restructuring fell disproportionately onto society's least powerful: alien workers, permanent noncitizen residents *(bidun)*, and women. The lines of contention formed by this "differential accumulation," Tétreault says, have remained in place despite the rise in oil prices in the year 2000 because the restructuring effort brought long-standing problems to the surface—everything from political corruption to inequitable rules for dispensing entitlements to nepotism in the composition of the civil service. The resulting potential to change the structure of power in Kuwait has rendered the status of women and their rights to the entitlements of citizenship a critical point of contention.

Among those groups for whom the status of women is especially threatening are men from the first educated generation of poor families, especially former bedouin, and the old elite for whom preferred treatment is no longer automatic. These groups, and especially the Islamists among them, exert social pressure and legal maneuvers to get women out of the workforce and out of the competition for jobs and admission to places in the university. While crime of all kinds has risen since the end of the Gulf War, there are now ongoing incidents of violence against women. The underlying reason is that women's emancipation not only threatens the long-standing advantage of men in the workplace, but also undermines popular ideas about the role of women in the family and their symbolism as icon of communal identity. Thus structural adjustment, Tétreault reminds us, is never a gender-neutral process: women are an easy scapegoat to identify and punish for social and political problems that are difficult to remedy.

Finally, in Chapter 10 Eleanor Doumato looks at the role of education as both a major stimulus for women to enter the job market and a major deterrent: a stimulant because education has disrupted the paradigm of women as belonging in the home just by virtue of giving girls a legitimate destination outside the home, while also raising women's expectations about their own capabilities; a deterrent because the traditional gender paradigm has been incorporated into the mandatory religious studies curricula to satisfy Saudi Arabia's powerful and culturally defensive ulama (Islamic scholars of religion), with the result that what was once a cultural understanding about keeping women segregated from men has become a moral imperative that is being more firmly instilled and more thoroughly defused throughout society.

At the same time, household income has dropped dramatically, the country as a whole suffers from very high unemployment, and with the drop in oil prices the state can no longer keep its unproductive citizens happy with oil-rent disbursements. Many women, therefore, need to work, and are entering the workforce in ever greater numbers. But how do these women reconcile the pull of conservative Islam and the push of globalization with its cultural and economic entailments? What are the practical implications of this paradox for job-aspiring women, and will the state respond to economic pressures by de-emphasizing legal impediments to women's working and reordering educational priorities? Doumato shows that the lead in gaining private-sector employment is taken by female elites, who succeed through a combination of discretion and personal connections. She suggests that the economic need for workers trained in practical skills will eventually force a revamping of the Saudi educational system, but that whatever the economic incentive, any expected change in the legal underpinnings of sex segregation would be a mirage.

Taken together, these chapters prove the central message of this book: that globalization is having a profound effect on gender dynamics in the Arab world. At the same time, women's responses to globalization are contributing to shaping its effects. As this dialectic unfolds, with both similarities and differences across individual countries, the critical importance of including gender analysis in the study of economy, politics, and culture is revealed.

Notes

1. We view the Middle East as extending geographically from Mauritania in the west to Iran in the east, and from Sudan in the south to Turkey in the north. Our emphasis on the Arab countries within this region reflects both theoretical concerns and practical realities. On the theoretical level, although we believe that the issues we are addressing here are equally relevant in Turkey and Iran, we do not see them applying to Israel, whose unique history as a Western implantation in the Middle East has implied a different economic, political, and cultural trajectory from the developing countries of the region. Practically, we were unable to include chapters on Turkey and Iran due to a combination of space and data limitations, and the unavailability of desired authors.

2. The literature on globalization is vast. See Rodrik, 1997; Garrett, 1998; and Held, 1999.

3. This is the phenomenon that Benjamin Barber (1996) refers to as "McWorld." Cf. Friedman.

4. Patriarchy as a factor in development is an issue of concern worldwide. See Moghadam, 1996.

5. The introduction of etatist economic policies in most countries in the area during the 1960s was encouraged by Gamal Abdul Nasser's promotion of Arab socialism. Similarly, although there were precursors elsewhere, it was Anwar Sadat's embrace of economic opening *(infitah)* in Egypt in the early 1970s that heralded the adoption of reform programs elsewhere.

Part 1

Women in Reforming
Middle Eastern Economies:
Employment, Production,
and Reproduction

Karen Pfeifer
Marsha Pripstein Posusney

Arab Economies and Globalization:
An Overview

The first part of this book focuses on various ways in which the economic aspects of globalization are affecting women in the Arab countries. A basic understanding of the nature of Arab economies and the processes of economic liberalization is a prerequisite to that discussion. Accordingly, this introductory chapter provides an overview of some basic economic characteristics of Arab countries and examines the history of development policy in the region in the post–World War II era. Next it surveys recent economic reform programs in the region and concludes with some general observations about the dilemmas of economic liberalization and its likely course in the region in the future.

Classifying Arab Economies

An analysis of the economic dilemmas faced by Arab countries typically begins by looking at the structure of their gross domestic product (GDP) and their exports.[1] One of the signposts of economic development is a diversified economy, where activity is dispersed among agriculture, manufacturing, mining, construction, and services, and where there are strong domestic linkages among industries in these various sectors. It is a sign of weakness when a high proportion of a country's economic activity is concentrated in a single sector, since adverse developments in that one sector—such as a severe drought in an agriculturally based economy like Morocco's, or a price shock in a single-export economy like Kuwait's—will seriously affect the rest of the economy.

Before World War II, Arab economies were predominantly agricultural. While industrialization took off in numerous countries after
independence, this happened in the context of the growing international importance of oil and the increased bargaining position of the
large oil-producing countries after the formation of OPEC. Today a
sizable number of Arab countries have economies that revolve
around hydrocarbon exports, rendering them vulnerable to the vicis-
situdes of the global oil market. Moreover, several of the countries
not dependent on oil are heavily reliant on the extraction and export
of other minerals, especially phosphates.

Table 1.1 classifies eighteen Arab countries according to the
importance of mineral exports for their economic well-being.
Countries in the top category typically earn 70 percent or more of
their export revenues from crude oil, natural gas, or refined products
made from oil and gas.[2] Extractive industries account for 20 percent
or more of their GDPs. Half of the countries in the sample fall into
this category, and most of these have substantial oil and gas reserves
and are significant players in the international energy market.
Yemen's oil exports are still comparatively limited, however; thus its
appearance in this category reflects the unusually low level of development of its other sectors, even relative to the other countries of the
region. Countries in the middle category earn between 20 percent
and 70 percent of their export earnings from mineral exports, with
extractive industries comprising between 6 percent and 20 percent of
their national output. While most of the countries in this category
export hydrocarbons, Morocco's extractive industry sector is based
on phosphates and phosphate products. The third category reflects
countries whose economies are the least reliant on hydrocarbon or
other mineral exports, with export earnings less than 20 percent.

For those countries that do export hydrocarbons, Table 1.2 provides an additional assessment of the importance of export revenues
to the domestic economy. It classifies oil exporters according to the
proportion of government revenues that derive from hydrocarbon
export earnings. Since fiscal revenues have historically been used by
countries in the region to finance infrastructural development and
other capital investment projects, this ratio offers further insight into
the overall dependence of their economies on the hydrocarbon sector.
The countries in the table are grouped, in descending order, according to the dependency ratio in 2000, with the statistics from 1990 and
1995 showing the direction in which the various economies are mov-

Table 1.1   Importance of Mineral Exports to Arab Economies, Middle to Late 1990s

Economies Earning 70% or More of Export Revenues from Mineral Exports, with Extractive Industries Composing 20% or More of GDP
   Algeria
   Bahrain[a]
   Iraq
   Kuwait
   Libya
   Oman
   Qatar
   Saudi Arabia
   Yemen

Economies Earning 20% to 70% of Export Revenues from Mineral Exports, with Extractive Industries Composing 6% to 20% of GDP
   Egypt
   Morocco[b]
   Syria
   Sudan[c]
   United Arab Emirates[a]

Economies Earning 20% or Less of Export Revenues from Mineral Exports, with Extractive Industries Composing 6% or Less of GDP
   Jordan[b]
   Lebanon
   Palestinian Territories
   Tunisia

Sources: Jahangir Amuzegar, *Managing the Oil Wealth: OPEC's Windfalls and Pitfalls* (London: I. B. Tauris, 1999), appendix, tabs. 4–5; and estimates based on data from: *Middle East and North Africa* (London: Europa Publications, 1998), pp. 426, 553, 666, 742, 834, 858, 963, 1006, 1129; State of Bahrain, Monetary Agency, *Quarterly Statistical Bulletin* 27, no. 2 (June 2001): 27; and World Bank, *World Development Report 2002* (New York: Oxford University Press, 2002), tabs. 1A, 3–4.
   Notes: a. Figures for Bahrain and UAE include reexports.
   b. Morocco and Jordan do not export hydrocarbons, but do have significant extractive industries in phosphates and phosphate products, and, in Jordan's case, potassium as well.
   c. Large reserves of oil were discovered in southern Sudan and were being commercially exploited before the year 2000, but no specific figures are available.

ing. By this measure, all of the Arab Gulf countries except Yemen again emerge as highly oil dependent, but the statistics show that Yemen's dependency is on a sharp upswing. Algeria and Libya also demonstrate high dependency, while Egypt alone emerges in the category of low dependency.
   A second important way of distinguishing among Arab countries

Table 1.2   Hydrocarbon Earnings of Oil-Exporting Countries, Percentage

	1990	1995	2000
High Dependency			
United Arab Emirates	88	84	87
Saudi Arabia	76	72	83
Qatar	65	65	79
Algeria	48	54	74
Kuwait	15	71	73
Libya[a]	N/A	53	73
Oman	83	75	72
Moderate Dependency			
Yemen[b]	38	51	64
Iraq[ab]	76	N/A	63
Syria	N/A	36	49
Low Dependency			
Egypt running out	12	8	4

Source: Courtesy of the Petroleum Finance Company (PFC).
Notes: Some countries' entries reflect fiscal year data. N/A indicates that data are not available.
a. Data in 2000 column is from 1999; 2000 data was not available.
b. PFC estimates.
    Indicates ammount of Diversification

is by the size of their domestic markets. This is indicated both by a country's total population, and by its citizens' aggregate purchasing power, measured by the gross national product (GNP).[3] Countries with small populations, even if they are relatively wealthy, cannot efficiently produce everything they need for local consumption. In order to develop, they need to rely more on imports to fulfill domestic needs while their local industries have to export some products to earn foreign exchange to pay for imports. By contrast, firms in larger countries, especially if they are protected from international competition at an early stage, may be able to prosper simply by selling to local consumers. Large countries are also more likely to enjoy diverse resource endowments that can reduce their dependence on imported goods.

In other words, smaller countries are more trade dependent. Those that are small but wealthy—in this case small countries endowed with substantial oil resources—are generally able to finance their import needs, although they remain susceptible to oil price shocks. Countries that have both small populations and low

GNPs, however, like Jordan, are in the most vulnerable position, since they are the most dependent on nonhydrocarbon exports and on the largesse of foreign donors and lenders.

Table 1.3 groups Arab countries according to domestic market size, by both population size and GNP. Only Egypt emerges as a large economy based on both a population exceeding 60 million and a GNP in excess of U.S.$95 billion. Algeria, Morocco, Tunisia, and Iraq can be considered to have medium market size by both measures, with populations of 10 million to 30 million and GNPs of U.S.$20 billion to 50 billion. Of the remaining countries of medium market size by population, Saudi Arabia has a large GNP, but the others—Yemen, Syria, and Sudan have small GNPs (below U.S.$20 billion). Finally, Jordan, Lebanon, Oman, Bahrain, Qatar, and the Palestinian

Table 1.3   Domestic Market Size of Arab Economies, 1999–2000

National income or Domestic product

Rank by Population Size		Rank by Aggregate GDP	
Large: > 60 million people		*Large: > U.S.$95 billion*	
1. Egypt	64.0	1. Saudi Arabia	139.4
		2. Egypt	95.2
Medium: 10–30 million people		*Medium: U.S.$20–$50 billion*	
2. Algeria	30.0	3. UAE	49.2
3. Sudan	29.7	4. Algeria	48.3
4. Morocco	29.0	5. Kuwait	34.5
5. Iraq	23.0	6. Morocco	33.8
6. Saudi Arabia	21.0	7. Libya	27.8
7. Yemen	18.0	8. Tunisia	20.1
8. Syria	16.0	9. Iraq	N/A
9. Tunisia	10.0		
Small: < 6 million people		*Small: < U.S.$20 billion*	
10. Libya	5.5	10. Lebanon	16.2
11. Jordan	5.0	11. Syria	16.0
12. Lebanon	4.0	12. Oman	15.6
13. Palestinian Territories	2.9	13. Qatar	14.5
14. UAE	2.9	14. Sudan	9.6
15. Oman	2.4	15. Jordan	8.2
16. Kuwait	2.0	16. Yemen	6.7
17. Bahrain	0.7	17. Bahrain	4.9
18. Qatar	0.6	18. Palestinian Territories	4.7

Sources: World Bank, *World Development Report 2002* (New York: Oxford University Press, 2002), tabs. 1, 1A; and IMF, *International Financial Statistics Yearbook 2001* (Washington, D.C.: IMF, 2001).

Adv.
Large tax base
Domestic market
Labor

Territories have both relatively few people (less that 6 million) and small GNPs. The remaining small-population Arab countries—Libya, Kuwait, and the United Arab Emirates (UAE)—are in the medium income category because of their oil export earnings.

The same statistics that indicate domestic market size also *suggest* the relative levels of an average citizen's material well-being within the various countries. GNP per capita, or national product divided by population, is an imprecise measure of a citizen's standard of living, both because of the various deficiencies associated with these aggregate measurements in general, and because GNP per capita does not capture variations among countries in the *distribution* of income among the population.[4] Nevertheless, it is a useful first cut at comparing average levels of well-being across countries in the region.

Table 1.4 uses the World Bank's fourfold classification—high, upper-middle, lower-middle, and low incomes—to categorize the countries of the region according to GNP per capita. The high-income countries, with an average income of U.S.$9,266 per person or higher, are those that combine substantial oil earnings with small populations; only Qatar, Kuwait, and the UAE qualify. The majority of Arab countries, having either high or moderate oil earnings but larger populations, or smaller populations but more diversified economies, fall into the middle range—with a GNP per capita range of U.S.$2,996–$9,265 for upper-middle income, and U.S.$756–$2,995 for lower-middle income. The only two low-income countries in the region, with a GNP per capita less than U.S.$755, are Yemen and Sudan.

The third significant aspect of a country's economic profile is its external position, reflected in its balance of payments account. This measures and classifies the inflows and outflows of currency for all purposes, usually converted to U.S. dollars. Countries with outflows greater than inflows in the trade category (imports of goods and services in excess of exports) need to staunch the foreign currency drain through inflows in other categories, such as transfer payments like foreign aid and worker remittances, direct or portfolio foreign investment, or borrowing. Lacking enough of these, the country risks depleting its foreign currency reserves to the point where it can no longer finance necessary imports for consumption and investment. This imperative has led countries with persistent current account

Table 1.4   Classification of Arab Economies by Per Capita Income, 1999–2000

High Income: > U.S.$9,266	
Qatar	24,121
Kuwait	20,349
UAE	18,060
Upper-Middle Income: U.S.$2,996–$9,265	
Bahrain	7,640
Saudi Arabia	6,900
Oman	6,720
Libya	5,026
Lebanon	3,750
Lower-Middle Income: U.S.$756–$2,995	
Tunisia	2,090
Jordan	1,680
Palestinian Territories	1,610
Algeria	1,590
Egypt	1,490
Morocco	1,180
Syria	990
Iraq	N/A
Low Income: < U.S.$755	
Yemen	380
Sudan	320

Sources: World Bank, *World Development Report 2002* (New York: Oxford University Press, 2002), tabs. 1, 1A; and IMF, *International Financial Statistics Yearbook 2001* (Washington, D.C.: IMF, 2001).

Notes: If purchasing power parity (PPP) measurement is used, GNI per capita is higher than is captured here in current dollars at the going exchange rates. For example, the UAE's GNI per capita becomes $19,430, Saudi Arabia's $11,050, Egypt's $3,690, and Yemen's $780. That is, the tourist or investor finds that his or her dollar stretches further in these countries than it does in the United States, Japan, or much of Western Europe. The income categories are defined on p. 241 of the *World Development Report 2002*.

deficits to borrow from private international banks, Western governments, and multinational agencies such as the World Bank. The International Monetary Fund (IMF) plays a different but equally crucial role as lender to cover short-term shortages of foreign exchange and as guarantor for renewed lending by private international banks through the negotiation of structural adjustment programs (SAPs) for debtor countries. The IMF is not itself a major long-term lender.

Oil reserves and domestic market size become particularly significant in this regard because those countries that have been able to export large quantities of oil at high or moderate prices can maintain positive trade balances. Highly oil dependent countries with more sizable populations, and those countries with little or no oil, regardless of population size, are more vulnerable to current account deficits, and are thus more dependent on the largesse of foreign creditors. In the Arab region, many countries have had to rely on foreign borrowing, including Tunisia, Morocco, Algeria, Egypt, Jordan, Yemen, and more recently Lebanon. Table 1.5 shows the extent of the debt burden in 1999 and the accompanying debt service burden (the percentage of the value of goods and services exports that must go to repay principal and pay interest on foreign debt each year). It shows Sudan, Syria, and Jordan to have the highest overall debt measured as a percentage of their GNP; however, when debt service obligations are contrasted with foreign exchange earnings from merchandise and service exports, Algeria, Morocco, and Tunisia emerge as the countries with the greatest vulnerability.

If a government takes out loans to use for productive purposes that will help its economy grow, for example, to extend and improve its road system, this borrowing is considered healthy because the debt service can be paid out of the resulting new national product. Debt is unhealthy for a country only if the borrowed funds are not used productively (e.g., if they are spent on unnecessary weapons), because new national product will not be generated and debt service will become harder to meet. While the countries mentioned above as well as the major Arab oil producers were often profligate in the use of borrowed funds for military purchases and unproductive displays (such as grandiose public buildings and lifestyles), they also borrowed funds for infrastructure development and other productive investment.

This is not to imply that the course of a country's economic development is predetermined by its population size and resource endowment. Rather, these factors should be understood as both constraints and opportunities that confront economic policymakers. The choices that governments make, in their context, also play a significant role in shaping a country's economic performance. Because the post–World War II period saw a high degree of commonality in the economic development strategies of various Arab countries, despite their otherwise wide differences in regime type and political orienta-

Table 1.5   Debt and Debt Service Obligations of Arab Countries, 1999

	Rank by External Debt as % of GNI	Debt Service as % of Goods and Services Exports
> 100%		
Sudan	183	6.5
Syria	138	6.4
Jordan	104	11.8
50–100%		
Algeria	64	37.8
Tunisia	59	15.9
Yemen	58	4.0
Lebanon	51	9.6
Morocco	51	24.4
25–50%		
Egypt	27	9.0
Oman	N/A	9.7
*< 25%*a		
Iraq	N/A	N/A
Palestinian Territories	N/A	N/A
*Negligible*b		
Bahrain		
Kuwait		
Libya		
Qatar		
Saudi Arabia		

(handwritten annotations: "b/c of self-inf loans" next to Algeria; "also similar to Algeria" next to Morocco; "more than a third of their exports" next to 37.8; "Debt good or bad depends on what it is used for")

Sources: UNDP, *Human Development Report 2001,* tab. 15, and *2000,* tab. 18 (New York: UNDP, 2001, 2002); and World Bank, *World Development Report 2002* (New York: Oxford University Press, 2002), tab. 4.

Notes: a. Due to political constraints, neither the Iraqi government nor the Palestinian National Authority were able to borrow on the international capital markets in the 1990s. However, Iraq still has debt hanging over from the 1980s and is also obliged by the United Nations to pay war reparations to Kuwait, while the PA received official development assistance from a number of sources that it has not been able to use.

b. All of these countries received some official development assistance in 1999, but no net debt was indicated. In fact, several of them may be net creditors via their overseas investment portfolios and their development aid programs.

(handwritten: "Concessionary Loan ~ Long Term")

tion, the region faces a common set of economic challenges at the start of the twenty-first century. At the same time, the distinctions among the Arab countries highlighted here are important factors contributing to the nature of their reform agendas.

Development Trends in the Arab Region

The heyday of economic development in Arab countries came between the early 1960s and the mid-1980s. While agricultural exports remained crucial to countries like Egypt and Sudan, the development process overall was increasingly fueled by the export of oil, natural gas, and phosphates, and by the increased volume of export revenues that followed sharp rises in the prices of these products on the world market in the 1970s. The main thrust of this development was the emergence of a set of political and economic institutions integrated around state-led development with a populist authoritarian cast.[5] This entailed the nationalization of resources such as hydrocarbons, phosphates, and the Suez Canal, and occasioned a powerful role for the state in central planning, in banking, and often in managing productive enterprises. These developmental states also promoted import-substitution industrialization and land reform, and installed programs providing universal social services like education and healthcare.

The coherence of the state-led development model, on the one hand, rested on an effective social contract among the major social and political forces in each nation, based on the expectation that economic development policy would explicitly address the material needs of all citizens, including poor peasants and urban workers. This was the model's populist aspect, an approach originally pioneered by Turkey, under Kemal Atatürk, in the 1930s. The price of this social contract, on the other hand, was the continuation or rapid emergence of authoritarian regimes, be they monarchies or republics, in virtually all Arab countries.

Among Arab countries, import-substitution industrialization (ISI) was first introduced as a pragmatic policy in Egypt during the global capitalist depression of the 1930s. It is an arrangement whereby governments promote the development of industries within a country by raising tariffs and quotas against imports. In the era of national liberation and decolonization following World War II, broader and more explicit versions of state-led development were elaborated, often expressed in the ideological form of populist nationalism and anti-imperialism. The two earliest and most dramatic expressions of radical economic nationalism in the Middle East were the nationalization of the Anglo-Iranian Oil Company in Iran in 1951 and of the Suez Canal Company in Egypt in 1956. Although Iran returned to a more liberal economic policy after the nationalist government of Mohammed Mossadeq was overthrown in a U.S.-engineered coup, Egypt's Gamal Abdul Nasser continued along a strict nationalist path, with the state taking over banks, insurance companies, and large industries, and committing resources to the development of new state-owned enterprises.

In the 1960s the state-led development model spread to Syria, Iraq, Tunisia, Algeria, and the former South Yemen (the People's Democratic Republic of Yemen [PDRY]), and then to Libya. The governments of these countries referred to their economic and political systems as "Arab nationalism" and "Arab socialism." With the advent of huge oil export revenues in the mid-1970s, even regimes that explicitly rejected this ideological orientation, such as Jordan, Morocco, and later the conservative oil-exporting monarchies like Saudi Arabia, Kuwait, and Oman, subsequently followed the same institutional pattern. They also began designing five-year plans, developing large public sectors and a wage labor force (much of it imported), and providing generous social programs and economic privileges to their citizens. Important parts of these plans, productive though they were, were financed by borrowing on international markets, a practice that eventually led to the buildup of debt. The sole clear exception to the pattern was Lebanon, which has maintained a semblance of a laissez-faire economy to the present.

The authoritarian populist Arab regimes declared the goal of national economic construction to be improvement of the standard of living of the majority of the populace, urban and rural. Rural dwellers, including a large number of poor and middle-class peasants, still constituted large majorities of the population of Egypt in the 1960s. Thus the peasantry welcomed the Nasser government's land reform because it claimed to eliminate large "feudal" landholdings as an obstacle to economic development and to enhance Egypt's independence from imperialist influence. The land reforms that followed in Syria, Iraq, and Algeria were similar in scope and rhetoric, while the South Yemeni regime (under secular socialist leadership) went the furthest. Significant redistribution did occur, and the political dominance of the landed elite was sharply curbed, but poor peasants and rural landless workers were granted less power and fewer benefits than official rhetoric claimed. Rather, middle-class peasants were often the main beneficiaries, even as agriculture became more commercialized and land-reform bureaucracies deepened state intervention in rural life. The direct promotion of modern agriculture in Jordan, Saudi Arabia, and Morocco generated similar end results without an antecedent land reform.

Urban workers in the formal industrial, clerical, and service sectors, especially in the greatly expanded public sector, also benefited from state-led development. In the Arab nationalist regimes, they were encouraged to join trade unions and national labor federations subordinated to the ruling party and the state, acceding to the regimes' rejection of the notion of class struggle. In return, union and federation members enjoyed job security, higher wages than average, shorter working days, health and unemployment insurance, and retirement security, while unorganized workers in small-scale and informal enterprises were not included in these programs. It was the urban middle class and an elite segment of the working class that benefited relatively more as the public sector expanded and government spending on education and other social services grew.

The legitimacy of the nationalist regimes depended on improving the standard of living of the common people, who suffered substantial violations of human rights and undemocratic rule in exchange. Political repression was common in both the republican nationalist and monarchical regimes. Denial of civil and labor rights to independent political action took the form of imprisonment, torture, and even execution. In many cases, collective action of workers and peasants that dared exceed authorized boundaries or challenged the regime was crushed or bureaucratically co-opted. The Egyptian Free Officers hanged two leaders of the aborted textile workers' strike at Kafr al-Dawwar in August 1952. In the first few years after independence in Algeria, the "revolutionary" National Liberation Front (FLN) government, socialist rhetoric to the contrary, turned workers' self-managed farms and businesses (the *autogestion* system) into centralized state-owned enterprises.

The model of growth and transformation led by public investment prevailed for about twenty-five years (1960–1985) while average investment and economic growth were relatively strong. However, the populist authoritarian model of state-led development gradually succumbed in the middle to late 1980s to a combination of external pressures and internal contradictions. The external pressures included a pronounced decline in the relative prices of primary exports, as well as rising real interest rates on world financial mar-

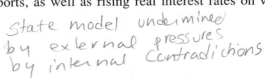

State model undermined
by external pressures
by internal Contradictions

kets, stemming from the monetarist policies of the governments of Margaret Thatcher and Ronald Reagan. The internal contradictions included declining investment and productivity growth, rising inequality in income distribution, and growing, unsustainable public deficits.

While the neoliberal logic of the IMF and the World Bank attributes these crises to the heavy hand of government intervention in the economy (see Handy et al., 1998; Maciejewski and Mansur, 1996; Nsouli et al., 1993, 1995), it was the mutual interaction between these internal and external factors that culminated in the foreign exchange shortages and debt crises of the late 1980s. These crises in turn tolled the death knell for the state-led development model.

Table 1.6 shows that these factors combined with population growth in the 1990s to produce average annual growth rates in per capita GDP of less than 3 percent; indeed, more than half the countries experienced negligible gains or declining per capita incomes. The economy of Lebanon was exceptional in that it experienced a surge of very high, but unsustainable, growth in the five years immediately following the end of its long civil war, bringing its average for the 1990s to over 3 percent.

An alternative model—of IMF-supervised, export-oriented growth led by private investment—arose out of the crisis and was applied in Arab countries in the 1990s, as elsewhere around the world. This neoliberal "Washington consensus" promotes economic stabilization in the short run by curbing government spending and subsidies, raising interest rates and prices, and devaluing the currency to stimulate exports. In the long run it promotes economic reform by means of SAPs, including liberalization of investment and trade and privatization of publicly held enterprises and resources. IMF staff studies repeatedly praise the policy changes that have taken place since reform began, especially the shift in investment lead, from the government to the private sector, even if investment by the latter remains small in scale, and the shift in development strategy, from inward-looking (ISI) to outward-looking (export-led).

The purpose of these various neoliberal policies and adjustments is the opening up *(infitah)* of these economies to private capital, both foreign and domestic, both real and financial, which is considered essential to attract investment capital to sustain growth in the short

Table 1.6   Macroeconomic Performance of Arab Countries

	Rank by Average Annual Growth Rate of Real GDP, 1990–2000	Per Capita GDP Growth, Annual Average, 1990–1999[a]
> 5%		
Lebanon	5.9	5.7
Syria	5.6	2.7
Jordan	5.0	1.1
3–5%		
Tunisia	4.7	2.9
Egypt	4.6	2.4
Oman[b]	4.2	0.3
Bahrain[b]	4.0	0.8
Yemen	3.5	−0.4
0–3%		
UAE	2.9	−1.6
Morocco	2.2	0.4
Algeria	2.1	−0.5
Saudi Arabia	1.6	−1.1
Kuwait[c]	1.0	0.7
Qatar	N/A	N/A
< 0%		
Libya[d]	−0.8	−3.0
Palestinian Territories	−2.2	−6.1
Iraq[e]	N/A	N/A
Sudan[e]	N/A	N/A

[handwritten annotations: "war Recovery period Starting from low base so growth is fast"; "→ standard of living"]

Sources: UNDP, *Human Development Report 2001* (New York: UNDP, 2001), tab. 11; World Bank, *World Development Report 2002* (New York: Oxford University Press, 2002), tabs. 1A, 3; IMF, *International Financial Statistics Yearbook 2001* (Washington, D.C.: IMF, 2001); and Karen Pfeifer, "The Material Basis of Palestinian Society: A Long-Term Perspective" (ms., 2002), tab. 2.

Notes: a. The GDP per capita growth rate is calculated as a compound annual average from the GDP per capita for the beginning and ending years of a period. It also equals the aggregate GDP growth rate minus the population growth rate.

b. In these cases, the aggregate GDP growth rate was surmised from adding the GDP per capita growth rate and the population growth rate.

c. Calculation is for 1989–1999, due to a large decline in GDP in 1990–1991. 1989 was a "normal" year from which to calculate a growth rate.

d. These calculations were made in current U.S. dollars at the published exchange rates (the Libyan dinar falling to half of its 1990 value relative to the dollar by 1999). If the rate of inflation in the United States had also been taken into account, the real drop in GDP would have been greater than the nominal drop.

e. No statistics were available, but due to the political conditions within each of these countries, it is commonly surmised that they experienced no real economic growth in the 1990s.

term, and to create jobs and raise living standards in the long term. The "free markets" in international capital are expected to send investment to the most deserving developing countries, those with the most attractive policies of taxation and currency conversion and the most favorable investment laws. These policies include, first, the freedom of foreign capital to repatriate not only profits but also proceeds from the sale of vested capital, and second, "flexible labor markets," the freedom of employers to hire and fire and to negotiate variable remuneration with employees.

Economic Reform and Its Consequences in the Arab Countries

The countries that have embraced standard stabilization and structural adjustment in the Arab world are Egypt, Jordan, Tunisia, Morocco, Algeria, and Yemen.[6] Their common impetus was the rise of public spending deficits and balance of payments strains leading to difficulties in servicing extant external debt. The governments of these countries have expressed adherence to the principles of neoliberal orthodoxy to varying degrees. While official criticism of the "Washington consensus" has become common, it typically focuses on the pace of the reform agenda, rather than its underlying philosophy. However, borrowing countries have little leverage. Over time, debt service payments themselves become an obstacle to achieving balance of payments equilibrium, prompting the debtor countries to seek relief from their creditors in the form of debt rescheduling or outright forgiveness. Because the IMF's seal of approval is required before Western lenders will sign off on debt relief, the Fund has the upper hand in negotiations.

Although there are important commonalities, the structural adjustment process has differed between the oil-poor and oil-rich countries. In this section we first examine the dilemmas of stabilization and structural adjustment, drawing on Egypt, Jordan, Tunisia, and Morocco, four illustrative oil-poor countries that have conducted their reforms under the tutelage of the IMF and the World Bank and been pronounced as successful by these agencies. Thereafter, we consider the economic reforms under way in the oil-rich countries that faced different constraints and followed a somewhat different path.

Economic Reform in the Oil-Poor Countries

Just as Egypt was a pioneer in state-led development in the Arab world in the 1950s and 1960s, so did Egypt pioneer liberal economic reform by inviting foreign capital under its *infitah* policy, begun in 1974. It succeeded, at least temporarily, in attracting foreign direct investment, ranking fourth among developing countries in total amount received during the 1981–1990 period, ahead of Turkey, Indonesia, the Philippines, and South Korea (World Bank, 1991–1992). Although the absolute quantity of new foreign capital was ultimately disappointing, the economy boomed in the following decade due to inflows of hard currency from U.S. aid, oil exports, tolls from the reopened Suez Canal, renewed international tourism, and remittances from migrant workers, as well as the accumulation of debt from foreign lenders.

After the boom ended, investment, economic growth, and the standard of living stagnated, leaving Egypt's per capita income about the same in 1995 as in 1985. The end of the oil boom in 1985–1986 led to shortages of foreign currency to finance imports of industrial inputs and consumption goods, and fueled the debt crisis that struck Egypt as elsewhere in the third world. Egypt signed a short-lived standby contract with the IMF in 1987, which was aborted after the country implemented only limited reforms. A second agreement was signed in 1991; this time Egypt had to enact most aspects of stabilization, and to commit itself to privatization, before the agency would approve the standby loan. A long-term structural adjustment program was then put into force.

Jordan's economic development was shaped by two main forces. The first was the influx of Palestinian refugees, mainly in 1948 and 1967, who became the majority population. The second factor was the rapid regional expansion that followed the rise in oil prices in the early 1970s. Jordan benefited from these two factors in part through increased aid from the oil-rich countries to the Frontline States. In addition, with a relatively high level of human resource development, professionals and laborers (mostly Palestinian) migrated to the Gulf to work. This émigré labor force became one of Jordan's main exports, and because the workers sent home much of their earnings, their remittances became one of the main sources of foreign exchange. The Jordanian government used these inflows of funds partly to expand public services—the government sector became the largest employer—and partly to invest in large-scale infrastructure construction. Jordan's per capita income doubled in the 1974–1982 period.

Two major shocks subsequently left Jordan's economy in disarray. First, the oil price decline of the late 1980s sent the oil-exporting economies into recession. That reduced the demand for émigré labor, curbed demand for Jordanian exports and transshipment of exports coming from elsewhere, and also reduced Arab foreign aid. The second major shock came with the Gulf crisis of 1990–1991. Trade with its most important partner, Iraq, fell by half as war and economic sanctions took effect. Further, the Gulf country allies halted their aid to, and trade with, Jordan in retaliation for its neutral stance in the conflict and expelled expatriate workers, especially Palestinians. Jordan's unemployment rate for 1991 is estimated to have risen to between 14.4 and 25 percent. Real GDP declined by an average of 2.6 percent per year between 1988 and 1991. Poverty, having declined from 24 percent in 1980 to 3 percent in 1986–1987, rose to almost 20 percent in 1991 (Maciejewski and Mansur, 1996: 58–59).

Morocco has manifested a pattern of vacillation between state-led development and economic liberalism. Postindependence state-led development was accompanied by a real GDP growth rate of 6.5 percent per year from 1956 to the mid-1970s, as per capita income grew at a rate of 2 percent per year. However, the capital-intensive nature of industry and the failure of exports to perform as expected contributed to growing problems such as unemployment and current account deficits. Postponement of the day of reckoning was facilitated by the sharp rise in the demand for, and prices of, phosphate-based fertilizers on the world market in the early 1970s. The consequent infusion of foreign exchange stimulated another government-led investment campaign, raising gross fixed capital formation from 14 percent of GDP in 1973 to 33 percent in 1977. Faster economic growth ensued, but so did rising import bills, along with fiscal and trade deficits, and a widening gap between savings and investment. Morocco, like so many other developing countries, turned to borrowing on the international markets to cover these gaps. Debt increased tenfold between 1970 and 1982, while debt service rose from 11 percent of goods and services exports in 1970 to 49 percent in 1982 (Bourguignon and Morrisson, 1989: 157).

Morocco's economy swerved again as the fall of phosphate prices in 1977 threw this economic development program into another crisis and led to a long series of IMF interventions. The Moroccan government entered into an unofficial agreement with the IMF in 1980 and an official stabilization contract in 1981, entailing stringent government budgets for each year of the 1981–1985 development plan. Another round of crisis ensued under intense pressure from its international creditors and, in exchange for debt relief, Morocco contracted an entirely IMF-administered structural adjustment program in 1983. This was imposed on an economy that had known real growth in per capita income of 2 percent per year on average since 1960, but in which per capita income in 1983 was still only U.S.$750 (Bourguignon and Morrisson, 1989: 156). In January 1984, when deregulation of food prices and partial removal of food subsidies led to sharp price increases, dramatic food riots broke out. Morocco negotiated no fewer than seven multilateral debt relief agreements with the IMF and private international creditors between January 1980 and September 1991. The frequency of, and highly concessional element in, these loans enabled Morocco to survive this long period of austerity and structural adjustment with less pain and more growth than other severely indebted countries. However, these loans did not significantly reduce the stock of outstanding debt and did not eliminate the contradiction between growth and structural adjustment (World Bank, 1991–1992, vol. 1: 25, 74, 78, 82; UNDP, 1991b: 161–164).

Tunisia provides an example of a small, reputedly successful economy that went into crisis early in its history and undertook its liberalization in incremental stages before it became a fashionable trend in the Middle East. Like other Arab countries, Tunisia pursued state-led development in the 1960s, with high investment levels and development of public enterprises at the core of the economy. It also established a widely admired and fairly implemented social contract, the most progressive in the Arab world in terms of women's rights. The economy as a whole and the private sector were also growing, fueled by the increase in oil prices of course, and by the growth of other exports such as phosphates and food products. The *infitah*, or liberalization, that began in 1971 attracted foreign capital and added to the number of factory jobs, while expanding exports to include manufactured goods. External debt decreased to 38 percent of GDP in 1981 and debt service, at 17 percent of goods and services, was then considered under control.

In the mid-1980s, Tunisia experienced a sharp economic crisis, due partly to a drop in productivity growth in public industry and partly to a fall in prices for natural resource exports, and it agreed to an IMF-supervised structural adjustment program. Liberal reforms ensued and were intensified in the 1990s, much to the praise of the IMF and World Bank. With the restoration of public investment to 23 percent of GDP in 1991, facilitated by debt rescheduling and renewed access to external borrowing, economic growth, both in the aggregate and per capita, was restored (Payne, 1993: 146–148).

Tunisia's successes, however, are constrained in ways peculiar to a small export-oriented economy. Tunisia remains beholden to Western agencies and banks to provide aid for programs and funding to cover current account deficits, and its growth is now directly dependent on sales of exports to Europe. Faster integration with the international trade system contains its own risks, in that the need to service debt and to pay for imports requires increases in exports and other sources of foreign exchange. Aiming to reduce international debt, Tunisia switched its emphasis from debt to equity finance. While Tunisia has had a relatively good record among Arab countries in this strategy, it must constantly find new ways to attract and hold private foreign direct or portfolio investment in a ferociously competitive international environment. In the 1990s many developing countries around the world, including giants China and India, have pursued the same strategy as Tunisia, producing the same products (e.g., textiles) and wooing the same multinationals by granting tax concessions and pushing down production costs.

Social Programs and Poverty in Oil-Poor Countries

Under structural adjustment programs, the phasing out of general subsidies for commodities like basic foods, fuel, and transportation can make low-income families worse off. Initially indifferent to this problem, the multilateral lending agencies began in the 1990s to advocate that countries undergoing structural adjustment develop new social safety nets to help soften the negative impact of reform on the poor. In place of the universal social protection programs previously in place, this approach, comparable in conception to the welfare programs of the Organization for Economic Cooperation and Development (OECD) countries, seeks to target income supports, food coupons, and healthcare subsidies only to those who need them most.

These measures have been implemented, to different degrees, in Egypt, Jordan, Tunisia, and Morocco. Their success has varied across the four countries, for at least two reasons. First, it is difficult in practice in a developing country to identify and reach the truly needy. Second, the transition from universal to targeted protection programs is politically difficult. Even if morally and economically justifiable, such programs amount to a withdrawal of accustomed benefits from some segments of the population, who may mobilize to protect the status quo, and who may, after the benefits are withdrawn, resist paying the domestic taxes necessary to continue to cover such public transfers to the needy.

By IMF standards, Egypt made significant strides in the realm of structural reform in the 1990s. These included a reduction in the central government's budget deficit and in the rate of price inflation, and management of the currency to keep the pound pegged to within 3 percent of the U.S. dollar. However, one of the contradictions of economic reform is that Egypt remains a low-income country with significant poverty. Less than 8 percent of the population is abjectly poor (living on less than U.S.$1 per day on the purchasing power parity formula). But consumption surveys comparing the early to middle 1990s showed that the overall poverty rate remained unchanged, with 44 percent of the population unable to spend enough to have a minimally adequate diet (Handy et al., 1998: 42).

Jordan dealt with the dilemma relatively effectively by protecting social services as much as possible during its adjustment period. Its social security system covers the one-third of all workers employed by private-sector companies with at least five employees (the public sector has its own system). However, in 1996–1997 the poverty rate, which had declined to 3 percent in 1986–1987, is estimated to have returned to its 1980 level, in the 20–30 percent range.[7]

International organizations and business give Tunisia's government high marks for promoting social welfare over the long run. Having spent 7.5 percent of GDP on education from 1975 to 1985 and 6 percent since 1988, Tunisia can boast 100 percent of primary school-age children in school and a literacy rate of 65 percent. Health indicators also improved, and Tunisia has had the lowest rate of population growth in the Arab world, less than 2 percent per year in the late 1990s, thanks to a long-running and highly successful family planning program. However, Tunisia's poverty rate in 1990 was greater than 20 percent of the population, according to International Labour Organization (ILO) estimates, a decline of less than one-tenth since the mid-1980s (Fergany, 1998: 7). Furthermore, agricultural policy under structural adjustment has mainly benefited large-scale commercial farmers at the expense of small farmers (King, 1999).

Privatization, Employment, and Labor Markets in Oil-Poor Countries

Privatization has become a central element of structural adjustment programs across the region. Its rationale is that state-owned enterprises (SOEs) tend to become bloated and inefficient, established as they were under ISI policies with generous subsidies on inputs and secure, relatively well-compensated workforces. With little motivation to innovate to raise productivity, many SOEs can neither meet domestic needs nor compete on international markets and therefore contribute too little to net export earnings. In the Arab countries, as in many other regions, the workforce of SOEs has indeed grown substantially, partly because governments have used them for job creation. Then, when payrolls and other expenses exceed earnings, the government or state-owned banks have assumed the debts of loss-making SOEs. Private firms are arguably more efficient because no agency will assume their debts when they make losses and the less efficient ones go out of business.

Yet privatization poses numerous dilemmas for reforming countries. Nationalist concerns have been a central controversy. The public sector in these countries was established primarily in the post-colonial era, and reflected the drive of third-world countries throughout the globe to achieve economic self-sufficiency along with political independence. While not all privatization schemes involve sales to Western-owned firms, the international financial institutions (IFIs) do promote this method for the Arab countries. Accordingly, leftist and nationalist opposition forces have charged that privatization will put foreigners in control of their countries' vital assets; they have particularly raised the specter of Israeli capitalists purchasing strategic industries.[8]

Privatization also engenders a variety of social concerns. Because the products of SOEs, even if inferior, were made available to citizens at controlled or subsidized prices, the elimination of the public sector generally means higher-priced goods for consumers. At

although argument is that
Competition in the private Sector
will drive down prices

the same time, because government employment has served as an alternative means of social protection in these countries, the elimination of public-sector jobs can mean throwing people onto the streets without benefit of unemployment insurance or welfare provision.[9] The private sector, even with structural adjustment, has proven unable to generate enough jobs for new entrants into the labor market, much less those who would be made redundant when SOEs are sold or liquidated. Unemployment rates for Tunisia and Jordan were about 15 percent in 1995, while those for Morocco and Egypt were about 20 percent (Handy et al., 1998: 43, tab. 17). The annual real GDP growth rates for these countries would have to rise to around 7 percent in order to absorb domestic labor force growth each year. Mass layoffs associated with privatization thus threaten to worsen an already severe unemployment problem.

There is also a disparity in job security and benefits between the public and private sectors. At the outset of the 1990s, Egypt, Morocco, Tunisia, and Jordan all had labor laws that made it very difficult for employers to fire workers hired under indefinite job contracts, except for serious job infractions. The laws also required formal-sector employers to provide health and accident insurance and pension plans to permanent employees. These protections did not obtain in the informal sector, however, and, at least in Morocco and Egypt, many private entrepreneurs in the formal sector as well were able to routinely evade these laws. As a consequence, at the advent of privatization, public-sector workers enjoyed job security and social protection that was not available to many of their private-sector counterparts.

Because of these political and social concerns, the governments in Egypt, Jordan, Tunisia, and Morocco all embraced privatization with caution, and serious efforts in this regard did not begin until the early 1990s in the Tunisian and Moroccan cases, and the latter half of the decade in Egypt and Jordan. There were also technical delays associated with the establishment, regulation, and expansion of capital markets and with the valuation of firms to be sold. Thus, despite the favorable reviews they have received from IFIs for their overall macroeconomic performance under structural adjustment, all four countries have been criticized by foreign lenders and business for the slow pace of their privatization efforts.

In Morocco, for example, the monarchy began to express concerns about the size of the public sector and the need for structural reform toward the end of the 1970s, but retreated in the face of popular resistance. Law 39 of 1989 finally authorized privatization of 112 firms, but due to technical and political delays the first sale did not occur until October 1992. By the end of summer 1996, with just twenty-five companies and seventeen hotels either completely or partly sold, Morocco led the Arab world in privatization proceeds, but the original privatization deadline expired with less than half of the planned sales completed. In the spring of 1999, parliament approved a bill to extend the program until 2001. However, the legislation removed about thirty companies from the intended sale list.

The first calls for privatization in Egypt were issued in 1973, but as late as 1988, President Hosni Mubarak was repeating earlier vows that he would neither sell off nor shrink the public sector. Revived openness to privatization began only in 1989, after the effective collapse of the aforementioned 1987 IMF standby agreement. Law 203, passed in June 1991, provided the legislative framework for divestiture, but the pace of sell-offs in the early 1990s was nevertheless slow, and rose to the forefront of new negotiations with the IMF in 1996. Accordingly, the government announced plans for more extensive and rapid privatization, and soon supplanted Morocco as the region's leader in this endeavor. As of spring 1999, 119 of 314 state-owned enterprises, mainly manufacturing ventures, had been fully or partially sold. The government has since pledged to offer utilities, public-sector banks and insurance companies, maritime and telecommunications firms, and prominent tourist hotels, but the program slowed considerably in late 1999 and 2000, with only an additional twenty or so transactions occurring.

As their privatization programs advanced, all four countries were encouraged by the IFIs to revamp their labor laws, since the prohibitions against mass layoffs made bloated firms less attractive to buyers. The Tunisian government revised its laws in 1994 and 1996 to accommodate retrenchments, while tripartite committees of government, business, and labor representatives were established in the early 1990s in Jordan, Egypt, and Morocco to consider possible reforms.[10] During these negotiations the labor leaders objected to the retraction of provisions for job security; Jordan's new law was passed in 1996 after the unionists had walked out of the talks. In both Egypt and Morocco, draft bills on which these committees agreed had yet to be enacted by the parliaments as of summer 2001.

Morocco's proposed legislation, agreed in 1997, would lessen the time allotted to the government to respond to mass dismissal requests, but makes the requirements for submitting such applications more cumbersome and increases the severance pay for dismissed employees. This compromise between labor and business falls well short of the desires of investors and multilateral lenders, and the latter have continued to push for changes to the draft. Egypt's proposed new law would still require that firms obtain government approval for any mass workforce reductions, but signals a sea change by stating explicitly that it is an employer's right to adjust the workforce according to economic conditions. In a compensatory concession to workers, the law also contains provisions for legalizing the right to strike, but would still render permissible work stoppages rare. The repeated delays in issuing the law suggest that the regime itself is not anxious to legalize labor protest in even this sharply limited manner.

These actual or impending legal changes notwithstanding, the governments in all four countries have taken steps to ameliorate the potential social disruptions associated with widespread layoffs. Jordan has for the most part avoided the latter by shifting redundant workers to other government employment. Egypt's government is endeavoring to make the SOEs more attractive to investors by streamlining the workforce prior to sale, using voluntary early retirement incentives negotiated between the trade union confederation and the authorities in 1996. An estimated 130,000 workers, or about 10 percent of the public-sector workforce in the early 1990s, had accepted early retirement packages by the late 1990s, but critics charge that many workers were coerced into the program, or accepted it only out of fear that they would later be fired by their new private-sector employers with no compensation whatsoever. In Morocco's mining, postal, and telecom sectors, a restructuring plan prior to privatization called for most redundant workers to be reassigned and others to be laid off with severance packages.

Workers nevertheless perceive privatization to be threatening. Privatization-related incidents were on the upswing in both Morocco and Egypt by the end of the decade, with Egyptian workers demonstrating a higher propensity for actual work stoppages as opposed to the symbolic gestures that had characterized earlier labor protests. In Morocco, the first half of 1999 saw 32 percent more strikes than the same period in 1998, with a 44 percent increase in the number of workers involved, and a 102 percent increase in workdays lost.

Export-Led Growth and the Role of Foreign Capital

One of the cornerstones of structural adjustment programs is to encourage export production both to ease balance of payments pressures and to generate greater equity in income distribution. Firms operating under ISI programs, heavily protected and geared toward the domestic market, often were unable or unwilling to generate export earnings. To overcome this problem, government policy in most Arab countries now encourages the expansion of export production. Governments can pressure domestic firms to become more competitive by removing tariffs and import quotas and by creating special export-processing zones where domestic and foreign companies may be granted tax holidays, freedom from restrictive labor laws, and other incentives to reward export production.

Success requires an increase not just in the volume of exports, but also in the diversity of exports, in expansion of trading partners, and in the generation of jobs and new sources of income. But this has proven difficult. Lebanon would like to return to its unique pre-1975 niche as the conduit for financial and commercial services for its Arab neighbors, but that role has been rendered obsolete by the rise of alternative suppliers. Jordan would like to return to its pre-1990 niche as trade channel to Iraq, but the scope of this trade has been restricted by economic sanctions on Iraq.

The World Bank and IMF often argue that increased equity in income distribution is generated by export industries, especially to the extent that their labor-intensive techniques, in industries such as textiles and electronics, create new jobs. In other regions of the world, especially Asia, such industries have also proven to be important avenues for female employment. However, the hiring of women is related to the fact that these enterprises tend to pay low wages and provide few protections, particularly in the special export-processing zones.

In Morocco, a careful study found highly inequitable conditions in some important export industries, including textiles and the citrus and vegetable sectors.[11] Greater equity can be found in those export industries that (a) use a labor-intensive technology or hire in a labor market without fierce competition on the supply side (inducing offers of higher wages), (b) have widespread private ownership of productive operations and thus broad dispersal of profits, or (c) distribute benefits widely via public spending on social goods like education.

The government-owned and -operated Moroccan phosphate industry is an example of the last (Bourguignon and Morrisson, 1989: 175–177). Thus exporting, in and of itself, does not necessarily lead to greater equity; rather, social and political arrangements are key.

Reform in Oil-Rich Countries

Integration into the global economy is not new for the oil-rich countries of the Arabian peninsula and Gulf, insofar as their modern development has been dependent on trade for decades. Recognizing their vulnerability to oil price fluctuations, most of these countries began efforts to diversify their economies during the oil price boom of the 1970s. However, the decline of oil prices that began in the mid-1980s diminished the resources available to them even as population growth led to increasing demand for social spending.[12] The effect was particularly noticeable in Saudi Arabia, where per capita income fell by more than half, from around U.S.$16,000 in the early 1980s—among the highest in the world—to about U.S.$7,000 in 1998. Thus, although they are less susceptible to influence from multilateral lenders than are the oil-poor countries, the Arab Gulf governments and Iran have been pressed by circumstances to adopt more market-oriented policies.

State-owned enterprises continue to dominate the peninsula economies, but steps have been taken to make them friendlier to domestic private and foreign investment. For example, Saudi Arabia liberalized its thirty-year-old law restricting direct foreign investment, and may also reduce its foreign corporate tax rates. In Kuwait, where there are no income taxes and no taxes on native-owned businesses, reforms to allow increased foreign participation in direct and indirect investment are under way. Bahrain, seeking to become a regional trading center, has steadily liberalized business laws and practices, and imposes no taxes on individual or corporate earnings. Even Oman, the most recent oil-rich economy to emerge, has a strategy for private-sector development.

Privatization is also in process. Oman appears to be the most advanced, with sell-off programs in electric power, telecommunications, air transport, and banking. The Kuwaiti public investment authority has divested itself of equity holding in the telecommunications and cement industries, and privatization is being considered in power, healthcare, food products, education, and housing. Saudi

Arabia is expected to privatize telecommunications and electric power, while Bahrain may sell government interests in several service areas, including transport, electricity, and water.

Curbing public expenditures on social programs is another important but difficult tool of economic liberalization. Several of the Gulf regimes have been endeavoring to reduce fiscal expenditures, although the recovery of oil prices in the year 2000 may have weakened their resolve. So far, only Saudi Arabia has reduced the generous subsidies and social protections instituted after the oil price boom, cutting price supports in the mid-1990s on wheat, energy supply, utilities, and air travel, and reducing expenditures on health, education, and other social services. Kuwait is considering a five-year plan to reduce subsidies and government employment to citizens, and has raised fees charged on healthcare and utilities to expatriate workers. Oman's government cut capital spending in 1997 and 1998 in order to reduce the deficit, although it increased spending on education and healthcare, both of which are still provided to the populace virtually free of charge. The Bahraini government financed its deficits in the late 1990s through domestic borrowing and liquidation of its overseas financial assets and thus avoided cutting public spending.

During the heyday of the oil boom, the oil-rich countries came to rely extensively on foreign workers for the performance of manual labor, at first from the poorer Arab countries and then increasingly from South, East, and Southeast Asia. The conditions faced by these expatriates, who were denied citizenship and organizing rights and sometimes treated as indentured servants, has been criticized by international labor and human rights organizations. Female domestic workers seem to have the least protection of all. While peninsula governments have resisted reforms in this regard, the recent pressures on fiscal budgets, along with domestic labor force growth, have prompted efforts to generate more private-sector employment opportunities for natives. In Saudi Arabia, the 1997 workforce included 2.5 million natives and 4.7 million non-Saudis. Efforts to curb the number of foreign workers make it more expensive for employers to recruit expatriates, and the government is offering soft loans and contracts to private companies that meet the targets for hiring Saudis. On a larger scale, about 90 percent of the workforce in the UAE is expatriate. Efforts to achieve the stated national objective of "Emiratization" have imposed minimum quotas for the employment of nationals and banned the import of unskilled labor from certain countries. Similarly, Oman has closed certain jobs to foreigners in its "Omanization" campaign. In Kuwait, where more than 90 percent of working citizens are employed by the government, the regime is now offering subsidies to private-sector employers who hire Kuwaitis.

Conclusion

Despite significant differences in their demographics and resource endowments, the developing countries of the Middle East and North Africa face a common set of economic pressures as they confront globalization. Throughout the region, growing integration with the international economy leads countries to promote exports, to open themselves to greater foreign investment and imports, to privatize key sectors of the economy, and to cut back on government employment at least in relative, if not absolute, terms.

The pressures to conform to neoliberal orthodoxy are greatest in those countries that have suffered chronic balance of payments difficulties and debt overhang. It is these countries that have adopted the most stringent programs of stabilization and structural adjustment. They have often cut social protection programs, lifted long-standing price controls on many items, privatized, and begun to reorient production toward greater and more diversified exports. In the oil-rich countries of the Arabian peninsula, where a significant consequence of government generosity to natives has been reliance on cheap imported labor to fill jobs from the menial to the professional, governments are undertaking campaigns to indigenize their labor forces.

Although proponents of economic orthodoxy promise that growth and prosperity will result from neoliberal policies, the evidence has been mixed. In the short run, numerous countries adopting stringent stabilization and structural adjustment programs—both in the region and elsewhere—have witnessed rising levels of poverty and growing gaps between rich and poor after several years of "structural adjustment," even as overall macroeconomic indicators show improvement.

For working women, the economic changes under way raise a number of questions. Will private-sector employers be as open to hiring females as governments have been? Will provisions for working women's gender-based requirements, such as maternity leave, time off for nursing, and subsidized daycare, be available in private-sector firms and export-oriented industries? If women released from civil service or public-sector positions cannot find alternative employment, will social and cultural pressures and the reduced opportunity cost lead them to bear more children? Such questions will be addressed, from several different angles, in the remainder of this book.

Notes

1. Gross domestic product is the total value of all the final goods and services produced within the geographic borders of a country in a given year, "domestic" referring to the location of production, regardless of who the producers are (e.g., General Motors' production in Egypt is counted in Egypt's GDP). *[Location]*

2. Export earning percentages will fluctuate based on annual production and price movements.

3. Gross national product is the total value of all the final goods and services produced by the corporations and citizens of a country wherever in the world they produce them; that is, GNP is defined by the nationality of the producers not by the place of production. Gross national income (GNI) is the value of all the employee compensation, profits, rents, and interest earned by the corporations and citizens of a country, wherever they earn it, that is repatriated to their home country (General Motors' repatriated profits from its production in Egypt are counted as U.S. GNI). Gross national income is by definition equal to gross national product, because the value of all the contributions to production must show up in the final value of the products they jointly make. The distinction between domestic product (or income) and national product (or income) can be significant. For example, for a country like Jordan, many of whose citizens depend for their livelihood on remittances from their relatives working abroad, the national measure is greater than the domestic measure, and gives a better indication of the standard of living. *[nationality] [nationality]*

4. For an explanation of the limitations to the use of GDP and GNP statistics, see Baumol and Blinder, 1999: 99–101.

5. This presentation follows, in part, the analysis by Joel Beinin (1999: 18–22).

6. For a critical evaluation of structural adjustment programs in other regions, see Rapley, 2002. The World Bank itself admits to some of the failures of SAPs in its *World Development Report 2000–2001*, pp. 64–72. *[TRUE]*

7. *Middle East Economic Digest* 41, no. 22 (May 30, 1997): 13.

8. Alternative forms of privatization and their implications are discussed in more depth in Posusney, 1999.

9. The discussion of privatization, unemployment, and labor laws that follows draws on Mikawy and Posusney, 2002; and Posusney, 2001.

Original sources are detailed in these works; only additional references are cited here.

10. Egypt's committee also had representatives from the International Labour Organization and the local legal community.

11. The measure of inequality used in the study is based on the relationship between Gini coefficients for consumption and for income derived from household surveys (Bourguignon and Morrisson, 1989: 161–162).

12. Information on the economies of the Arab Gulf countries is drawn primarily from quarterly country reports published by the Economist Intelligence Unit and annual country reports released by the Bureau of Economic and Business Affairs, U.S. Department of State.

Zafiris Tzannatos
Iqbal Kaur

2

Women in the MENA Labor Market: An Eclectic Survey

The purpose of this chapter is to review two critical aspects of women in the labor market in the Middle East and North Africa (MENA): labor force participation rates and employment dissimilarity between women and men.[1] After highlighting some of the socioeconomic characteristics of MENA, we examine the level and trends of female labor force participation rates, as well as the degree of gender segregation in the labor market, comparing the MENA statistics to data for other world regions. Though highly aggregate, the results contain some implications worthy of more detailed research.

MENA in a Global Context

The economies in the MENA region are predominantly middle income. With the exception of Yemen, average per capita income ranges from U.S.$1,250 to U.S.$3,560. The regional average of U.S.$2,050 compares favorably to most other world regions (see Table 2.1). In terms of social indicators, life expectancy at birth is relatively high in MENA, but fertility and adult female illiteracy also remain high (see Table 2.2). These aggregate figures mask, however, some significant differences between countries. For example, illiteracy rates are relatively low in Jordan and Lebanon, but this is not so for Morocco and Yemen (see Table 2.3).

There are significant gender differences in most social indicators in the MENA region. For example, there are typically twice as many illiterate women as men (Table 2.3). These gender differences are not unique to MENA, however, as similar differences are found in other world regions (see Table 2.4 and Figures 2.1 and 2.2).

55

Table 2.1   Average Per Capita Income in MENA Economies and Other Regions, 1998

	Per Capita Income (U.S.$)	PPP Per Capita Income (U.S.$)
Country		
Algeria	1,550	4,380
Egypt	1,290	3,130
Iran	1,770	5,360[a]
Jordan	1,520	3,230
Lebanon	3,560	6,150
Morocco	1,250	3,120
Tunisia	2,050	5,160
Yemen	300	740
Region		
EAP	990	3,400
ECA	2,190	4,240
LAC	3,940	6,780
MENA	2,050	4,220
SA	430	1,610
SSA	480	1,430

Source: World Bank, *World Development Report 2000* (New York: Oxford University Press, 2000).

Notes: Purchasing power parity (PPP) per capita income is GNP divided by mid-year population and converted to international dollars using PPP rates. PPP data come from the International Comparison Program (ICP), which is coordinated by the UN regional economic commissions and other international organizations. An international dollar has the same purchasing power locally as the U.S. dollar in the United States.

EAP = East Asia and Pacific, ECA = Europe and Central Asia, LAC = Latin America and Caribbean, MENA = Middle East and North Africa, SA = South Asia, SSA = sub-Saharan Africa.

a. Refers to 1997 data.

Table 2.2   Selective Regional Social Indicators, 1990s

	Fertility Rate Per Woman	Adult Female Illiteracy Rate	Female Life Expectancy at Birth
EAP	2.2	24.0	69.8
SA	3.5	64.5	62.4
SSA	5.6	52.5	53.5
MENA	4.2	50.1	67.7
LAC	3.0	14.5	72.6

Source: World Bank, *World Development Indicators 1999* (Washington, D.C.: World Bank, 1999).

Table 2.3 Adult Illiteracy Rates by Country

	Male (percentage of males age 15+)		Female (percentage of females age 15+)	
	1985	1995	1985	1995
Algeria	37.3	26.1	64.9	51.0
Egypt	40.4	36.4	70.5	61.2
Iran	40.9	21.6	63.7	34.2
Jordan	14.3	6.6	38.0	20.6
Lebanon	14.1	10.0	31.2	20.0
Morocco	45.7	43.4	70.5	69.0
Tunisia	32.2	21.4	52.7	45.4
Yemen	52.9	46.7[a]	79.5	73.7[a]

Source: World Bank, *World Development Indicators 1999* (Washington, D.C.: World Bank, 1999).
Note: a. Data from 1990.

Table 2.4 Adult Illiteracy Rates by Region

	Male (percentage of males age 15+)			Female (percentage of females age 15+)			Total		
	1985	1990	1995	1985	1990	1995	1985	1990	1995
EAP	18.5	15.1	9.5	40.5	34.6	24.1	29.4	24.5	16.9
ECA	3.0	2.0	2.0	7.0	6.0	5.0	5.0	4.0	4.0
LAC	15.5	13.6	12.4	19.6	17.3	14.5	17.6	15.1	13.4
MENA	38.2	33.0	28.0	64.6	57.5	50.1	51.4	45.1	38.7
SA	44.5	41.0	37.6	72.5	68.3	64.5	58.1	54.1	50.6
SSA	44.9	41.3	33.5	67.9	64.2	52.5	56.7	53.0	44.0

Source: World Bank, *World Development Indicators 1999* (Washington, D.C.: World Bank, 1999).

An area where MENA lags behind other regions is maternal mortality. Figure 2.3 plots the regression line between country per capita income and maternal mortality. Of course, there are many factors other than income underlying this aggregate relationship (such as availability of and access to medical services as well as household demand for different medical services for different household members). However, after controlling for income differences, maternal mortality in MENA economies is significantly higher than in countries in other regions.

Figure 2.1   Primary Education Enrollment, 1995

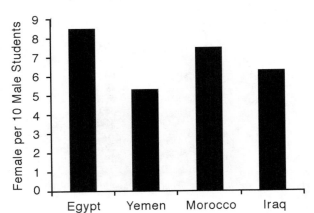

Source: World Bank and *UNESCO Statistical Yearbook 1997* (New York: UNESCO, 1997).

Figure 2.2   Gender Gap by Region, 1997

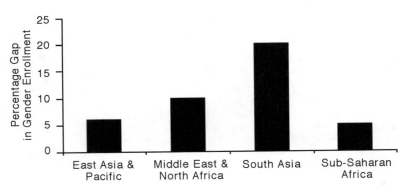

Source: SIMA database, World Bank.

There are additional dimensions of development not captured in these selective indicators. For example, women in MENA (as often elsewhere) have little access to ownership of land and other productive assets, due to a variety of reasons ranging from family and social arrangements to government regulations and laws. An example here

Figure 2.3   Maternal Mortality Rates

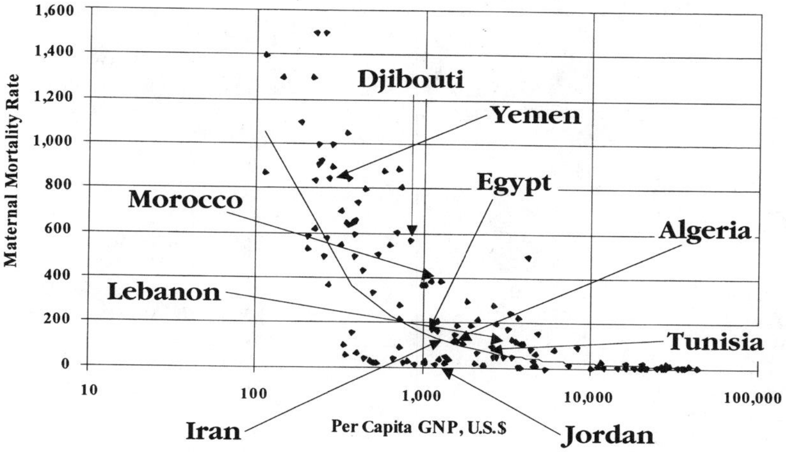

Source: World Bank, *World Development Indicators,* various years.

is Egypt, where a survey of 2,000 households showed that less than 3 percent of females own land (see Table 2.5).

At a more aggregate level, female socioeconomic indicators are summarized in the gender development index (GDI) and the gender empowerment index (GEM). The GDI takes into consideration gender disparities in life expectancy at birth and education attainment. The GEM uses variables constructed to measure the empowerment of women relative to men in political and economic spheres.[2] Table 2.6 presents the rankings for MENA economies in 1998 in terms of these two measures as well as the human development index (HDI).[3]

Table 2.5   Female Landownership in Egypt

Number of females owning land	105
Total number of females over age 15	4,750
Percentage of all females over age 15 who own land	2.2
Mean size of land owned by females (acres)	0.7

Source: Egypt Ministry of Agriculture (PCUWA)/World Bank Survey of Rural Egypt, 1995–1996.

Table 2.6   Human Development Index, Gender Development Index, and Gender Empowerment Index, 1998

	Rank HDI	GDI Rank	GDI Value	HDI Rank Minus GDI Rank[a]	GEM[b] Rank	GEM[b] Value
Algeria	107	91	0.661	−2	93	0.241
Egypt	119	99	0.604	0	88	0.258
Iran	97	84	0.691	−3	87	0.261
Jordan	92	N/A	N/A	N/A	97	0.211
Lebanon	82	74	0.718	−4	N/A	N/A
Morocco	124	103	0.570	−1	82	0.302
Tunisia	101	86	0.688	−3	74	0.345
Yemen	148	133	0.389	−10	N/A	N/A
World	N/A	N/A	0.706	N/A	N/A	N/A
LDCs	N/A	N/A	0.427	N/A	N/A	N/A
Developing (all)	N/A	N/A	0.634	N/A	N/A	N/A
Middle East	N/A	N/A	0.612	−13	N/A	N/A

Source: UNDP, *Human Development Report 1995, 1998, 2000* (New York: UNDP, 1995, 1998, 2000).

Notes: HDI refers to 174 countries. The GDI and the GEM are, however, available for fewer countries due to lack of country data on specific variables. For example, the GDI is available for 143 countries, and the GEM for 102 countries. The HDI ranks used in this table are recalculated for 143 countries for which GDI results were obtained. The value of GDI ranges from 0.932 (Canada) to 0.280 (Niger).

a. A negative figure in this column indicates that the GDI rank is lower than the HDI rank; that is, a country's position in terms of gender differences is lower than in terms of general development.

b. The value of GEM ranges from 0.790 (Sweden) to 0.121 (Niger).

Overall, the MENA region's human development index was 0.6443 in 1995, higher than that of South Asia or sub-Saharan Africa, but lower than that of Southeast Asia and Latin America (UNDP, 1995: 216).

In summary, the MENA economies are on average in the middle and upper-middle range of socioeconomic development. Although they are not the lowest in terms of female indicators, gender differences are somewhat greater than the average for other countries in these same development categories. To the extent that gender differences are the result of past norms and practices that no longer reflect current country realities and individual preferences, they can impede individual country development and the region's integration into the world economy. In this respect, female access to the labor market and patterns of employment can be key in breaking up the vicious circle of low productivity and poor outcomes for women.

Female Labor Force Participation

Globally, most men during prime age are in the labor force. Male labor force participation is typically 90 percent or more with little variance across countries. In contrast, female labor force participation rates (i.e., the percentages of women who are officially classified to be in the labor force) are much lower and also more variable than men's (see Table 2.7). However, men's labor force participation rates have shown a tendency to decline over time (due to longer education enrollment or retirement opportunities), while women's labor force participation rates are on the rise. Lower male and increasing female participation rates are also found in the MENA economies. But female labor force participation rates in the MENA region remain the lowest in the world (see Table 2.8). This may be due to several factors whose effects have not been fully analyzed.

For example, setting aside measurement issues, cultural and reli-

Table 2.7   Average Regional Labor Force Participation Rates, Ages 20–59 Years, Percentage

	Number of Countries	Earliest Census, 1950s/1960s		Latest Census, 1980s/1990s	
		Male	Female	Male	Female
East/Southern Africa	8	92	35	90	45
West Africa	6	91	61	90	57
East Asia and Pacific	20	93	35	89	51
South Asia	4	94	39	91	29
East and Central Europe	9	94	62	90	76
Rest of Europe	26	95	37	90	54
Middle East	8	93	12	92	23
North Africa	5	93	N/A	91	14
Americas	38	94	33	90	47
Total	124	94	36	90	48

Source: Zafiris Tzannatos, "Women and Labor Market Changes in the Global Economy: Growth Helps, Inequalities Hurt, and Public Policy Matters," *World Development* 27, no. 3 (1999): 555–569, based on ILO census data.

gious determinants of female labor force participation can be significant. Noneconomic analyses on this issue are abundant and here we report the results of a simple cross-country regression of the female participation rate on a country's major religion (see Table 2.9). Major religion is defined as the religion that is followed by more than half the population (a country with no majority, such as a distribution of 40 percent Protestants and 40 percent Catholics, is defined as having "no major religion"). Though the economic determinants of female labor force participation are well researched and established, this

Table 2.8   Female Labor Force, Percentage of Total, by Region, 1996

EAP	44
ECA	46
LAC	33
MENA	26
SA	32
SSA	42
High income	43

Source: World Bank, *World Development Indicators 1999* (Washington, D.C.: World Bank, 1999).

Table 2.9   Percentage Increase/Decrease of Female Labor Force Participation Rate, by Country's Major Religion

Hinduism	−1
Buddhism	−1
Confucianism	−7
Roman Catholic	−15
Islam	−26
No major religion	+10

Source: Zafiris Tzannatos, "Women and Labor Market Changes in the Global Economy: Growth Helps, Inequalities Hurt, and Public Policy Matters," *World Development* 27, no. 3 (1999): 555–569.

Notes: Based on a simple regression of the female labor force participation rate on religion: (a) omitted religious category: others (i.e., not listed in the above); (b) no other variable included in the regression; (c) the coefficients on Hinduism, Buddhism, and Confucianism are insignificant; (d) results are based on data for 124 countries in 1980/1990s; (e) the dependent variable is the official female labor force participation rate and the independent variable is a 0–1 variable, 1 if the majority of the country's population follows the specific religion; (f) the constant term was 0.49 and R2 of the regression was 0.36.

simple regression "explains" one-third of the cross-country variance of female labor force participation and suggests that some religions (a proxy for different norms and social values) have a significantly greater association with the level of the officially measured female labor force participation rate than others.

Notwithstanding their low levels in the MENA region (and somewhat related to this), the female participation rates in MENA are increasing faster than in any other region. The average female labor force participation rate for the MENA countries was 23 percent in the 1990s and constitutes a substantial increase (near doubling) over the 1950s and 1960s, compared to a world increase of one-third.[4] This increase can be generally confirmed by examining the change in the share of the labor force that is female in a given country (see Table 2.10). Despite the low levels of female labor force participation in the MENA economies, women are entering the labor market at greater rates than before and the most recent estimates suggest that approximately one-third of women (fifteen years and older) are in the labor force (see Table 2.11).

Patterns of Female Employment

As a global characteristic, most women are employed in only a few industries (such as light manufacturing or services), certain occupations (such as unskilled or clerical), and types of work (such as infor-

Table 2.10 Female Labor Force, Percentage of Total, 1985 and 1996

	1985	1996
Algeria	21	25
Egypt	27	29
Iran	21	25
Jordan	16	22
Lebanon	25	28
Morocco	34	35
Tunisia	29	31
Yemen	31	29

Source: World Bank, *World Development Indicators 1998* (Washington, D.C.: World Bank, 1999).

Table 2.11   Female Labor Force Participation Rate, 1998 (ages 15+)

	Female Labor Force Participation Rate (%)	Relative to Male Rate (%)
Algeria	28	36
Egypt	34	43
Iran	28	35
Jordan	25	32
Lebanon	29	37
Morocco	34	51
Tunisia	36	46
Yemen	30	36

Source: UNDP, *Human Development Report 2000* (New York: UNDP, 2000).

mal activities). This leads to considerable gender-segregated patterns of employment (Sayed and Tzannatos, 1999).

Employment by Industry

Agriculture is still the largest employer of women. With the exception of Lebanon, the share of women workers in agriculture is generally in excess of 40 percent and more than 60 percent in Yemen, Iran, and Morocco (see Table 2.12). However, if we consider women's engagement in informal types of activities in agriculture, the actual percentage could be much higher. In terms of changes over time, the trend of female employment in agriculture between 1980 and 1994 is negative, except for the case of Egypt, which is discussed in more detail below. Excluding Egypt, male agricultural employment appears to be declining at a slightly faster rate.

Services constitute a sizable and growing sector of employment for women. The service sector already employs more than half of female workers in Jordan and Lebanon and one-third in Algeria and Egypt. The trend is positive and strong. In contrast, the share of men in the service sector seems to have been stable or rising but, if so, more slowly than in the case of female workers.

The industrial sector remains weak in the MENA region and this is reflected in the low shares of manufacturing in employment and also in these shares' rather anemic changes over time. This applies to both female and male workers. For example, the shares have been

Table 2.12   Shares of Employment by Industry

	Agriculture				Industry				Services			
	Male as Percentage of Male Employment		Female as Percentage of Female Employment		Male as Percentage of Male Employment		Female as Percentage of Female Employment		Male as Percentage of Male Employment		Female as Percentage of Female Employment	
	1980	1994	1980	1994	1980	1994	1980	1994	1980	1994	1980	1994
Algeria	27	18	69	57	33	38	6	7	40	44	25	36
Egypt	43	32	8	43	20	23	10	9	32	38	56	31
Iran	36	30	82	73	28	26	6	9	35	44	12	18
Jordan	11	10	58	41	27	28	3	4	62	63	39	55
Lebanon	13	6	20	10	29	34	21	22	58	59	59	68
Morocco	48	35	72	63	23	28	14	19	29	37	14	18
Tunisia	33	22	53	42	30	33	32	32	37	44	16	26
Yemen	60	50	98	88	19	22	1	6	21	29	1	7

Source: World Bank, *World Development Indicators 1998* (Washington, D.C.: World Bank, 1998).

practically the same for women in Algeria, Egypt, Jordan, Lebanon, and Tunisia, and have generally increased slightly in the other countries. Similarly for men, the shares remained almost the same in Iran and Jordan, and increased in Algeria, Lebanon, and Morocco with smaller changes in Egypt, Tunisia, and Yemen.

Level and Type of Employment

Almost half of the women in the formal sector of MENA's labor markets are engaged in lower-level white-collar jobs such as typists and clerks. At the same time women tend to be underrepresented in professional and managerial positions, and are overrepresented in unskilled jobs. A few women hold administrative and managerial positions (see Table 2.13). In Algeria and Tunisia the respective shares are 6 percent and 13 percent, in Egypt 11 percent, and in Jordan 5 percent. These figures are in general below the 40 percent mark in advanced countries and 15–20 percent in developing countries (UNDP and NIP, 1998). A higher share is obtained for women who work in professional and technical positions, but this often means occupations such as nursing, teaching, and social and clerical

Table 2.13   Women's Share in Administration/Management Positions and in Parliament, Percentage

	Administration and Management	Parliamentary Seats
Algeria	5.9	3.2
Egypt	11.5	2.0
Iran	3.5	4.9
Jordan	4.6	1.7
Morocco	25.6	0.7
Tunisia	12.7	6.7

Source: UNDP, *Human Development Report 1998* (New York: UNDP, 1998), tab. 3, p. 134.

work. Women's share in total professional and technical workers ranges from 18 percent in Tunisia to 26–28 percent in Egypt and over 33 percent in Jordan.

Formal and Informal Sectors

Although women in the MENA region have been entering the labor force in record numbers, much of the increase has come from the informal sector. The significance of this sector for women's employment (especially through subcontracting arrangements) is widely cited, but difficult to accurately document and analyze in the absence of relevant statistics: most official information relates to formal forms of employment. Nevertheless, when data exist, they suggest that many new female entrants to the informal sector tend to be the less educated young, who belong to households that have recently migrated from rural areas to urban centers. For example, a study done by the International Food Policy Research Institute (IFPRI) in 1997 on the status of women in rural Egypt indicated that more that 50 percent of informal-sector female workers were originally migrants from rural areas. The vast majority of women who sought employment in the informal sector (perhaps as high as 80 percent) came from families with very low incomes, were young (fourteen to thirty-four years of age), and had little or no education (Adams, 1997).

Informal-sector employment has traditionally been widespread in agriculture. However, this trend is slightly changing with increasing urbanization in most MENA countries. Even though underreported in official statistics (Moghadam, 1998), the urban informal sector is a significant employer for women, especially for the self-employed, unpaid family laborers, part-time workers, and domestic workers. In some cases, the informal sector is increasing; for example, a study in 1994 (as cited in Said, 1994) found that 70 percent of all new jobs created in urban areas in Morocco during the period 1986–1990 came from the expansion in self-employment, mainly home-based workers and unpaid family workers who were predominantly female. But in other cases the converse is true. In Tunisia, the informal sector constituted about 47 percent of total employment in 1980 but only 42 percent in 1984, falling to 35 percent in 1989 (World Bank, 1995).

In Egypt, the growing informal private sector (firms with fewer than ten employees) encompasses 90 percent of total private-sector employment outside agriculture and has generated many jobs for women (in the form of casual labor). However, after 1985, wages fell for the jobs dominated by women, discouraging their participation in private nonagricultural jobs and resulting in a negative annual rate of growth of 1 percent between 1988 and 1998 (see Table 2.14). At the same time, female agricultural employment increased at 4.1 percent annually. Most of the changes in both cases occurred among non-wage workers, with an 82.4 percent growth in female employment and a 28.6 percent reduction in male employment in this category (Assaad, 2002). Unlike agriculture, where nonwage work among women is growing, nonwage work outside agriculture is responsible for practically all of the decline in female private nonagricultural employment. Female wage work in this sector has in fact grown, albeit rather slowly. The growth in wage labor in the private nonagricultural sector has even outpaced the growth of male employment in the fast-growing government sector. This indicates considerable dynamism in the private sector, though it seems to be limited to males.

Employment Patterns: An International Comparison

The statistics on employment patterns in the MENA economies indeed suggest that the region has relatively fewer women workers in professional, technical, and administrative occupations than other regions (see Table 2.15). This may be the result of a vicious cycle

Table 2.14   Employment Growth in Egypt, 1988–1998, Percentage

	Male		Female		Total	
	Share of Growth	Annual Rate of Growth	Share of Growth	Annual Rate of Growth	Share of Growth	Annual Rate of Growth
Public Sector						
Government	55.6	4.5	28.1	5.4	41.8	4.8
SOEs	−11.2	−2.3	−2.9	−4.1	−7.0	−2.6
Subtotal	44.4	2.6	25.2	4.3	34.7	3.0
Private Agriculture						
Wage Work	2.7	0.6	−3.5	−6.3	−0.4	−0.2
Nonwage Work	−28.6	−3.1	82.4	4.4	27.4	1.9
Subtotal	−25.9	−1.9	78.9	4.1	26.9	1.6
Private Nonagriculture						
Wage Work	61.0	4.7	2.6	1.6	31.6	4.3
Nonwage Work	20.5	2.6	−6.8	−2.7	6.7	1.3
Subtotal	81.5	3.9	−4.1	−1.0	38.3	3.0
Total	100.0	1.9	100.0	3.4	100.0	2.5

Source: Ragui Assaad, "The Transformation of the Egyptian Labor Market: 1988–1998," in Ragui Assaad, ed., *The Labor Market in a Reforming Economy: Egypt in the 1990s* (Cairo: American University in Cairo Press, forthcoming 2002).
    Note: Figures are period averages and are subject to rounding.

reflected in the low female labor force participation rates in the region (i.e., there is an interdependency between low attachment to the labor force and occupational attainment). This interdependency affects both sides of the labor market, women and their families on the one hand and employers on the other.

To put these statistics into an international context, worldwide industrial and occupational data can be used to show the levels and changes in employment segregation in the MENA region. Using the Duncan index of segregation (Duncan and Duncan, 1955; Tzannatos, 1990), which varies between 0 (no segregation) and 1 (no men and women work in the same sector), suggests that: (1) MENA has the highest gender segregation in employment, and (2) segregation is increasing in MENA while decreasing or remaining the same in all other regions (see Table 2.16). In fact, the Duncan index for all regions/sectors has the highest value (0.49) for employees in MENA (see Tzannatos, 1999: 557).

Table 2.15   Women's Share in Major Occupational Groups by Region, 1990 (women per 100 men)

	Professional, Technical, and Related Jobs	Administration and Management	Clerical Service	Sales Workers	Production Workers
Industrialized Countries					
Western Europe	50	18	63	48	16
Other	44	32	69	41	22
Eastern Europe	56	33	73	66	27
Developing Countries					
Sub-Saharan Africa	36	15	37	52	20
Oceania	41	18	52	53	17
Latin America	49	23	59	47	17
Caribbean	52	29	62	59	21
Eastern Asia	43	11	48	42	30
Southeast Asia	48	17	48	53	21
Southern Asia	32	6	20	8	16
MENA					
Middle East	37	7	29	12	7
North Africa	29	9	22	10	10

Source: UN, *The World's Women 1995: Trends and Statistics* (New York: UN, 1995).

Table 2.16   Employment Dissimilarity (Duncan Index) by Occupation and Industry

	Occupation		Industry	
	1950s/ 1960s	1980s/ 1990s	1950s/ 1960s	1980s/ 1990s
Africa (excluding North Africa)	0.23	0.23	0.28	0.25
EAP	0.32	0.32	0.27	0.22
SA	0.20	0.20	0.15	0.20
ECA	0.27	0.26	0.21	0.26
Rest of Europe	0.41	0.40	0.34	0.30
MENA	0.36	0.46	0.38	0.40
Americas	0.52	0.45	0.45	0.37
Total	0.39	0.38	0.34	0.31

Source: Zafiris Tzannatos, "Women and Labor Market Changes in the Global Economy: Growth Helps, Inequalities Hurt, and Public Policy Matters," *World Development* 27, no. 3 (1999): 555–569.

Note: Figures are period averages.

Gender segregation is therefore a very significant issue for MENA. However, additional data will be required to shed more light on its origins and implications, as well as on education and training, wage determination mechanisms, and the interaction between work and household choices on the one hand, and family formation on the other.

Conclusion

This chapter has presented some key socioeconomic characteristics in the MENA countries and region as a whole and assessed two key aspects of the labor market from a gender perspective: the labor force participation rate and employment segregation. Although the factors underlying these aspects and the dynamism of the regional economies could not be fully addressed, this chapter points to the following:

- The MENA region is well positioned amid middle-income countries in terms of its overall social indicators.
- Although some gender differences are also found elsewhere, they tend to be more pronounced in MENA; in particular, rates of maternal mortality and the educational achievement of girls are lagging behind other regions.
- Female labor force participation rates in MENA are among the lowest in the world, though this may in part be a reflection of differences in statistical conventions and practices. However, female participation in the labor force is increasing faster in MENA than in other regions, partly because these rates are so low to begin with.
- Cultural norms may have a greater influence on female labor force participation in MENA than in other developing regions.
- Employment segregation is more acute in MENA than in other regions.
- Contrary to the case of labor force participation (which moves in a favorable direction), segregation seems to be on the rise.

These findings mask complex underlying relationships and in some cases can be interpreted differently in a gender context. For example, a high female labor force participation rate may, on the one hand, provide women with higher income and generally contribute to their empowerment. On the other hand, if women's additional employment is not accompanied by measures that alleviate work in the home, or if women cannot retain their income from work, high labor force participation can create a double burden on them. Also, some of the measured segregation identified in this chapter may reflect optimal household choices.

The statistics measured in this chapter reveal little about what is happening in the invisible part of the economy, and norms and practices that appear paradoxical at face value may be relevant in some or many respects of economic and social life. Still, some of the observed gender differences give prima facie reasons for concern, such as the gender gaps in education and the high rates of maternal mortality. This gives rise to the need for more research, which will in turn require more and better data—a deficiency particularly characteristic of the MENA region. Good data and analysis are in order before any firm policy conclusions can be drawn.

Notes

The findings, interpretations, and conclusions in this chapter are entirely of the authors and should not be attributed in any manner to the World Bank, to its affiliated organizations, or to the members of its Board of Executive Directors or the countries they represent.

1. For the World Bank, the MENA region includes Algeria, Djibouti, Egypt, Jordan, Iran, Lebanon, Morocco, Tunisia, the West Bank and Gaza, and Yemen, all of which are active borrowers, as well as Bahrain, Iraq, Kuwait, Libya, Malta, Oman, Saudi Arabia, Syria, and the United Arab Emirates. Given limitations on the availability of data, this chapter focuses on the former group.

2. The variables used to reflect economic participation are the percentage shares of administrative, managerial, professional, and technical jobs, and the variable used to reflect political participation and decisionmaking power is the percentage share of parliamentary seats.

3. HDI is calculated using three indicators: longevity, as measured by life expectancy at birth; educational attainment, as measured by a combination of the adult literacy rate and the combined gross primary, secondary, and tertiary enrollment ratio; and standard of living, as measured by GDP per capita (purchasing power parity [PPP] in U.S. dollars).

4. These figures and trends can be misleading for a number of reasons, however, such as differences in national definitions of work or in the cultur-

al acceptability of female employment. For example, according to the Turkish census of 1980 there were only 40,000 carpet weavers, while the number of looms in the country was probably in excess of half a million at that time (Berik, 1987). Similarly, in Sweden only 8 percent of farmers declared that their wives worked in 1960, but the corresponding figure for 1965 was 56 percent—this was due to the adoption of a broader (and more appropriate) definition of "work" (Nyberg, 1993).

Jennifer Olmsted # 3

Reexamining the Fertility Puzzle in MENA

Population and fertility issues are quite contentious in the Middle East and North Africa (MENA). Governments, development agencies, and community groups often have disparate views of what constitutes appropriate population policies for the region. Economists and development agencies have generally pushed for strong family planning and population control measures, arguing that economic growth and sustainable development are more attainable when population growth rates are slower. Researchers examining the situation in MENA have been alarmed by growing population rates, and have stressed the impact these rates will have on government resources and labor markets (see, e.g., Galal, 1995; Qudsi, 1996). Rising illiteracy rates and high unemployment are two outcomes that policymakers in the region fear. Some have argued though that fertility is not a problem in the region, either citing declining fertility or focusing more on a critique of population control policies, with the argument that such policies do not make good economic sense or are merely the articulation of racist, imperialist ideas emanating from the West. Some governments, particularly those representing the oil-exporting nations, have argued that higher fertility rates are important and necessary to ensure a large indigenous labor force for the future. Leaders from both the left and the Islamic communities have argued that policies aimed at reducing fertility rates not only are racist and imperialist, but also fail to address the appropriate concern: global income-distribution disparities. Feminist scholars, while sometimes agreeing with these critiques, have added another dimension, arguing that scholars and policymakers often ignore the asymmetrical impact that fertility costs and benefits, as well as economic policies, have on women and men.

While not rejecting the argument that some population policies may be racist, or may undermine the political goals of particular groups, I begin with the premise that reducing fertility is a desired goal, primarily because large families put a strain not only on infrastructure and economic resources, but also on individual women's bodies and energy. At the same time, policies in general, and structural adjustment policies in particular, may undermine attempts to reduce fertility rates. The impact of structural adjustment may reverse some of the downward trends in fertility rates that we are currently seeing in the region. As such I will ask a two-part question: What factors may be facilitating or impeding fertility declines, and how have economic conditions, gender norms, and policies contributed to changes in fertility patterns? Following the lead of other feminist scholars, I argue for a holistic approach that does not take fertility reduction to be the only goal of a fertility policy, but rather suggests that the improvement of family conditions, and particularly for women, should be an important part of fertility programs as well.

Linking Fertility to Other Socioeconomic Factors

The Economics of Fertility

Economic theory has generally approached fertility as a cost/benefit and budgeting problem, suggesting that parents choose the number of children they have based on their income, as well as the benefits and costs of children. As the cost/benefit of a child increases, the number of children will drop or rise. As income rises (holding the benefits and costs constant), families can afford more children, suggesting a positive correlation between income and fertility (see, e.g., Becker and Tomes, 1976, for an economistic discussion of children). Throughout the world, though, rising national income has been linked to declining fertility rates. This phenomenon is explained by the fact that as income has risen, the costs of having children have also risen, while the benefits have declined, particularly as industrialization has occurred.

The costs of having children include the direct costs of paying for shelter, clothing, and education, as well as the costs of foregone opportunities, particularly in terms of paid employment. Since women have generally been held responsible for most of the reproductive and productive burden of bearing and raising children, they are usually the ones who must forgo paid employment opportunities, as they find it difficult to juggle market employment and child-rearing simultaneously. Increased wage-based employment opportunities, by pulling women into the labor market, have thus contributed to reducing fertility rates.

Industrialization and modernization have also reduced the economic importance of children to families. Children historically have contributed to family well-being by providing labor and contributing income, both as children and as adults. Industrialization has led to a decrease in the importance of the family-based economy and therefore the role of child labor. However, children may provide economic benefits to parents later in life as well. As parents age, they may rely on their children for economic support, particularly if no publicly provided social safety net for the aged is in place. The more recent involvement of the state in providing social safety nets, including old-age support, further diminishes the need for parents to raise many children (see Folbre, 1994, for a historical treatment of some of these issues).

A related factor that affects both fertility and the cost of fertility is the perceived need for and cost of education. The cost of child-rearing increases as children are expected to stay in school longer and families bear at least part of the cost of schooling. As such, families may opt to have fewer children and provide them with higher levels of education. For girls there is a further link between education and fertility. Staying in school generally leads to the postponement of childbearing as well as to an increase in women's earning power or potential wages. Thus, increased education and reduced fertility are generally positively correlated.

The economics of fertility are complex, obviating a simple cost/benefit analysis. Economic factors are intertwined with cultural or policy factors, and their impact is not always clear. The flow chart represented in Figure 3.1 provides a guide to these interactions: the number of children a woman has in her lifetime (or total fertility rate) is determined by, among other things, whether she participates in the paid labor market, her level of education, and her income. At the same time, fertility is a determinant of education, labor force participation, and income. Finally, there is a causal link between working and education. As such, causality flows in both directions between work, education, and fertility. Having more children makes it more difficult for women to work or go to school, but women may have more children because they do not have access to employment or schools. Education affects fertility both directly and indirectly, as an increase in schooling may shorten the time a woman is married and thus reduce the number of children she has, and higher education may alter a woman's preference for family size. At the same time, education indirectly affects fertility by increasing a woman's likelihood of participating in the labor market.[1]

Public Policy and Fertility

Policy outcomes contribute to fertility outcomes in two ways. First, population policies may directly affect women's fertility. The availability of abortions and birth control and the funding of fertility research, for example, may affect family size. Policies that are not targeted at fertility, such as taxation, spending, and regulatory decisions, though, can also affect fertility policies. Women's employment options and even their access to the labor market may be linked to government decisions, such as policies controlling the size of the public sector, or governing the treatment of mothers in the labor market. Tax incentives may encourage or discourage large family size.

Figure 3.1   Linking Fertility, Policy, and Socioeconomic Indicators

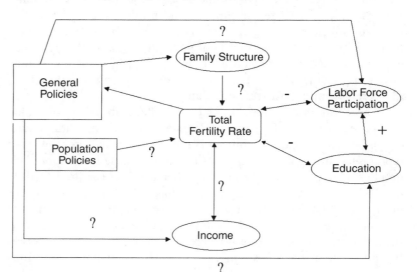

Similar arguments can be made when looking at educational outcomes. Laws outlawing child labor or mandating child education can
impact the cost/benefit of raising children. Government decisions
about spending are also important for ensuring the availability and
adequacy of schools.

Structural adjustment policies aim to increase marketization of
the economy and encourage freer trade. These policies also often
emphasize cuts in government spending, which may imply less
spending on social safety nets (poverty programs, old-age support,
etc.), infrastructural development, education, and a smaller public
sector. Decreased spending on social safety nets, public-sector
employment, and education may adversely affect families, particularly women, and indirectly lead families (and women) to perceive the
need to have more children.

Culture and Fertility

Cultural contexts also contribute to fertility patterns. For instance,
women's access to education and the labor market may be partially
defined by cultural conceptions of women's roles. Expectations
about how and when the government should interfere in markets, and
whether and how much the government should assist the poor, the
disabled, and the aged, are also influenced by culture. Finally, views
about the role and value of families are a function of culture. One
particular institution that has often been important in defining much
of the cultural rhetoric around fertility and family size is religion.
Interpreters of religion, throughout the world, have often articulated
a stand against population control policies. Community leaders and
peer groups may also help shape notions of acceptable family size.

What Can We Learn from Existing Data Trends?

Table 3.1 presents socioeconomic and demographic statistics from
the countries of the MENA region, including population, life
expectancy, literacy, total fertility rate, infant mortality, per capita
gross domestic product (GDP), unemployment, age at marriage, and
contraceptive use, as well as correlation coefficients that quantify the
relationship between total fertility rates and various other socioeconomic indicators, including income, literacy, and women's labor

Table 3.1 Basic Fertility Indicators

Country	Population in Millions	Per Capita GDP	Life Expectancy	Infant Mortality per 1,000	Unemployment	Female Labor Force Activity	Literacy	Female Literacy	Contraceptive Use	Average Age of Marriage	Total Fertility (TFR 1)	Total Fertility (TFR 2)
High Income/High Fertility												
Oman	2.0	11,710	70	30		9	35.0			19.2	7.2	6.9
Libya		9,782		68			72.4	57.4			6.4	6.4
Saudi Arabia	3.9	9,880	65	29		9	60.6	46.3		21.7	6.4	5.5
High Income/Low Fertility												
Kuwait[a]	1.8	8,326	75	13		27	76.9	72.9		22.4	3.1	3.6
UAE[a]	1.8	21,830	74	19		23	77.7	77.3		23.1	4.2	
Bahrain[a]		14,590		18		17	76.7	76.7		25.5	3.8	
Qatar[a]	0.5	22,380	72	20		19	78.1	77.4		22.7	4.3	3.6
Medium Income/High Fertility												
Syria	13.7	4,960	68	39	20.0	16	67.7	51.6	14	22.3	5.9	6.9
Iraq	19.0	3,413	66	58		23	54.6	40.9	35	24.7	5.7	6.7
Jordan[a]	4.1	4,270	70	36	25.0	10	83.9	75.4	65		5.6	4.6
Iran[a]	64.2	5,420	68	36		19	64.9	55.0			5.0	

Medium Income/Low Fertility

Tunisia	8.7	5,160	68	43	15.0	26	62.8	50.2	50	25.0	3.2	3.4
Algeria	26.7	4,870	67	55	21.4	8	57.4	44.1		23.7	4.0	4.3
Morocco	25.9	3,370	64	68	15.0	21	40.6	27.7			3.8	4.0
Egypt	56.4	3,540	64	67	15.0	9	49.1	36.1	46	22.0	3.9	3.6
Lebanon[a]	3.9	2,500	69	34	25.0	25	91.4	89.0			3.1	
Turkey[a]	59.6	5,230	67	65		45	80.5	70.1	63	21.5	3.4	2.9
Low Income/High Fertility												
West Bank and Gaza[a]		2,000				14	69.0	62.0		19.5	6.4	6.2
Yemen	13.2	2,410	51	119	26.0		41.1				7.6	
Sudan	26.6	1,620	53	78	10.5	26	42.7	30.6	9	24.1	5.7	6.1
Correlation Coefficients												
TFR 1	-0.12	-0.48	0.38			-0.51	-0.46	-0.29		-0.49	1.00	0.91
TFR 2	-0.07	-0.31	0.24			-0.26	-0.37	-0.35		-0.56	0.91	1.00
GDP	1.00	0.56	-0.61			-0.06	0.31	0.49		-0.10	-0.12	-0.07

Sources: UNDP, *Human Development Report 1995* (New York: UNDP, 1995); Marianne Heiberg and Geir Ovensen, *Palestinian Society in Gaza, West Bank, and Arab Jerusalem: A Survey of Living Conditions,* FAFO report no. 151 (Oslo: Fafo Institute for Applied Social Science, 1993); World Bank, *Developing the Occupied Territories: An Investment in Peace* (Washington, D.C.: World Bank, 1993); and Sulayman al-Qudsi, Ragui Assaad, and Radwan Shaban, "Labor Markets in the Arab Countries: A Survey," paper presented at the First Annual Conference on Development Economics, Cairo, 1993.

Notes: Due to the small number of observations, correlation coefficients were not calculated for unemployment and contraceptive use.
a. Female literacy rates are relatively similar to overall literacy rates (within 10 percent).

force participation rates. There is a great degree of variability across countries in all these indicators. The wealthiest country, Qatar, is fourteen times richer than Sudan, which has a per capita income of only U.S.$1,620. Total fertility rates in the region also vary a great deal, ranging from 2.9 to 7.6.[2] Literacy rates vary from 35 to 91 percent, with women's literacy having a slightly larger spread, from 27.7 to 89 percent. Women's labor force participation rates range from 9 to 45 percent. The rich Gulf countries are split between those with high and low total fertility rates, while the same is true for the poorer countries. The correlation coefficient between per capita GDP and total fertility rate is negative, suggesting that the pattern seen in the rest of the world, where rising income is linked to declines in fertility, is also occurring in MENA. The small coefficient (-0.12), though, suggests that the link remains quite weak.[3] Countries that have reduced their fertility rates to an average of 4 or fewer children per woman include Kuwait, Bahrain, Lebanon, Turkey, Tunisia, Egypt, and Morocco. The first two have high per capita income, but the other five are developing countries with mid-range incomes. North African countries, with the exception of Sudan and Libya, although relatively poor, have been strikingly successful in reducing fertility rates compared to other parts of the region. Only in Sudan, Yemen, and the small Gulf countries do we see strong evidence that rising income is leading to falling fertility in the region. Poverty is linked to high fertility, but observed patterns in the Gulf suggest that for some countries increased income is still leading to increased fertility, although this conclusion has not been widely tested at the microeconomic level.[4] At the same time, some poor countries have experienced decreases in fertility rates, despite low income levels.

Literacy and labor force participation seem somewhat more closely linked to changes in fertility, but a look at individual countries suggests that the evidence is mixed. The correlation coefficient between literacy and fertility is -0.46, suggesting that increasing education is one important way of reducing fertility. Certainly the examples of the smaller Gulf countries, Turkey and Lebanon, suggest that this negative relationship is possible, but education alone is no panacea.

One of the important distinctions that must be made is between overall literacy and female literacy. The data suggest that women's literacy has lagged behind men's. A disturbing, although not universal, trend is evident when one examines female literacy rates in the region, which suggests a significant gender gap. The average female literacy rate in the Arab world is 40.7 percent, and female literacy as a percentage of men's is only 62 percent, which is similar to rates among the least developed countries, although few MENA countries are in this category. Countries such as Saudi Arabia and Syria are examples where the gap remains disturbingly large, while Lebanon, Kuwait, the United Arab Emirates, and Qatar have been able to narrow the gap considerably.[5] Dropout rates, particularly among girls, remain quite high in Egypt, Morocco, Tunisia, and Yemen (World Bank, 1997: 4). Even more problematic is the fact that the correlation coefficient between women's literacy and fertility is much weaker, −0.29, than the correlation between fertility and overall literacy. The second set of correlation coefficients suggests a somewhat weaker relationship between overall literacy and fertility, but a somewhat stronger relationship between female literacy and fertility.

While data at the macro level are somewhat discouraging in terms of the relation between fertility and women's literacy, at the micro level there is substantial evidence that more education leads to smaller families. Philippe Fargues (as cited in Khlat, Deeb, and Courbage, 1997) states that women's education is a clear determinant of fertility decline in the region. I found that higher education of women (but not men) was linked to reduced family size among Palestinians (Olmsted, 1998a). Susan Cochrane, Ali Khan, and Ibrahim Khodair Osheba (1990) report that education is negatively correlated with desired fertility rates in Egypt. Somewhat contradictorily, Aida Hudson (1998) found no correlation between contraceptive use and education in a West Bank village.

In looking at female labor force participation, we also see a fairly strong negative relationship between fertility and women's paid work. In fact, one factor that can explain high fertility rates in MENA compared with other parts of the world is low women's labor force participation, since MENA has some of the lowest labor force participation and highest fertility rates in the world. Still, there are a number of outliers. Iraq and Sudan, for instance, are two countries with relatively high rates of labor force participation and fertility. At the same time, Egypt and Algeria have low fertility rates and low labor force participation rates. And while for most of the other statistics, Egypt, Algeria, Tunisia, and Morocco look quite similar, in this case they look quite different. Labor force participation rates thus tell only a partial story.

Differences in the age of marriage in the region may also explain some of the fertility differences. The correlation coefficient between age of marriage and fertility rates is -0.50. Yet it seems unlikely that the difference between an average age of marriage in Kuwait of twenty-two and in Oman of nineteen can explain fertility differences of almost four children. Studies using household data sets also confirm that women who marry later have fewer children and obtain more education (Olmsted, 1998a, 1998b). Again, this variable provides only a partial answer, while reinforcing the need to look at how all these economic and social factors interact. The age at which a woman marries may be closely linked to the number of children she bears, as well as to her educational achievements and likelihood of participating in the labor market.

The data suggest that education and women's work provide important explanations of fertility, but none alone provide a complete answer. The interaction between each of the socioeconomic variables is further complicated by the two-way causality and the complex interactions between them. Are women marrying young because they have no educational opportunities, or is the early age of marriage shortening the time they spend in school? Are they staying out of the labor force because of their high fertility rates, or are they having more children because of their limited labor-market options? Are low education levels causing high fertility rates, or vice versa? In fact, all of the variables—literacy, labor force participation, income, and fertility—are interdependent. As Fargues (1995) has argued, researchers cannot look at any single factor in isolation. Education cannot be considered without also looking at women's access to labor markets. At the same time, women's access to labor markets is linked to the number of children they have already had, which in turn may be a function of their level of education.

By examining the data trends we can gain some insight into fertility patterns in the MENA region, but cannot necessarily address all the issues contributing to fertility outcomes. It is also important to examine the interaction between policy and culture and economic outcomes, and in particular, the reasons for women's continued lack of economic independence and how this contributes to fertility outcomes. Women's low labor force participation and literacy rates certainly do contribute to this outcome, but these trends are in turn linked to factors such as the strength of patriarchy, the ideology of Islam, and the shortsightedness, ineptitude, or recalcitrance of policy.

Linking Economy, Culture, and Policy in Explaining MENA Fertility

Women's Employment

Reasons given for low recorded labor force participation rates for women include high fertility (again suggesting the symbiotic relationship), low education levels, patriarchy, Islam, wage discrimination, the type of economic development, and lack of employment opportunities.[6] While a commonly held belief is that low labor force participation rates are somehow linked to Islam, some scholars have disputed this claim. A number of Islamic countries, particularly those outside the Middle East, do not have low female labor force participation rates. Ivy Papps (1993) found that even within the region religiosity was not a factor in predicting people's attitudes about women's economic roles among groups in four countries: Egypt, Jordan, Morocco, and Turkey. She concludes that culture and the strength of patriarchy in the region are far more important considerations than religion.

Nadia Hijab (1988) discusses the role of gender ideology in constraining women's access to the public sphere and more specifically to wage labor in the Arab world. She argues that women's access to employment remains contested, but that researchers have often overstated the importance of culture and religion. At the same time, it is clear that, given certain cultural norms, the types and locations of employment available to women are important. Families still view certain kinds of work, such as work outside the public sector, as unacceptable for women. Low education may also in part explain low labor force participation rates. There is ample evidence both regionally and globally that increased education leads to higher labor force participation rates for women. But even compared to other countries with similar female literacy rates, the MENA region lags behind.

Others have emphasized the importance of economic structure in determining women's employment. Valentine Moghadam (1995c) argues that development patterns in the region have not been conducive to female employment. MENA economies have generally been based on the extraction and heavy-manufacturing sectors, where women's employment opportunities may be limited. High unemployment may also discourage women from entering the labor force. As can be seen in Table 3.1, a number of countries in the region have been experiencing high unemployment rates. Women may be particularly vulnerable to unemployment for a number of reasons. First, as in other parts of the world, they are likely to face sex-based discrimination. In addition, unemployment in the region is concentrated primarily among new entrants to the labor market, who are more likely to be women than men. Yet despite high levels of unemployment women remain hopeful about job prospects and continue entering the labor market at high rates. Female labor force growth rates throughout the region average 4.49 percent annually, with Jordan in the lead, at 6.06 percent, and Bahrain coming in last at 3.49 percent (Qudsi, Assaad, and Shaban, 1993).

The Role of Patriarchy

Patriarchy has been recognized as a force that restricts women's access to paid employment and more generally determines the level of women's economic well-being in many parts of the world. Patriarchy is generally defined as a system where men dominate women, primarily through the enforcement of strict gender-role ideologies, with the argument that women are responsible for reproductive labor and are more limited in their access to the public sphere. Patriarchal systems often marginalize women by defining them as economic dependents and nonproductive members of society. Feminist scholars have pointed out that far from being dependents, women provide vital labor and care. In patriarchal societies women and men are mutually dependent, since men require reproductive labor to function in the public sphere and women require the fruits of men's market labor to manage the reproductive sphere. Unfortunately, this division of labor contains a power asymmetry because of men's greater access to money.

In MENA, traditional gender roles prevail and as such women's economic dependency rates continue to be very high. Because women's labor force participation rates are low and their unemployment rates are high, their income-generating abilities remain limited.[7] In addition, state-sponsored safety nets remain limited. While the degree of control over women's labor differs in the region, most women have trouble obtaining their own income.

A simplistic interpretation of patriarchy would be to argue that high fertility levels among certain populations are merely a result of men imposing their desires for large families on women against their will. This argument is contradicted by evidence on desired fertility rates for the region. On the issue of who articulates a desire for large families, for instance, Rahma Bourqia (1995) interviewed rural Moroccan women and found that their desired fertility levels averaged between four and five children, not far from the actual rate of 5.5. Cochrane and her colleagues (1990) found that couples in rural, upper Egypt had a desired fertility rate of five children, with wives desiring more children than husbands. This number is considerably higher than measured total fertility rates for Egypt, which are closer to four. All these numbers indicate that desired fertility rates, particularly among certain subpopulations in the region, remain quite high. Homa Hoodfar (1997) too finds that poor women (in Cairo) express a desire to have many children, but she goes beyond simply linking poverty and fertility rates, pointing out the role of social expectations and status in determining fertility. Poor women, she states, articulate a desire to have many children because they believe it stabilizes their marriages and decreases the likelihood of divorce, as well as increasing their status in the community.

Hoodfar's conclusion that women have children to maintain their marriages and increase their status does not preclude an economic explanation of these outcomes, but rather suggests that the patriarchal structure of society determines women's economic dependency and hence their desire and need for large families. For most Egyptian women their economic well-being is linked to the presence of a male provider, beginning with a father, then a husband, and finally one or more male children to support them economically. In much of MENA, and patriarchal societies in general, women who do not have children are not only vulnerable to the threat of divorce, as well as reduced social status due to being childless, they are also at a much higher risk of poverty, particularly in old age.

The data on the average age of marriage presented in Table 3.1 also suggest tight control of women's sexuality, which is generally a component of patriarchy. Although data on the percentage of women who are married are unavailable, anecdotal evidence suggests that the rate of marriage is very high in the region. Thus the structure of marriage and the perceived need to control women's sexuality are important parts of the fertility story.

Does Islam Play a Role?

Some scholars have argued that Islam plays a role in reinforcing patriarchal control in the region and that its presence can explain higher than average fertility rates. This conclusion is problematic for two reasons. First, it does not explain why fertility rates differ across Islamic countries. Second, it presents Islam as a monolithic force, without problematizing different views within Islam. Certainly there is evidence from around the world that religion plays a role in attitudes about birth control. In the case of MENA, although Islam is not the only religion practiced in the region, it does dominate the culture and ideology. The position of Islam on population control and fertility has been articulated by religious leaders and followers in MENA in different ways.

First, interpretations of whether birth control is acceptable within Islam are quite varied. Proceedings from a conference in Rabat, Morocco, which included scholars and political leaders from throughout the Islamic world, provide ample evidence that both birth control and abortion can be interpreted as permissible within Islam (International Planned Parenthoood Federation, 1971). And yet much of the rhetoric in MENA suggests that at least those who are vocal about the subject are often those who are against birth control. Saad Eddin Ibrahim (1995), for instance, finds that part of the reason population control in Egypt has not been more vigorously pursued is that imams, even those working in state mosques, do not consider population growth a problem in Egypt. In contrast, they generally view attempts to reduce population as Western propaganda. Ibrahim also provides some insight into when birth control is not practiced due to religious reasons. In his survey of 503 women, he found that 31 percent found birth control "religiously or morally repugnant," and therefore did not practice it. Clearly, more research is needed to understand how widespread the perception is that Islam does not condone birth control and how much this affects actual fertility rates in the region. In addition, one might ask whether less extreme views of birth control within Islam are widely articulated, and if not, why this is the case.

What does seem to emerge in looking at a few case studies is that religious leaders interpret the question of birth control through their own political lens. While there is generally a political, anti-Western rhetoric around the pronatalist policies of many Islamist groups, views on birth control have also evolved over time.[8] What still needs further illumination, though, is how important conservative Islamic rhetoric is in the determination of fertility outcomes. Ibrahim's research in Egypt suggests that conservative Islamic forces may be somewhat effective. By contrast, Hudson (1998) surveyed West Bank Palestinian villagers and found that only 7 percent felt family size was determined by God, and only 3 percent did not use birth control for religious reasons. Georges Sabagh, Jodi Nachtwey, and Mark Tessler (1998) found that religious practices such as veiling were weak predictors of fertility outcomes and desires, and that while some were linked to higher fertility outcomes, some were linked to lower outcomes, suggesting that the influence of Islam on fertility behavior is complex and ambiguous. While rhetoric opposing birth control exists within Islam, its effectiveness is questionable.

The Current and Potential Influence of Policy

While most development scholars argue that fertility reduction should be a goal in the region, a number of MENA governments continue to pursue pronatalist policies. Both the official articulation of pronatalist policies, and actual government policies that encourage large families by providing citizens with incentives, such as tax relief and income subsidies, may be contributing to high fertility outcomes. Even among countries that do articulate the need to reduce fertility rates, success varies.

Abdel Omran and Farzaneh Roudi (1993) categorized MENA countries into four groups: those that want to increase, maintain, or reduce fertility, and those that have no intervention policy. Omran and Roudi further divided the countries by access to contraception. Egypt, Jordan, and Yemen were among the countries advocating reducing fertility and supporting the provision of birth control. Upon examining their total fertility rates, it seems that only Egypt has been successful. Iraq and Kuwait were endorsing policies aimed at increasing fertility, and in Iraq the state was limiting access to contraception. The data suggest that Iraq's policy has been more successful than Kuwait's. Stated policy in Oman, Qatar, and Saudi Arabia was to maintain existing fertility levels, and not to encourage birth control use. Given the current high levels of fertility in Oman and Saudi Arabia, this is tantamount to encouraging high total fertility rates. Bahrain, Lebanon, and Syria, while not having official policies on fertility, did support access to birth control, but with differing results. In Bahrain and Lebanon the fertility rate is relatively low, below 4, while in Syria the fertility rate is 6.9.

Thus direct government policy at the national level is not a good predictor of fertility rates. Among countries with population control programs, one aspect that explains the ineffectiveness of government policy is implementation strategy, particularly dissemination of information about availability and use of contraceptives. Ibrahim (1995) argues that while official policy may articulate support for population control, implementation of the government line may be sporadic, as is the case in Egypt, where local staff, particularly doctors and local politicians, are often quite unsupportive of the government program.

Another aspect that is often ignored by policymakers is the impact of indirect policies on fertility outcomes. As Table 3.1 suggests, it is important to identify not only those policies that directly impact fertility, such as family planning and population control, but also those that have an indirect impact, which may be the result of a lack of government-provided social safety nets, shifts in macroeconomic policy, or other factors. Perhaps direct fertility policies have been unsuccessful in part because of the impact of indirect policies. One way to reduce fertility may be to focus more on general policies, such as spending in the areas of public-sector employment, social safety nets, and education.

While targeted family planning is important, a far more holistic approach to fertility, which keeps in mind the role of social safety nets, economic insecurity, and particularly the economically dependent position of women, will be more effective than one that simply pushes for contraceptive access and education. In particular, policymakers need to be especially aware of the impact of structural adjustment programs (SAPs), which have led to increased economic hardship for many families and particularly for women. Feminist scholars such as Diane Elson (1991) have argued that SAPs increase both the productive and the reproductive demands on women's time, as well as increasing their economic insecurity. How SAPs will affect women's fertility rates remains to be seen, but as to whether increased economic hardship is causing women to have more children, or whether the reduction in resources and increase on women's work is causing women to restrict their fertility, certainly economic theory suggests that the former is a possibility.

Unfortunately, not many studies have addressed the specific record concerning the impact of cuts in government spending on women's economic dependency in MENA, in part because SAPs are a recent phenomenon and in part because the gender implications of SAPs have often been ignored. There is ample evidence that women employed in the paid labor market are overrepresented in the public sector in MENA (Qudsi, Assaad, and Shaban, 1993) and therefore that they will be hardest hit by reductions in government employment. Looking at the case of Egypt, Mervat Hatem (1994) argues that policymakers' emphasis on reducing government spending has asymmetrically affected women, who are more likely to be employed in the public sector. Although Hatem does not address the fertility implications of this policy, one could argue that when employment opportunities become less available to women, they are pushed back into the home and experience increased economic dependency on male household members, as well as the reduced opportunity costs of having children. It is too early to see the effects of SAPs on fertility in Egypt and other countries in the region, but future research must address the question of whether SAPs could lead to a stagnation or even an increase in fertility rates. More generally, the MENA region has provided very little in the way of social safety nets, the absence of which has doubtless kept fertility rates high. Without these in place, women's economic position could worsen if fertility rates decline.

Another dangerous result of these policies is that due to increased economic and social instability in the region, political instability has increased. Political protests to economic reforms have occurred in many countries, including Morocco, Algeria, Tunisia, Sudan, Egypt, and Jordan (Seddon, 1993; Richards and Waterbury, 1996). In part as a reaction to increased economic hardship, there has been a rise in the popularity, or at least in the visibility, of Islamist groups. Another, even more indirect outcome of SAPs that may impact women's economic position is the increasingly popular articulation of a type of political Islam that advocates a return to more rigidly defined gender roles, and the reassigning of women to the reproductive sphere, simultaneous with a reduction in their access to education, employment, and so forth. Thus the importance of political Islam, a movement that has provided both a political and an economic critique of the current economic system and reform attempts, must also be taken into account when discussing the current socioeconomic and political conditions in the region. If government policies are increasing economic uncertainty, reducing women's educational and employment options, as well as providing fuel for conservative social movements in various countries, this could discourage further reductions in fertility rates.

Conclusion

Reducing fertility rates is the goal of policymakers, as well as development planners, feminist scholars, and others, in many MENA countries. In a recent article, Fargues (1994) argues that alarm over the slow decline in fertility rates in the region is overstated since more recent evidence suggests that many countries in the region have "turned the corner" and that rapid decline is likely in the next few years. While I agree with some of Fargues's optimism, I have argued that it is important to keep in mind the role of economic signals in determining the speed at which fertility rates decline. Policymakers need to be aware of how changes in economic conditions may impact fertility decisions. The policy outcome I am most concerned about is how cuts in government spending due to SAPs have created particular hardships for women. Women's access to the formal labor market, particularly to public-sector jobs, as well as girls' access to education, have been or are likely to be affected by these cuts. These changes may slow the decline in fertility rates that has been observed.

In addition, the rise of political Islam, which is often fueled by the economic hardship resulting from SAPs, has reinforced the rigid gender roles in MENA, emphasizing women's roles as reproducers and as economic dependents who must rely on fathers, husbands, and male children for economic support. Given the levels of economic insecurity in the region, as well as women's tenuous position as economic dependents, which has in many cases been exacerbated by SAPs, women have a particular interest in maintaining high fertility rates, because of both the economic security and the improved social status it offers them. Yet government policies that could lessen some of this patriarchal control are under threat because of SAPs.

Researchers need to understand fertility patterns as being embedded in the greater structure of economic dependency, and need to recognize that women themselves often articulate the desire to have large families. A better understanding of social constraints, household dynamics, and gender ideology is necessary. As such, a feminist analysis can provide additional insights into the question of fertility. The lack of social safety nets for families, and for women in particular, has always been a problem in MENA, but SAPs are likely to worsen this problem. While SAPs may appear to be a short-run solution to the problems of government debt and economic stagnation, these programs could prove shortsighted if the strain on government and natural resources increases in the long run because of large population cohorts. A more longsighted strategy would involve increasing current spending on education, employment, and poverty relief to ensure smaller cohorts of future citizens, which will reduce the government burden in the long run.

Notes

An earlier version of this chapter was prepared for the Brown University Workshop on "Economic Restructuring and Women in the Middle East: Gender, Jobs, and Activist Organizations" in April 1998. A revised version was presented at the Western Economics Association meetings in Tahoe, Calif., June 30, 1998.

1. Economistic explanations of fertility greatly oversimplify the determinants of family size. At a minimum, researchers have pointed out that the costs of preventing pregnancies (which have varied considerably across time and culture) must be incorporated into the analysis. In addition, economists have been critiqued for ignoring institutional, cultural, and technological factors. While not discounting these factors, I argue that it is important to keep in mind the economic costs and benefits of children, as well as the asymmetrical distribution of these factors by sex.

2. Reported total fertility rates may also be problematic. Estimated rates for Kuwait range from 3.1 to 5.9 percent. Reported rates for Syria range from 4.2 to 5.9 percent. These two examples present the largest discrepancies, but varying figures have also been reported for other countries. In Table 3.1 two estimates for each country are reported, where available.

3. I will primarily discuss the correlation coefficients associated with the first set of TFR estimates, because that set contains more data points and as such may be slightly more accurate, assuming that the TFR measures are relatively accurate. The second correlation estimate suggests an even weaker relationship between income and fertility. Patricia Alonso-Gamo and Mohamed El-Erian (1997: 23) estimate a somewhat stronger correlation coefficient between income and fertility (-0.35), using data from the International Monetary Fund rather than from the United Nations. They also find a correlation of -0.57 between income and infant mortality and 0.58 between income and life expectancy.

4. In my own work, looking at fertility rates among Bethlehem-area Palestinians (Olmsted, 1998a), I found that income and fertility were positively correlated.

5. Statistics on female literacy in Oman are unavailable.

6. There is considerable evidence in the region that women's contributions to productive labor are underestimated, but this argument is less relevant to the discussion here as the labor in question is informal-sector or rural, both of which are more conducive to women's needs to combine their reproductive and productive roles.

7. There is also some evidence that women face wage discrimination, further diminishing their gains from entering the labor market. See UN, 1995, and Olmsted, 2001.

8. Notably, and most recently, the Islamic government of Iran has reversed its stand on birth control and has begun encouraging family planning.

Part 2

Case Studies

Egypt: Structural Adjustment and Women's Employment

Women in developing countries in general and in Egypt in particular are considered the first victims of economic changes. Macroeconomic policies, including economic structural adjustment programs, concentrate mainly on the reallocation of resources to achieve both stability and growth rather than on microeconomic issues and gender differentiation. These policies are male-biased as they fail to take into account the specific conditions of women, particularly in the labor market. This is the result of the long-term neglect of the role of gender in institutional theories about structures of internal labor markets, dual labor markets, and labor-market segmentation.

The purpose of this chapter is threefold. The first section offers a conceptual framework for analyzing the effects of economic reform and structural adjustment programs (ERSAPs) on women. The second section examines the impact of ERSAPs on employment of women in Egypt. Finally, the third section recommends policy measures to absorb the effects of ERSAPs on women.

ERSAPs and Gender Segmentation of the Labor Market

Theoretical Background

Labor-market theories were developed emphasizing the segmentation of the labor markets by race, color, religion, economic activity, age, geographical location, regulation, educational level, wage system, and occupational structure. More recent research has shown how the structure of the female labor market differs from that for men: "It

95

differs in terms of distribution by occupation, by sector as well as by work status. In some empirical work it was stated that women are more likely to be secondary workers than men, more likely to be primary subordinate workers and less likely to be independent primary workers such as craft workers, managers, professionals" (Brown and Peckman, 1987). Internal labor markets treat workers as members of groups and tend to treat workers within these groups differently, segregating women and men into different jobs nationally rather than paying them unequally for the same job.

In addition to this gender segmentation of the labor market at the national level, there is gender segmentation at the enterprise level. Men and women might have different labor-market experiences within the same institutions, although national labor laws treat workers in the same job category equally:

> Workers of different gender having similar occupational characteristics might not experience similar earnings or mobility prospects at the enterprise level. Entry-level jobs are likely to be different for men and women so that segregation will be maintained throughout one's career in the firm and women's job ladder may be shorter. Institutionally, that type of differentiation could be aided by placing women in job titles that differ from related jobs that men hold. Clerical jobs that are feminized constitute a secondary system with many points of entry, high turnover and low wages in contrast to managerial jobs that are organized along craft or industrial lines. (Bergman, 1995)

Such observations suggest that the effects of internal labor markets differ for men and women in spite of consistent legal rights. Recognition of gender segmentation of the labor market highlights three socioeconomic factors responsible for the male bias in economic policies and in ERSAPs in particular (Elson, 1991):

1. *The sexual division of labor.* Some kinds of work are socially constituted as women's work while other kinds of work are socially considered as men's work. This is a result of the prevailing pattern of social values, the division of labor inside as well as outside the household.

2. *Nonrecognition of unpaid work.* This includes work required for the process of reproduction and maintenance of human resources, as well as the work done by women outside the house to help their husbands, especially in the agricultural sector. The explicit exclusion

of this work by different economic policies leads to the subordination of women to men.

3. *Women's responsibility within the household.* In some cases economic policies add to women's responsibility within the household through an increase in the costs of living, without adding to the resources women require to undertake their responsibilities, whether inside or outside the household. Price liberalization policies and the rise in the cost of living accompanying ERSAPs, in particular, lead to increased electricity fees and kerosene prices. This places an additional burden on working women, given their traditional role in the household: while they will be compelled to save money by cutting back help in the household, whether human or electrical, to manage the financial obligations of the family they will also need to have a job outside the house to compensate for the decrease in family income.

Gender Segmentation of the Egyptian Labor Market

Applying the previous discussion to the Egyptian situation, and reviewing the literature on the structure of the Egyptian labor market, one readily concludes that gender, as well as age, have been totally neglected in past analyses of labor segmentation. Type of ownership remained for a long period the most important segmentation factor of the Egyptian labor market due to the extensive number of employees in the government and the public sector in Egypt since the 1960s. The public/private divide has been closely connected to the degree of labor-market regulation in both urban and rural sectors. In addition, the classification of the labor market by skills and various occupations has historically been related to the public/private segmentation of the economy. With the growth of the private sector since the mid-1970s, this factor became more important due to different wage determinations in both sectors as well as different labor skills (Aly, 1994). Education was also regarded as a critical factor for the division of the labor market in terms of differentiation in wage level, social status, as well as fringe benefits.

Previous surveys thus belittled or ignored the labor force participation of females. Currently, however, with the increase in poverty, child work and women's employment have both become significant sources of household income and therefore important phenomena that should be studied. At the same time, the improvement in survey techniques has made such studies more feasible. In particular, gender segmentation can be analyzed by considering not only the gender-neutral socioeconomic factors that affect the female labor market, but also the particular characteristics of female employment and unemployment, and through a redefinition of economic activities that leads to an increase in the participation rates of females in economic activities (CAPMAS, 1991).

Women in the Egyptian Labor Market

Although the women's labor market has its own characteristics, it is difficult to separate it from the general employment conditions in Egypt. Egypt's current employment problem is characterized by inadequate labor absorption of graduate students and an underutilization of unskilled human resources. Additional problems are overstaffing in the public sector, coupled with declining real wages and negative implications for employee productivity.

Several factors have led to the difficult situation in the labor market. On the supply side, these are: the population growth rate, estimated at 2.2 percent over the period 1980–1995; an overall labor force participation rate estimated at 47.2 percent over the period 1986–1992; and the substantial increase in the number of graduates from higher education over the period 1960–1985, a result of the expansion in free education (CAPMAS, 1995a).

On the demand side other factors have been relevant. In the first half of the 1960s Egypt witnessed a fairly rapid economic growth in terms of gross domestic product (GDP) at 6.1 percent, and a decline in the unemployment rate from 2.70 percent in 1960 to 1.15 percent in 1966. However, this low rate of unemployment was a result of the government's guaranteed employment policies pursued in 1961. These policies led to a sizable increase in the labor force in the public sector as well as the government sector, due to the rapid growth of these sectors after nationalization.

Egypt's labor market during the 1960s, 1970s, and the first half of the 1980s suffered from a low labor-absorptive capacity in the industrial sector, estimated at 12 percent, due to increasing capital intensity in industries protected by import-substitution policies. In the rural areas, push factors developed because of the use of a strict quota system, fixed prices of input and output, and a biased investment policy that led to a decline in the labor-absorptive capacity of the agriculture sector from 52.8 percent between 1959–1960 and 1965–1966, to 31 percent in 1995 (CAPMAS, 1995a)

Despite an economic boom over the period 1973–1981, the unemployment rate was estimated at 7 percent in the 1976 census. This reflected a decline in the growth rates of productive sectors over the 1970s. The two main labor-absorptive sectors were the nontradable sector and the construction sector (Handoussa and Potter, 1991). Two additional mechanisms were developed to absorb surplus labor: the informal sector in urban areas, and external migration to the oil-rich economies.

With the implementation of the first phase of structural adjustment programs in 1987 the government attempted to reduce the wage bill, which reached 26.1 percent of total public expenditure in 1986, through the abolition of employment guarantee policies in the public sector, the deceleration of growth in nominal wages, and the reduction of real wages for government and public-sector employees. Other means were adopted to decrease the size of the public payroll, which reached U.S.$2.3 million in 1986–1987, such as extending the waiting period for guaranteed jobs offered to secondary and postsecondary graduates, and introducing many complications in the application procedures for employment in the government, such as the condition of yearly registration in the labor offices (Nassar, 1996a). All these measures aggravated the employment problem in Egypt, leading to an unemployment rate of 11 percent from 1986 through 1996.

All these conditions affected the situation of women in Egypt's labor market. On the supply side, the officially reported participation rates of females in the labor force increased from 4.8 percent in 1960 to 22 percent in 1996, according to the census data. On the demand side, females, like all members of Egyptian society, were affected by the low absorptive capacity of the industrial sector. The majority of females working in the formal sector were mainly absorbed into the service sector, which became overstaffed. Meanwhile, due to the massive migration of peasants to the Gulf countries in the late 1970s and the resultant increase in the real wages of agricultural workers, a significant proportion of women in rural areas replaced men in work.

Economic conditions in Egypt since the 1980s have led to limited job opportunities, particularly in paid employment for women, who turned to self-employment activities especially as street vendors, in petty commodity production, and in personal services. These activities were regarded by a significant number of females as important means to increase their incomes. In addition, migration to become schoolteachers was a resort for some professional women. The increase in the number of female-headed households as a result of the external migration of men as well as the mortality patterns by which females outlive males (sixty-six years for females versus sixty-four years for males; UNDP and NIP, 1998) affected the participation rates of females positively.

However, the visible improvement in female participation in the labor market masks a fundamental reality: socioeconomic conditions continue to restrict women's participation in the economy and limit their mobility. The negative effects of the recent economic policies on women include growing unemployment, declining real wages, unsatisfactory working conditions in the private sector, persistent occupational segregation, discrimination in promotional procedures, duality in role performance, as well as underestimation of women's contributions to the labor market.

Table 4.1 shows various estimates of female participation rates in economic activities. Until the 1980s, data on females' contribution to economic activities suffered from an obvious underreporting by the Central Agency for Public Mobilization and Statistics (CAPMAS). These low figures for female participation were the result of the following data-collection factors (Anker and Anker, 1989):

- reliance on precise words or phrases such as "main activity, work, and occupation," which resulted in ambiguity for respondents (an activity schedule was not used);
- neglect of females' activities in agriculture as active work;
- lack of specification in the questionnaires of different types of activities that women perform;
- reliance on a single labor force definition.

Substantial increases in reported female employment occurred after 1983 with the redefinition of an "economically active person" to include activities in the formal as well as the informal sector. These changes led to an increase in the reported proportion of working females aged twelve to sixty-four years from 7 percent in CAPMAS's Labor Force Sample Survey in 1975, to 18.7 percent in 1984. CAPMAS's Labor Force Sample Survey in 1998 indicated a figure of 14.1 percent for female participation in the labor force. A

Table 4.1 Female Participation Rates in Economic Activities

Source	Year	Percentage
Census data[a]	1976	8.0
	1986	10.0
Labor Force Sample Survey[b]	1975	7.0
	1984	18.7
	1998	14.1
Labor Force Information Project 1988[c]	1988	31.0
Arab League & Cairo Demographic Center[d]	1993	
Paid work		11.3
Unpaid work		21.0
Diverse economic activities outside the house and domestic work		70.0
Human Development Report of Egypt[e]	1998	14.0
Survey on Monitoring Social Development in Egypt[f]	1994	13.8

Sources: a. CAPMAS, *Census Data* (Cairo: CAPMAS, 1986, 1996).

b. CAPMAS, *Labor Force Sample Survey* (Cairo: CAPMAS, 1975, 1984, 1998).

c. Malak Zaalouk, *Women, Labor Force Information Project* (CAPMAS: Cairo, 1991).

d. M. Hassan et al., *Women in the Labor Market* (Cairo: Arab League and Cairo Demographic Center, 1995).

e. UNDP and NIP, *Human Development Report of Egypt* (Cairo: UNDP and NIP, 1998).

f. CAPMAS and Social Fund, *Monitoring Social Development in Egypt* (Cairo: CAPMAS, 1995).

similar figure was given by CAPMAS's Survey on Monitoring Social Development in Egypt, 1992–1995, and the Human Development Report of Egypt.

Regardless of such definitional changes, most national official surveys are still gender biased and fail to recognize much of women's work in Egypt. Two other important national surveys, which enlarged the concept of women's contribution to economic activities, indicated a significantly higher level for economic contribution by females in Egypt. The CAPMAS Labor Force Information Project in 1988, which was a special round of the Labor Force Sample Survey, showed a 31 percent participation rate for women. This figure is the result of the global definition of work used in this survey, as well as different methods of sampling in data collection. The definition of females' work, in accordance with international trends, was broadened to include paid and unpaid labor so that women who were employed for at least one hour during the reference week of the survey, in either a formal or an informal basis, were included in the labor force. In addition, activities such as producing and processing primary commodities in agriculture, forestry, hunting, mining, and quarrying were included, whether for personal or marketing reasons. Meanwhile, production for market purposes in the nonprimary sectors was also included (Zaalouk, 1991).

In 1993 the Cairo Demographic Center analyzed a subsample of 1,900 individual questionnaires from 9,700 originally collected for the Egypt Use Effectiveness of Contraceptives Survey (1991). Data were collected in time-distribution schedules for every married woman aged fifteen to forty-nine years on the time and days spent in work outside and inside the home, as well as time spent caring for the family. In a reference period of one week, depending only on paid work, the percentage of working females reached 11.3 percent of the total labor force. Extending the definition of work to include paid and unpaid work, the last percentage reached 21.0 percent. This figure is similar to the estimation reported in Anqing Shi and Changpo Yang's study of the long-term demographic trend in Egypt (1996). But taking all activities into consideration, including domestic activities, the estimates by the Cairo Demographic Center of the participation rate of females in economic activities reached 70 percent (Sayed and Wahishi, 1995).

The Impact of ERSAPs on Women's Employment in Egypt

The withdrawal of the government from the employment process and the shrinking of job opportunities in the public sector, through attrition as well as privatization, will affect women in particular. This is due to several reasons related to the gender segmentation of the labor market: gender segregation by occupation, the feminization of government employment, changes in job status and working conditions, the particular effects of unemployment on women, and the vulnerability of women in the labor market.

Occupational Gender Segregation

Table 4.2A presents gender differences by occupation as of 1995. Women are squeezed into a limited number of jobs on the lower rungs as well as the highest rung of the occupational ladder. More than one-third of the employed females are working as agricultural workers; another third are working in professional, legislative, mana-

Table 4.2 Employment Status of Females, 1995

A: Percentage of Household Individuals 6 Years and Older Working During Last Week by Occupation and Gender

Occupation	Male	Female	Total
Legislative officials and managers	11.9	8.5	11.3
Professionals	9.6	20.3	11.6
Technical and associate professionals	3.9	4.8	4.1
Clerks	5.8	16.4	7.7
Service workers and sales workers	9.5	6.7	9.0
Skilled agricultural and fishery workers	32.8	37.3	33.6
Crafts and related trades	14.6	3.3	12.6
Plant and machine operators	6.7	1.3	5.7
Elementary occupations	3.7	1.3	3.3
Unknown	1.5	0.1	1.2
Total	100.0	100.0	100.0

B: Percentage of Household Individuals 6 Years and Older with Previous Job by Economic Activity and Gender

Economic Activity	Male	Female	Total
Agriculture, hunting, and fishing	33.8	37.6	34.5
Mining and quarrying	0.5	0.1	0.4
Manufacturing	14.5	7.7	13.3
Electricity, gas, and water	1.0	0.6	1.0
Construction	7.3	0.6	6.1
Commerce, restaurants, and hotels	10.0	10.4	10.6
Transport, storage, and communication	10.7	1.1	5.0
Financial, insurance, and real estate	5.9	1.2	1.3
Communications, social, and personal services	1.3	40.6	27.2
Activities not adequately defined	24.2	0.1	0.6
Total	100.0	100.0	100.0

C: Percentage of Household Individuals 6 Years and Older Who Worked During Last Week by Sector and Gender

Sector	Male	Female	Total
Government	23.9	39.4	26.7
Public	9.4	3.9	8.4
Private	66.2	56.4	64.5
Investment	0.3	0.3	0.3
Cooperation	0.1	0.0	0.1
NGO	0.0	0.0	0.0
Foreign	0.0	0.0	0.0
Total	100.0	100.0	100.0

D: Percentage of Household Individuals 6 Years and Older Who Were Paid for Work During Last Week by Number of Workplaces and Gender

Number of Workplaces	Male	Female	Total
Current job	78.1	88.5	79.9
Two jobs	3.5	1.4	3.1
Three jobs	1.5	0.5	1.3
Four jobs	0.7	0.6	0.7
Five jobs	0.4	0.1	0.4
Six or more jobs	15.8	8.9	14.6
Total	100.0	100.0	100.0

Sources: CAPMAS, Program of Surveys for Monitoring Social Development in Egypt, 1992–1995; and Priority Survey, 1995.

Notes: The complete survey was conducted in 1993; a smaller sample was resurveyed in 1995 for in-depth analysis. Totals may not equal 100 percent due to rounding.

gerial, and technical occupations; and only 11.3 percent are employed as production workers and sales workers. These percentages reflect educational status: despite the fact that most working females in the informal sector are illiterate (43.9 percent), most educated working females have achieved secondary or university grade levels (41.4 percent [Sayed and Wahishi, 1995]). The occupational structure for men is more evenly distributed: one-third are working in agricultural occupations; one-fourth are working in legislative, managerial, professional, and technical occupations; and one-third are employed as craft workers, sales workers, and plant and machine operators.

The distribution of females by economic sector, presented in Table 4.2B, reflects the previous occupational structure of working females. More than half the females are absorbed in the service sector, in its broader definition, with agriculture serving as the second main absorbing sector. The agricultural and service sectors are reversed for males, who are also relatively more absorbed than females in the manufacturing, construction, transportation, storage, and communication sectors.

This kind of occupational segregation is a result of the sexual division of work. The specific occupations in which females are engaged are suited to their prescribed social and reproductive roles in the society. Females do not penetrate economic activities designed for men, such as construction and mining. They are usually assigned to inferior or secondary roles as clericals. These occupations are the most vulnerable when privatization is implemented.

However, the occupational segregation of men and women did decline somewhat starting in the 1970s as a result of the entry of more women into the so-called male occupations (e.g., managerial and professional jobs). This trend had its roots in the 1960s, when the economy began to diversify and females began to enter nonagricultural occupations such as manufacturing, tourism, commerce, and government services.

There is currently a gender-biased professionalism in Egypt. Some professional occupations are dominated by females. Social services, teaching, nursing, and medical services employ women more than other fields. The female shares of these occupations are high: 68 percent of nurses, 40 percent of teachers, and 27 percent of medical doctors. Females constitute almost 50 percent of the graduates of faculties of medicine, pharmacy, and dentistry (Moghadam, 1995a).

In the manufacturing sector, women still constitute a limited share. This might be explained by their low representation in vocational education. Women working in manufacturing are concentrated in labor-intensive industries, such as textiles and garments, food processing, and pharmaceuticals, which employ, respectively, 43 percent, 14 percent, and 13 percent of all female workers in the industrial sector. However, some of these industries have become feminized, as women now represent 60 percent of the total number of workers in the Nasr Company for Textiles and almost 50 percent of the workers in the pharmaceutical industries (Alliance for Arab Women, 1995).

The service sector is the destination for a significant share of females. However, their absorption into the various service occupations is different. Females are concentrated in social services (80 percent of total employment, versus 52 percent for males), with very low representation in transportation and communication services (4 percent versus 18 percent for males). Female representation is relatively better in commerce, hotels, and restaurant services (8 percent), but still lower than the male share (33.3 percent). No significant gender differences exist in the occupation rates of real estate, banking, and insurance services.

Moreover, gendering of agriculture appears to be a function both of men's physical strength and of men's historically dominant role (Toth, 1991). Culturally, there is a strict boundary between men's and women's work in agriculture. Females' engagement in agriculture was always regarded as part of their role as housewives, but for long periods it was not counted as economic activity. Thus, in this sector the basic problem facing women is not a lack of work opportunities, but the fact that they are working constantly without any financial evaluation of their contributions to this sector (Nassar, 1995b). For example, during peak periods almost one-third of working females in rural areas work the whole week, versus only 7.3 percent of working females in urban areas (Sayed and Wahishi, 1995). In addition, the number of females in this sector has traditionally varied according to the circumstances that men face. During the oil boom men left Egypt to seek work in oil-producing Gulf states. Those who had been employed in agriculture were replaced by women and children.

When men returned, females were withdrawn from various job opportunities. However, the substitution of women for men is today encouraged by a desire to reduce costs, especially after recent changes in the Agricultural Reform Law. The new land reform legislation stipulated an immediate increase in land rent of seven to twenty-two times the land tax. More important, the new law gave landowners the right to evict tenants after a transitional period of five years that lapsed in October 1997.

Feminization of Government Employment

Policies aimed at eliminating overstaffing in the government sector will affect women more than men, due to the so-called feminization of the government sector. Most job opportunities for females in the formal sector have been concentrated in government, and to some extent in the public sector (see Table 4.2C). The percentage of the total female labor force working in the government sector (39.4 percent) exceeds that for males (23.9 percent). The equal opportunity environment prevailing in the government sector has resulted in some progress for women in access to senior positions. Women have made significant advances in the government sector as compared to the private sector, and enjoy a secure wage setting, equal regulations, and comfortable working hours. However, females in the public sector currently face a number of problems, including a deterioration in the status of government employees, as real wages declined by 51 percent over the period 1986–1993 (Nassar, 1995b).

Second, privatization is having a negative effect on working females in the public sector, because among public-sector redundancies the percentage of females is high. Women tend to work in the clerical, secretarial, and administrative fields, which are already saturated. In the case of dismissal, they will be the first to go, as working conditions in the private sector are unsuitable for most married females. Meanwhile, the persistence of occupational segregation elsewhere renders the vocational training process that accompanies mass dismissals from the public sector more suitable for men than for women. Moreover, women's household maintenance and childcare responsibilities affect their productivity and result in persistent barriers against their engagement in the private sector. In the Egyptian privatization case, more women are accepting early retirement than men.

Job Status and Working Conditions

ERSAPs might have an effect on the increase in transitory employment and changes in work status. As a solution for overstaffing, this is unsuitable for women who prefer permanent jobs. The high percentage of the total female labor force working in permanent jobs reflects their desire for the social protection and stability that is offered to them in permanent work. Questions of mobility were addressed in the Labor Force Sample Survey in 1988, and it was clear that females are more reluctant than men to change their employment status from permanent to temporary. Those women who reported voluntary changes cited family reasons as opposed to personal aspirations, as was the case for most men.

Women are rather less able than men to work in more than one job. Table 4.2D indicates that only 11.5 percent of working females work in more than one job, in comparison to 21.9 percent of men. Women's responsibilities at home are obstacles against increasing their livelihood through dual employment. This means that women are more likely than men to lose their sole source of income in the case of dismissal from their jobs.

The informal sector has served as an unplanned mechanism to absorb surplus labor in general. The relatively high proportion of the total female labor force working in the private sector results from the increased engagement of women in the informal sector. For illiterate females this is the most suitable sector, and for educated females it has become a last resort. However, working conditions in the informal sector are poor, given the absence of social insurance, long working hours, and minimal sanitary and safety regulations. Females in the informal sector, similar to all workers in this sector, do not have any trade unions or legal protection and do not enjoy any labor rights such as paid holidays, fixed working hours, or healthcare. Given that most of the workers in this sector are illiterates with no training or work experience, they may be subject to exploitation. When educated women resort to this sector it is due to shrinking job opportunities in the formal sector, unsuitable working conditions there, or the need for extra income without fixed working hours.

The Impact of Unemployment on Women

Although unemployment is a common problem affecting every member of society who needs and is able to work, its impact on women is more intensive due to the fact that women are more vulnerable in the labor market. The unemployment rate for females increased from 17 percent in census 1976 to 22 percent in census 1996 and is higher than the national figure in that year (8 percent). The limited demand for female labor results in part from a gender bias among employers. One of the field surveys quoted a man saying, "No woman will accept a job which her idle husband can take; he should replace her" (Masry, 1993: 12). As one analyst observed, "Egyptian women have become the redundant bargaining chip in the political triangle involving their rights, state policies, and the pressure of conservative elements who blame working women for the country's unemployment problems" (Peter, 1995: 5).

At the same time, the supply of job-seeking females is growing in part because of the effects of ERSAPs. Accompanying ERSAPs, the percentage of the poor in accordance with the lower poverty line decreased in rural areas from 28.6 percent in 1990–1991 to 23.2 percent in 1995–1996 and increased in urban areas from 20.2 percent to 28.6 percent over the same period. In accordance with the higher poverty line the percentage of the poor increased in rural areas from 39.2 percent in 1990–1991 to 50.2 percent in 1995–1996 and from 39.0 percent to 44.9 percent in urban areas over the same time period. The two poverty lines differ in their estimation of food-basket expenditure, as the lower poverty line takes the cost of total expenditure into consideration to estimate the nonfood expenditure, while the higher poverty line considers only the cost of food expenditure. This trend accompanied an increase in the prices of food, electricity, and transportation due to a reduction in subsidies, which led to an increase in the cost of living. Many poor women can no longer afford to stay at home. The need for a steady flow of income as a buttress against the insecurity of unemployment and inadequate or nonexistent financial support from male partners and kin networks has pushed women to develop a variety of strategies to increase their incomes. In addition to seeking employment outside the home, many women are taking on extra jobs producing home handicrafts for sale and networking among kin and friends to obtain money.

Table 4.3 presents the characteristics of unemployment of females as of 1995. Duration of unemployment is longer for females than for males. It reaches four years and over for 43.1 percent of unemployed females and 36.4 percent of unemployed males, while it is less than twelve months for 14.5 percent of females and

Table 4.3   Unemployment Conditions by Gender, 1995

A: Percentage of Unemployed Individuals 6 Years and Older by Duration of Current Unemployment and Gender

Duration of Current Unemployment	Male	Female	Total
Less than 6 months	8.9	6.5	7.7
6–12 months	11.1	8.0	9.6
1–2 years	8.1	6.4	7.3
2–3 years	19.4	20.0	19.7
3–4 years	16.2	16.0	16.1
4+ years	36.4	43.1	39.7
Total	100.0	100.0	100.0

B: Percentage of Unemployed Individuals 6 Years and Older by Type of Unemployment and Gender

Type of Unemployment	Male	Female	Total
With no previous job	90.7	98.6	94.6
With previous job	9.3	1.4	5.4
Total	100.0	100.0	100.0

C: Percentage of Household Individuals 6 Years and Older Working During Last Week by Occupation and Gender

Occupation	Male	Female	Total
Legislative officials and managers	1.1	3.8	1.5
Professionals	2.3	19.2	4.5
Technical and associate professionals	5.1	3.8	5.0
Clerks	6.8	11.5	7.4
Service workers and sales workers	14.2	26.9	15.8
Skilled agricultural and fishery workers	6.3	3.8	5.9
Crafts and related trades	36.4	15.4	33.9
Plant and machine operators	9.1	7.7	8.9
Elementary occupations	16.5	7.7	15.3
Unknown	2.3	0.0	2.0
Total	100.0	100.0	100.0

D: Percentage of Household Individuals 6 Years and Older with Previous Job by Sector and Gender

Sector	Male	Female	Total
Government	6.3	24.0	8.5
Public	4.5	0.0	4.0
Private	85.8	72.0	84.1
Investment	1.7	0.0	1.5
Cooperation	0.0	4.0	0.5
Foreign	1.7	0.0	1.5
Total	100.0	100.0	100.0

E: Percentage of Unemployed Individuals 6 Years and Older by Last Week of Job Seeking and Gender

Job-Seeking Nature	Male	Female	Total
Search for job	71.6	52.2	62.1
No search for job	28.4	47.8	37.9
Total	100.0	100.0	100.0

Sources: CAPMAS, Program of Surveys for Monitoring Social Development in Egypt, 1992–1995; and Priority Survey, 1995.

Notes: The complete survey was conducted in 1993; a smaller sample was resurveyed in 1995 for in-depth analysis. Totals may not equal 100 percent due to rounding.

20 percent of males (see Table 4.3A). This reflects the fact that women's work can be interrupted for years by maternity responsibilities. It also indicates the impact of the dual role of females on their status in the labor market. Females might be forced to leave their jobs to undertake family responsibilities, which is not the case for males.

Due to the tight conditions of the labor market as well as privatization, reentry becomes a difficult task. This is particularly true for females who previously worked in the public sector and now have to face the competitive conditions of work in the private sector, compounded by increased responsibilities at home after childbirth. Employers are more likely to offer jobs to males rather than females due to the extensive maternity leaves granted to females. Another problem is that the length of unemployment might affect the accumulation of talents, such that a female who stays at home for five years to raise her children will lose her efficiency as a worker in the labor market.

Table 4.3B indicates that unemployment falls heavily on graduates and new entrants to the labor market. This is more apparent for females than males, as 98.6 percent of unemployed women do not have any work experience, compared to 90.7 percent for men. The distribution of unemployed persons by occupational structure, presented in Table 4.3C, shows significant differences among sectors. Women in agriculture rarely suffer from unemployment as they are performing jobs complementary to their housework. The highest percentage of female unemployment is among service and sales workers, followed by professionals, craft and trade workers, and clericals. This means that the main absorbing occupations of females are saturated and are starting to release workers. The higher percentage of females who worked in the private sector prior to their unemployment, compared to females who worked in the government sector, reflects the fact that work in the latter is more stable (see Table 4.3D) and that working conditions in the private sector may be unsuitable for many women.

Almost half of unemployed females are not searching for a job (see Table 4.3E). Although they are willing to work, their chances for searching for a suitable job are limited either by their parents, by their families, or by their ignorance of various ways to obtain a job. Females prefer to wait for employment opportunities in the government sector. As work of men is usually regarded as a necessity at both the societal and the household level, a relatively higher percentage of unemployed men than unemployed women (71.6 percent versus 52.2 percent) are searching for a job.

Thus unemployment has a relatively greater impact on women than men, as women's unemployment rates are higher, their unemployment periods are longer, and they are reluctant to search for jobs. They may wait years for an employment agency to provide them with the permanent jobs they need to achieve security. As long as this process is undergoing a structural change to free the market, women will be left with no jobs.

The Vulnerability of Women in the Labor Market

The negative impact of ERSAPs on women's employment will intensify due to several factors that lead to female vulnerability in the market: wage discrimination, discriminatory employment conditions, lack of childcare and transportation, the dilemma of maternity leave, women as unpaid workers, and lack of representation in trade unions.

Wage discrimination.   Women in manufacturing perform repetitive tasks. Their lack of education and inferior status in the labor market results in limited access to technical, vocational, and entrepreneurial training and reduces their chances to be engaged in more capital-intensive industries with higher salaries. For these reasons, women's wages are far below men's in the same industrial branch. This is clearly evident in Table 4.4, which shows that women's wages are only about two-thirds those of men. This gap does not reflect inequities in pay scales, as the manufacturing sector is still dominated by public enterprises that face uniform wage setting for both sexes. Rather, the main explanation for this gap is the difference in entry jobs based on gender. In the public sector, the low level of initial appointment is the primary form of discrimination that women complain about, according to the Labor Force Information Project of 1988. Following appointment, women face different promotional chances and limited opportunities to advance through vocational training. In addition, due to restrictions from their husbands or parents, as well as their household responsibilities, women are less likely to work overtime. In the private sector, according to the Labor Force Information Project, women reported wage differentials as the second most serious form of discrimination they faced. Women

Table 4.4   Wages by Sector and Gender, 1985–1992 (earnings/week, £Egyptian)

	1985	1986	1987	1988	1989	1990	1991	1992
Nonagricultural Activities								
Total	32	34	38	43	49	55	59	64
Men	32	35	39	45	50	57	61	66
Women	27	28	31	36	42	46	50	56
Manufacturing								
Total	29	33	38	41	46	54	55	62
Men	30	34	39	43	48	56	57	64
Women	22	25	28	31	34	38	41	48
Agriculture								
Total	25	22	25	25	29	34	39	41
Men	25	22	26	25	29	34	40	41
Women	21	18	22	25	26	32	39	41

Source: ILO, *Yearbook* (Geneva: ILO, 1996).

working in agriculture, where work is also quite repetitive, ranked wage differentials as the most significant form of discrimination.

Women's lower salaries are also a reflection of the difficulties they face in career advancement. In manufacturing, women are located at the bottom of the hierarchy and rarely become supervisors. In the public industrial sector, only 5 percent and 7 percent of the working females in the textile and food industries, respectively, could reach the highest administrative positions. For the public sector as a whole, 0.57 percent of working females could climb the occupational ladder versus 0.98 percent for working males (Alliance for Arab Women, 1995).

Even in the service sector and in teaching occupations, in which a significant proportion of the females are engaged, their share in administrative jobs is far below their share in employment. In primary education, preparatory schools, agricultural schools, and teachers' schools, the shares of females in employment reach 51.76 percent, 44.04 percent, 23.38 percent, and 49.10 percent of total employment, respectively, but their shares in administrative occupations are 33.75 percent, 26.48 percent, 5.73 percent, and 37.05 percent (Alliance for Arab Women, 1995). This kind of discrimination might be intensified with ERSAPs, as women will not be able to compete with men for administrative positions in the private sector.

Discriminatory employment conditions. According to the Labor Force Information Project, females reported facing different kinds of discrimination, including ill treatment by male colleagues, directors, supervisors, and employees (41.7 percent); harassment by the public (32.8 percent); sexual harassment (65 percent); the absence of transport facilities (4.7 percent); being asked for informal favors (2 percent); and malicious gossip (1.3 percent). Denial of opportunities for work-related travel abroad also figures high; in the government sector this was the most important form of discrimination, followed by the difficulty of attaining high-ranking posts and then the type of work given to women (Zaalouk, 1991).

Lack of childcare and transportation. Egyptian labor law provides for numerous forms of assistance for working women. However, this law is not always implemented. Law 137 of 1981 "requires employers having 100 or more female employees to set up a nursery close to the workshops far from noise, pollution, wastes and to allow for breastfeeding twice a day for not less than one half hour" (Moghadam, 1996). In spite of this law, however, only 16.2 percent, 23 percent, and 23.4 percent of the surveyed females in the government, public, and private sectors, respectively, reported the existence of daycare centers in urban areas (Zaalouk, 1991). The situation is almost the same in rural areas, where only 7.9 percent, 31 percent, and 31.6 percent of the employees in the government, public, and private sectors, respectively, reported the existence of daycare centers.

Labor legislation also protects women from hazardous work as well as most types of night work. When night work is allowed, as in the tourism sector, the law requires employers to provide transportation for women after 8 P.M. (Moghadam, 1996; Zulficar, 1995). Again, however, the data suggest that implementation is lagging behind regulations. In general, women complain of transportation difficulties as one of the main challenges in their employment. Females who enjoy employer-provided transportation in their work do not exceed 17.3 percent, 68.1 percent, and 9.4 percent in the government, public, and private sectors, respectively, in urban areas, and 3 percent, 31.2 percent, and 14.7 percent in rural areas (Zaalouk, 1991). Moreover, surveys by the Arab League and the Cairo Demographic Center indicate that 55.4 percent and 42.3 percent of the working females in urban and rural areas, respectively, need one to two hours to reach their work (Sayed and Wahashi, 1995). This represents a burden especially for working married females with families.

The dilemma of maternity leave.   Given that Egyptian labor law provides for maternity leaves, childcare centers, and nursing breaks, women are an expensive commodity for their employers. In the government and public sectors, "women workers are entitled to three months paid maternity leave and up to two years unpaid maternity leave available up to three times. For the private sector, Law 137 of 1981 allows for one year's unpaid maternity leave" (Moghadam, 1996). Although these provisions generally favor women, they may lead to discrimination in the labor market, as employers are opposing lengthy maternity leaves. A recent study, conducted by looking at job opportunities in the official newspaper *Al-Ahram* in September 1996, found that 72 percent of private-sector employment advertising was specifically targeted to males (Nassar, 1996b).

Yet it is not clear that modifying these provisions will benefit women. Currently, the labor law is being revised to unify labor rights in the various sectors of the economy. For women this is expected to entail a reduction of maternity-leave benefits, in both the public and the private sector, to one year's unpaid leave taken twice instead of three times. In addition, leave will be available only after ten months of service. This will lead to more equal working conditions for women in the two formal sectors, and may therefore reduce formal private-sector employers' resistance to hiring females. However, the implementation of these changes will lead to more women leaving the private sector for the informal sector due to the former's long, inflexible working hours and its limitations on maternity leaves.

Women as unpaid workers.   Table 4.5 indicates that unpaid work is relatively more visible among working females than working males. Females are the more vulnerable group, as more than a quarter of them are unpaid in comparison to only 10 percent for men. Moreover, work belonging to an establishment is an indicator of socioeconomic development and of better working conditions and protection by the labor laws. The same survey shows that the percentage of the total female labor force working in establishments (48.3 percent) is less than the similar percentage for men (54.8 percent), which means

Table 4.5   Employment Status by Gender, 1995

Percentage of Household Individuals 6 Years and Older Who Worked During Last Week by Employment Status and Gender

Employment Status	Male	Female	Total
Self-employed, unemployed, other	11.9	9.8	11.6
Self-employed, employed, other	18.5	6.8	16.4
Family worker without wages	10.2	26.2	13.1
Wage earner, government/public sector	33.2	43.2	35.0
Wage earner, private sector	26.1	14.0	23.9
Total	100.0	100.0	100.0

Sources: CAPMAS, Program of Surveys for Monitoring Social Development in Egypt, 1992–1995; and Priority Survey.

that a relatively higher percentage of working females are not covered by social insurance. This might be explained by the relatively higher percentage of men engaged in the formal manufacturing sector and the relatively high percentage of the unpaid working females in agriculture. Despite the fact that unpaid working females might not be influenced by ERSAPs, the number of entrants in this category will increase with privatization and the elimination or cut in employment in the formal public sector. As females working in this capacity are neither protected by social regulations nor paid, more women will be rendered vulnerable in the labor force.

Lack of representation in trade unions.   The impending new employment law gives the right of collective negotiation to workers. However, women, as a minority in the twenty-three unions of the Egyptian Trade Union Federation (ETUF), are not well positioned to take advantage of this right. Women's representation in the trade unions is still limited to ordinary positions and to working females in the formal sector. Moreover, women represent only a small proportion of union leadership. Female officers are represented in all unions of the ETUF, but they constitute only 3.5 percent of all officers (621 females versus 17,441 males in the trade unions). The largest numbers of women union officers are employed in public services (94), education (55), commerce (42), public utilities (38), and tourism and hotels (37) ('Abd al-Hady, 1996). Women have reached a leading position in only four of the federations that make up the ETUF. Only four women, in comparison to 479 men, are federation officers, a proportion of less than 1 percent. Just one woman sits on the executive board the ETUF, compared to twenty-two men.

Despite the fact that the ETUF has a women's unit, and that women's rights as workers are protected by law, those rights may not be interpreted from a female perspective. For example, women may not always obtain union support in combating such problems as occupational segregation. Moreover, trade union representation is not available for women working as domestic servants, in trade, or (generally) in the informal sector. There are no associations of women workers in the informal and agricultural sectors (Moghadam, 1995a).

Policy Recommendations

The implications of ERSAPs on women's employment in Egypt cannot be separated from the prevailing social norms and existing socioeconomic policies in Egypt, which point to females' vulnerability in general, a sexual division of labor, and the neglect of unpaid work outside as well as inside the household. Females' vulnerability is reflected in the specific occupations they are engaged in, which are suited to their reproductive role in the society, such as teaching and nursing. Their presence in agricultural work is subsumed by their responsibilities at home, which are unpaid, while the informal sector is the last resort for the illiterates and those who are forced to work by economic conditions. Meanwhile, the employment problems females face cannot be separated from the general conditions of the labor market, which ERSAPs threaten to worsen.

A number of policies can be implemented to improve the status of women in the labor market during economic restructuring:

1. *Conducting periodic, gender-sensitive surveys*. Studies are needed to provide information about the extent and characteristics of women's contributions to economic activities, as well as the demography of women and the problems and challenges they face. The definition of women's contributions to economic activities should differ from the traditional definition of work to include all activities of women, whether inside or outside their homes. Women's work in the informal and agricultural areas should be studied to examine female

vulnerability from all aspects. These surveys are also needed to understand women's working careers, entry points, and turnover rates in various institutions.

2. *Increasing women's participation in the formal private sector.* Participation can be enhanced by providing childcare centers to reduce the burden of conflicting roles for working mothers. To help reduce poverty, community childcare projects should provide nutrition and health services for children.

3. *Implementing antidiscrimination legislation.* Such legislation should ensure that discrimination against women in the workplace is illegal, especially given the wave of privatization under way in Egypt.

4. *Adopting affirmative action measures.* The affirmative action measures that have been adopted in some countries are effective in protecting women from the negative effects of ERSAPs. For example, in Bangladesh a portion of government jobs were reserved for women (UNDP, 1996). Such measures should be implemented in the private sector in Egypt.

5. *Requiring a sector-focused strategy to enhance self-employment.* As a channel to increase the contribution of women in the labor market, this strategy would seek to address the specific problems confronting the various enterprises and the self-employed within one or several economic sectors, industries, trade groups, or occupations. An organization must become an active participant by undertaking a range of interventions in marketing, input, supply, technology training, and credit.

6. *Providing credit.* Lack of assets is a constraint against productive employment for the poor—the vulnerable groups of ERSAPs. Thus, credits for the female poor are effective measures to enable them to obtain needed assets. Mobile credit offices, especially in rural areas, are an efficient means to lower transaction costs. Group lending may be a solution to lack of collateral, in addition to simplified application procedures for obtaining credit. Hiring staff from client communities facilitates communication with the borrowing community. Additional effective measures include the extension of short-loan terms, the extension of small loans to meet day-to-day financial requirements of women's businesses, the opportunity for full repayment of one loan to bring access to another, the limitation of time between application and disbursement, and the development of a public image that credits are for the poor. Credit cooperatives

provide women with the necessary capital, producer cooperatives help women to get better prices for their goods, and legal services enable women in the informal sector to protect their rights.

7. *Initiating training programs.* Training is effective in increasing the abilities of women to obtain productive employment opportunities and to alleviate job segregation in the private sector.

8. *Establishing self-employed women's associations (SEWAs).* In many developing countries, such as India, SEWAs have been successful in assisting poor women. SEWAs are an important step in developing sustainable programs of poverty alleviation. Drawing their female membership from the very poor, like petty vendors and casual laborers, these organizations aim to enhance women's income-earning opportunities as well as their working environment by providing credits, training, and appropriate technology.

9. *Implementing an area-focused strategy.* To help poor women enter the labor market, such a strategy should offer a comprehensive range of services to a target group of females to enable them to participate in economic activities. The area that is selected may be expanded over time. The program must provide, or identify externally, a wide range of services, including skills training, credit, marketing assistance, basic education, family planning, and health and nutritional services.

10. *Implementing safety net programs.* Safety nets are needed for those excluded from the market during ERSAPs.

11. *Increasing the awareness of the importance of women's contribution in economic activities.* Productive employment for women should be regarded not only as a condition for the survival of their households, like the unpaid work that most women undertake in rural areas, but also as an expansion of their role and status in the society. Only when women's role in increasing the welfare of their families is recognized will society be ready to protect them during socioeconomic restructuring.

Ragui Assaad 5

Gender and Employment: Egypt in Comparative Perspective

The international literature on structural adjustment and gender makes a strong case that the effects of economic restructuring and structural adjustment are not gender neutral. The burden of the elimination of food subsidies, falling incomes, and cutbacks in basic public services is borne disproportionately by women because of their position at the interface of the household and market economies and their disadvantaged position within the household (Haddad et al., 1995; Afshar and Dennis, 1992; Beneria, Lourdes, and Roldan, 1987; Sparr, 1994; Aslanbeigui, Pressman, and Summerfield, 1994). The literature also stresses that women's vulnerable position in the labor market makes them less able to cope with the changes imposed by structural adjustment. For instance, a number of authors argue that because women (especially more-educated women) are disproportionately represented in the public sector, the loss of public sector jobs through government retrenchment and privatization affects them disproportionately (Haddad et al., 1995; Sparr, 1994; Afshar and Dennis, 1992; Moghadam, 1998). Others argue that because women's mobility is constrained by social norms and household responsibility, they are less able to respond to the relative price changes brought about by structural adjustment programs (Tanski, 1994; Haddad et al., 1995). The literature also points out that female employment opportunities often expand under structural adjustment, albeit in low-wage, unstable jobs, because the labor-intensive, export-oriented industries spurred by adjustment policies tend to hire women disproportionately (Joekes, 1995; Sparr, 1994).

While the conditions described in the literature apply quite broadly, there are important differences among countries in the

119

extent to which women are disadvantaged in the labor market. Middle Eastern and North African countries stand out in terms of their low female participation in wage labor, their relatively high unemployment rates, the extent to which the employment of educated women is dependent on the public sector, and their relatively poor record in promoting labor-intensive, export-oriented industries. This chapter uses the case of Egypt, in comparison with other countries in the region and elsewhere, to illustrate these propositions.

Continuing Public-Sector Dominance in the Employment of Educated Workers

From the early 1960s to the late 1980s, the public sector played a major role in shaping the Egyptian labor market along educational and gender lines. Through the long-standing application of the employment guarantee scheme for graduates, the public sector has been the dominant employer of graduates, the fastest-growing category in the Egyptian labor force.[1] Although the public sector's role in employment creation has been somewhat attenuated in recent years as a result of the suspension of the employment guarantee scheme, it continues to have a major impact on the structure of the Egyptian labor market. This inertial impact is due in part to the role of public-sector employment in shaping the employment expectations and aspirations of graduates, and in part to the driving demand for certain types of educational qualifications that are of little value to private-sector employers.

It appears that employment expectations among young new entrants to the labor market are in fact changing. There is some evidence that young educated males are no longer remaining unemployed while queuing for public-sector employment. They seem to be increasingly willing to take on even casual employment in the private sector. Some of the evidence pointing to this is the higher proportion of private-sector wage and salaried jobholders among young male workers than among their older counterparts, and lower proportions of public employment among educated males over time. It is also supported by the apparent stability of male unemployment rates in the 1990s. However, young female new entrants are finding it difficult to join the private sector because of what appear to be significant barriers to the entry into wage work for young women. This is reflected in very low rates of wage employment in the private sector, continued high unemployment rates for educated females, and a large gender wage gap in the private sector.

Despite the slowdown in the growth of public-sector employment in Egypt, it continues to play a dominant role in the Egyptian labor market. First, the public sector is the primary employer of educated workers, and because of the strong relationship between education and labor force participation for women, it is also the dominant employer of female workers. As shown in Table 5.1, the public sector employs about one-third of all male workers and half of female workers. In urban areas, the role of the public sector is even more dominant. It employs over 60 percent of female workers in the metropolitan governorates, and close to 70 percent in urban upper and lower Egypt. The public sector's more limited role in rural areas is explained by its limited direct role in agricultural production.

The dominant role of the public sector is primarily attributable to its role in employing educated workers among both males and females. The proportion of workers employed in the public sector increases steadily as the educational level rises. As shown in Table

Table 5.1   Type of Employment by Gender and Region, 1997 (employed population ages 12–65)

	Metropolitan	Lower, Urban	Lower, Rural	Upper, Urban	Upper, Rural	Total
Males						
Public, salaried	39.4	36.7	28.8	43.1	22.3	32.3
Private, salaried	14.9	6.0	7.0	13.0	4.2	8.6
Self-employed	18.3	27.3	11.5	18.5	10.5	15.5
Casual	27.2	25.2	25.3	22.0	35.5	27.5
Farming	0.0	4.5	27.4	3.7	27.7	16.1
Total	100.0	100.0	100.0	100.0	100.0	100.0
Females						
Public, salaried	60.8	68.8	29.4	71.4	26.3	49.7
Private, salaried	12.7	3.2	3.5	10.5	2.6	6.9
Self-employed	9.0	11.8	10.0	9.5	28.9	12.1
Casual	16.3	7.5	20.4	8.6	19.7	15.6
Farming	1.2	8.6	36.8	0.0	23.7	15.7
Total	100.0	100.0	100.0	100.0	100.0	100.0

Source: Egyptian Integrated Household Survey 1997.
Note: Totals may not equal 100 percent due to rounding.

5.2, the public sector employs about 15 percent of male workers with less than a primary education, compared to 66 percent of workers with a university education. The pattern is even stronger among females, where less than 10 percent of employed women without an education work for the public sector, compared to 86 percent of employed women with a university education. The proportion of employed women working for the public sector rises sharply at the technical secondary level, which is the level at which graduates become eligible for the public-sector employment guarantee (see Assaad, 1997a, for a more detailed discussion of the employment guarantee policy).

Although the public sector remains an important employer of educated workers, there is evidence that its role is declining some-what for young male workers. Among employed males, the propor-tion of workers aged twenty to twenty-nine who are salaried public sector workers is about 20 percent, which is less than half the per-centages for other prime-age males thirty to fifty-nine years old (see Table 5.3). The public sector continues to be quite important in the

Table 5.2   Proportion of Employed by Sector of Employment, Educational Attainment, and Gender, 1997 (ages 12–65)

	Public, Salaried	Private, Salaried	Self-Employed	Casual	Farming	Total
Males						
Less than primary	15.3	5.0	17.7	35.2	26.9	100.0
Primary/preparatory	32.6	8.3	16.2	31.2	11.7	100.0
Secondary and						
postsecondary	46.0	12.5	13.4	20.8	7.2	100.0
University and above	66.1	14.8	10.7	5.9	2.6	100.0
Other	75.0	7.5	15.0	0.0	5.0	100.0
Total	45.1	11.2	14.0	21.7	8.0	100.0
Females						
Less than primary	6.5	3.4	25.0	26.3	38.8	100.0
Primary/preparatory	27.1	16.7	18.8	27.1	10.4	100.0
Secondary and						
postsecondary	77.4	8.5	3.4	8.5	2.6	100.0
University and above	86.6	4.5	3.6	6.3	0.0	100.0
Other	86.7	13.3	0.0	0.0	0.0	100.0
Total	74.3	8.6	5.1	9.8	2.7	100.0

Source: Egyptian Integrated Household Survey 1997.
Note: Totals may not equal 100 percent due to rounding.

Table 5.3   Type of Employment by Gender and Age, 1997

	Public, Salaried	Private, Salaried	Self-Employed	Casual	Farming	Total
Males						
12–19	1.33	6.00	13.33	57.67	21.67	100.00
20–29	19.63	12.57	15.84	33.77	18.32	100.00
30–39	39.55	11.08	15.37	23.68	10.20	100.00
40–49	45.12	5.56	16.50	20.88	11.78	100.00
50–59	53.28	3.83	12.84	12.02	17.76	100.00
60–65	17.02	2.84	22.70	17.73	39.72	100.00
Total	32.31	8.55	15.55	27.51	16.09	100.00
Females						
12–19	7.55	7.55	9.43	50.94	24.53	100.00
20–29	44.83	13.79	10.92	16.67	13.22	100.00
30–39	61.83	4.30	9.14	14.52	9.68	100.00
40–49	62.42	3.36	13.42	7.38	13.42	100.00
50–59	38.81	4.48	11.94	8.96	35.82	100.00
60–65	14.29	0.00	64.29	7.14	21.43	100.00
Total	49.69	6.85	12.15	15.58	15.73	100.00

Source: Egyptian Integrated Household Survey 1997.
Note: Totals may not equal 100 percent due to rounding.

employment of young females, however, retaining nearly 45 percent of working females aged twenty to twenty-nine. Further evidence along these lines comes from a comparison of results from the October 1988 Labor Force Sample Survey (LFSS) carried out by the Central Agency for Public Mobilization and Statistics (CAPMAS), and the Egyptian Integrated Household Survey (EIHS) of 1997.[2] The October 1988 LFSS data show that nearly 60 percent of male graduates and 80 percent of female graduates were employed by the public sector at that time. The corresponding figures from the EIHS of 1997 are 52 percent and 81 percent, respectively. This confirms a pattern of more private-sector employment for educated males but no change for educated females. If we disaggregate the graduates further into secondary school and university graduates, we see that the declining share of the public sector is limited to male secondary school graduates, of whom only 46 percent are found in the public sector in 1997 compared to 55 percent in 1988. The share of the public sector among educated females remains close to the 80 percent range for both secondary and university graduates.

The dominance of the public sector in the employment of graduates, particularly female graduates, is not unique to Egypt. Although data disaggregated by sector of ownership are generally not easy to come by for most Arab countries, the data that are available show that there is a general tendency for female workers to be concentrated in the public sector. In Jordan, for example, 54 percent of employed females worked in the public sector in 1987 compared to 44 percent of males. In Algeria in 1990, 85 percent of employed females worked for the public sector compared to 50 percent of males (Said, 1994). These similarities reflect a similar commitment on the part of these two countries to provide public-sector jobs for graduates. With the slowdown of public hiring in these countries, a crisis in providing employment to the growing number of educated females entering the workforce is bound to arise unless other socially acceptable employment opportunities emerge.

The experiences of Tunisia and Morocco are instructive in this respect. Both countries have managed to substantially increase female participation in private-sector employment by providing opportunities in export-oriented, labor-intensive manufacturing, such as textiles, garments, and leather goods. As a result, Morocco and Tunisia have much higher proportions of females among production workers and among manufacturing workers than Egypt, Algeria, Jordan, or Syria. In fact, the shares of female production and manufacturing workers in Tunisia and Morocco are similar to those of the newly industrialized countries (NICs), such as Mexico, Malaysia, and South Korea (see Table 5.4).

Segmentation of the Private Labor Market by Gender

The flip side of the public sector's dominant role in employing educated female workers is the apparent inaccessibility of the private labor market to female workers of all educational levels. Several pieces of evidence point to this:

1. Women have limited access to wage employment in the private sector.
2. Female unemployment rates are much higher than male rates.
3. Female wages in the private sector are significantly lower than male wages in that sector and are also much lower than female wages in the public sector.

4. Female workers are heavily concentrated in a small number of industries and occupations.

This section systematically examines some of the evidence available on these four points, relying on results from the EIHS of 1997 as well as other existing studies on the Egyptian labor market.

Limited Access to Wage Employment in the Private Sector

The main characteristic determining women's labor force participation in general, and participation in wage work in particular, is schooling. In fact, the structure of women's employment by educational level in Egypt is quite stark. Women with less than a secondary education simply do not work for wages at any significant rates, and only then as casual workers. Women with a secondary education or higher have significant rates of participation in wage work, but most are employed by the public sector.

Table 5.4   Percentage of Females Among Production and Manufacturing Workers

	Production Workers		Manufacturing Workers	
	Year	Percentage	Year	Percentage
Algeria	1987	2.5	1985	6.9
Egypt	1995	5.5	1995	10.9
Jordan	1993	—	1993	7.8
Morocco	1982	23.0	1992	38.3
Syria	1991	3.2	1991	7.6
Tunisia	1994	22.1	1994	46.3
Indonesia	1995	—	1996	45.4
Malaysia	1995	25.4	1995	41.7
Mexico	1995	19.5	1995	29.9
Pakistan	1995	6.9	1995	11.1
South Korea	1992	27.3	1995	36.8
Turkey	1995	—	1995	16.8

Sources: ILO, *Yearbook of Labor Statistics 1998* (Geneva: ILO, 1998). Data for Algeria are from Valentine Moghadam, "The Political Economy of Female Employment in the Arab Region," in Nabil Khoury and Valentine Moghadam, eds., *Gender and Development in the Arab World: Women's Economic Participation— Patterns and Policies,* pp. 6–34 (London: Zed Books, 1995).

According to the EIHS of 1997, only 12 percent of out-of-school females aged twelve to sixty-five who have less than a secondary education are economically active. Among those, about 80 percent are employed and 20 percent unemployed. Of those who are employed, 34 percent are engaged in farming, 26 percent are casual workers, 24 percent are self-employed outside farming, 10 percent are public-sector salaried workers, and only 6 percent are salaried workers in the private sector. As a proportion to all working-age women with less than a secondary education who are out of school, salaried workers thus constitute no more than 1.5 percent of the total, of whom 1 percent are in the public sector and 0.5 percent are in the private sector. An additional 2 percent are casual wageworkers. In comparison, the equivalent proportions for males are 18.5 percent employed in the public sector, 5 percent employed as salaried workers in the private sector, and 30 percent casual wageworkers. These results strongly suggest that wage work in general, and private-sector salaried work in particular, are currently very limited options for women with less than a secondary education in Egypt.

The rates of overall labor force participation for women with at least a secondary education are much higher, but nonetheless their opportunities for wage employment in the private sector remain extremely limited. Female labor force participation rates increase significantly once women acquire a secondary education and remain high thereafter. According to the EIHS of 1997, the participation rate for out-of school women aged twelve to sixty-five with a secondary education or higher is 68 percent, on average. Multivariate analysis shows that the probability of participating in the labor force is not affected significantly by education until the secondary school level. A vocational secondary degree increases this probability at the margin by 45 percentage points and a university degree increases it by as much as 62 percentage points, keeping other characteristics such as age, marital status, and location constant. However, a significant proportion (38 percent) of these educated women who are economically active are unemployed. Of those who are employed, 81 percent are salaried workers in the public sector, 7.5 percent are salaried workers in the private sector, and a similar proportion are casual wageworkers. Thus for every ten educated women in public-sector jobs, fewer than one educated woman works in a salaried private-sector job and one works in a casual wage job. As a proportion of all educated women, three out of ten work for the public sector and six out of one hundred work for the private sector either as salaried or casual workers.

Unemployment Rates

Further prima facie evidence of the strong barriers to entry faced by women in the private labor market are the significantly higher unemployment rates for women in general and for educated women in particular. According to the EIHS of 1997, female unemployment rates average nearly five times those of men—32 percent compared to 7 percent.[3] Again, the fact that female unemployment rates are higher than male rates is not unique to Egypt. This is a common occurrence across many countries (see Table 5.5). However, the gap is much larger in Egypt than in other comparable countries. Egypt is most similar in this respect to Syria and Pakistan, two countries with relatively closed economies and few opportunities for female labor outside the public sector.

Table 5.5   Unemployment Rate by Gender, Selected Countries and Years (ages 15–64)

		Unemployment Rate		
		Male	Female	All
Algeria[a]	1991	22.5	22.7	22.5
Egypt[b]	1995	7.4	23.8	11.1
Jordan	1991	14.5	34.2	17.1
Morocco[c]	1992	12.8	24.7	15.7
Syria[d]	1991	5.2	14.0	6.8
Tunisia[a]	1989	14.7	21.9	16.2
Indonesia[d]	1996	3.4	5.1	4.1
Mexico[b]	1996	3.5	4.1	3.7
Pakistan[d]	1995	4.1	13.7	5.4
South Korea[a]	1996	2.3	1.6	2.0

Sources: ILO, *Yearbook of Labor Statistics 1998* (Geneva: ILO, 1998); and, for Jordan, Mona Said, *Public Sector Employment and Labor Markets in Arab Countries: Recent Developments and Policy Implications* (Washington, D.C.: International Monetary Fund, 1994).

Notes: a. Ages 15+.
b. Ages 12–64.
c. Ages 12+.

The gender difference in unemployment in Egypt remains even after the age and educational composition of the labor force are taken into account. According to the EIHS of 1997, women are significantly more likely to be unemployed than men at all ages and at all education levels. Although educated women are only somewhat more likely to be unemployed than uneducated women, the vast majority of unemployed females (75 percent) have a secondary school education or higher because of the strong association between female labor force participation and the attainment of at least this level of education.

Even though uneducated female workers are virtually shut out from wage employment in both sectors, they normally don't consider themselves unemployed when not working. For people to declare themselves unemployed, they must at least aspire to a "job," which typically means wage employment. Since this is such a remote prospect for most uneducated women in Egypt, they typically do not express a desire for such employment, nor do they search for it when not working, and are therefore considered outside the labor force rather than unemployed. For these reasons, limited employment opportunities for females in the private sector would tend to show up as lack of participation in the labor force for uneducated females and unemployment for educated females. Because the latter can in theory obtain wage employment in the public sector, they aspire for such work and report themselves to be unemployed when not working.

Data from the LFSS show that the most serious open unemployment problem is experienced by females with intermediate levels of education (mostly commercial secondary degrees), especially those living in rural areas. Unemployment rates for this subgroup increased from 36 percent to 40 percent from 1991 to 1995 in urban areas, and from 59 percent to 64 percent in rural areas. In comparison, unemployment rates among males with similar levels of education appear to have either remained stable or declined slightly over the same period.

Although open unemployment rates are drastically different among males and females in Egypt, underemployment, defined as working fewer than forty hours per week and being available for additional work, is not. Data from the EIHS of 1997 show that 9 percent of working males are underemployed compared to 6 percent of working females (see Table 5.6). The same survey indicates that the majority of the underemployed males (55 percent) are casual wage-workers, followed by farmers (24 percent) and self-employed work-

Table 5.6   Underemployment Rates by Type of Employment and Gender, 1997 (ages 12–65)

	Public, Salaried	Private, Salaried	Self-Employed	Casual	Farming	Total
Males						
Part-time, available	1.4	1.3	8.4	20.6	14.8	9.5
Part-time, not available	7.7	6.7	14.0	18.4	33.3	15.2
Full-time	90.9	92.4	77.6	60.9	52.3	75.3
Total	100.0	100.0	100.0	100.0	100.0	100.0
Females						
Part-time, available	2.6	0.0	2.9	16.3	16.4	6.0
Part-time, not available	13.8	2.9	42.6	28.8	67.2	25.3
Full-time	83.6	97.1	54.4	53.8	17.9	68.6
Total	100.0	100.0	100.0	100.0	100.0	100.0

Source: Egyptian Integrated Household Survey 1997.
Note: Totals may not equal 100 percent due to rounding.

ers (14 percent). Among females, the largest groups of underemployed are also casual wageworkers (39 percent) and farmers (33 percent), but a significant proportion are public-sector salaried workers (24 percent) because of the predominance of this form of employment for women. These visibly underemployed salaried public-sector workers constitute only 2.6 percent of the female public-sector workforce, however.[4] The only categories with significant numbers of workers seeking additional work were casual workers, 21 percent of males and 16 percent of females, and farming, 15 percent of males and 16 percent of females. Unlike the openly unemployed, most of the underemployed are poorly educated. Although they have a tendency to be young, like their unemployed counterparts, they are more broadly distributed over age groups. Finally, most underemployed casual workers live in rural areas.

Wages in the Private Sector

One possible explanation for the low female participation rates in wage employment in the private sector and the high female unemployment rates presented above is that Egyptian women have a strong preference for public-sector employment due to its attractive nonwage attributes. Short of that, according to this interpretation, they would rather care for their families or engage in self-employment. In economic terms, their reservation wage is hypothesized to be somewhere below the public-sector wage but above the private-sector wage. They are therefore willing to queue to enter the public sector, but refrain from working in the private sector, which typically involves more stringent working conditions.

However, evidence on female wages in the private sector contradicts this "preference" interpretation. If this interpretation were true, female private-sector wages would be fairly comparable to male wages. However, there is strong evidence that they are much lower, even after correcting for differences in human capital. Earnings equations estimates on data from the EIHS of 1997 show that the earnings of female salaried workers are nearly 30 percent lower than those of males with similar levels of education and experience in the private sector, compared to a 15 percent gap in the public sector. Among casual workers, the gender gap in earnings is even larger, at nearly 40 percent. Similar estimates from the October 1988 LFSS produce even larger wage gaps. They point to a 50–60 percent gender wage gap in the private sector after correcting for experience and education (Assaad, 1997a). These data also show that although the public-private wage differential is largely negative for males, especially for males with lower levels of education, it is strongly positive for females, even after correcting for worker characteristics. Female public-sector wages are more than twice as high as private-sector wages, and the gap is largest at the intermediate level of education, the level at which females experience the highest rates of unemployment (Assaad, 1997a).

The most reasonable interpretation for these results is that high barriers to entry prevent the entry of females to most private-sector jobs. This results in crowding into the few occupations and jobs that are deemed acceptable for women, thus increasing the supply of labor to these jobs and depressing wages. Thus the wages of both males and females in these "feminine" jobs are likely to be depressed. For instance, the rates of return to schooling are negative for holders of vocational secondary school certificates who work in white-collar jobs, irrespective of gender, but positive, albeit low, for those working in blue-collar jobs (Assaad, 1997a). Female wageworkers are strongly concentrated in these white-collar occupations requiring vocational secondary school certificates. This also happens to be the level of education where female unemployment rates are by far the highest.

High Employment in Certain Industries and Occupations

Further investigation of the "barriers to entry" hypothesis requires an examination of direct evidence on the concentration of females into a small number of industries and occupations in the private sector. EIHS data only allow for the classification of employment by broad industry groups, but contain no information on occupation. Table 5.7 shows that the employment of females is concentrated in services, followed by the agricultural sector and then manufacturing and trade. The distribution of males by industry is more even, with agriculture, services, and manufacturing being the most important. For both

**Table 5.7   Type of Employment by Gender and Industry, 1997
(employed population ages 12–65)**

	Public, Salaried	Private, Salaried	Self-Employed	Casual	Farming	Total
Males						
Agriculture	7.1	4.0	3.9	26.8	95.0	25.9
Mining	0.7	1.2	0.0	0.0	0.0	0.3
Manufacturing	18.1	45.8	27.6	19.9	0.0	19.5
Utilities	3.2	3.2	2.6	2.2	0.0	2.3
Construction	6.1	5.5	8.0	21.9	0.0	9.7
Trade	0.8	11.5	28.3	5.7	0.0	7.2
Transport	7.1	6.3	11.5	10.6	0.4	7.6
Finance	1.9	2.0	0.2	0.5	0.0	0.9
Services	50.3	15.8	7.2	6.3	1.1	20.6
Personal services	1.3	2.0	4.3	1.5	0.0	1.7
Other	1.7	2.8	2.2	1.4	0.0	1.5
Not recorded	1.6	0.0	4.3	3.4	3.6	2.7
Total	100.0	100.0	100.0	100.0	100.0	100.0
Females						
Agriculture	4.7	6.8	0.0	32.0	87.3	21.5
Mining	0.0	0.0	0.0	0.0	0.0	0.0
Manufacturing	6.0	38.6	24.4	18.0	0.0	11.2
Utilities	1.3	0.0	0.0	0.0	0.0	0.6
Construction	0.9	4.5	0.0	2.0	0.0	1.1
Trade	0.6	6.8	55.1	15.0	0.0	10.0
Transport	1.3	0.0	0.0	2.0	0.0	0.8
Finance	3.1	4.5	1.3	0.0	0.0	2.0
Services	77.7	27.3	6.4	20.0	1.0	44.5
Personal services	2.2	11.4	9.0	3.0	0.0	3.4
Other	0.9	0.0	0.0	0.0	0.0	0.5
Not recorded	0.9	0.0	5.1	8.0	11.8	4.2
Total	100.0	100.0	100.0	100.0	100.0	100.0

Source: Egyptian Integrated Household Survey 1997.

sexes, services is the dominant sector for public-salaried workers, manufacturing for private-salaried workers, and trade and manufacturing for the self-employed, the association between self-employment and working in trade being particularly strong for females.

Data from the October 1988 LFSS do provide information on occupation and reveal that female wageworkers in the private sector are significantly more concentrated than their male counterparts in a small number of occupations. Moreover, among the most prevalent occupations among male and female workers, very few are common for both males and females, confirming that most occupations are gender-typed. Among female nonagricultural wageworkers in the private sector, 37 percent are in the three most prevalent occupations and 46 percent are in the five most prevalent.[5] The equivalent proportions for males are 20 percent and 31 percent, respectively. The five most prevalent occupations among female nonagricultural wageworkers in the private sector are salesperson (15 percent), domestic servant (14.5 percent), typist/secretary (7.6 percent), primary schoolteacher (4.6 percent), and dressmaker (3.6 percent). Of these occupations, only two are blue-collar and therefore open to women with less than secondary certificates. The only one of these occupations that shows up among the top five male occupations is salesperson.

Likely Causes for Gender Segmentation of the Private Labor Market

The barriers that women face in obtaining employment in the private sector are due to a complex set of causes related to prevailing social norms about women's domestic responsibilities and their participation in the public sphere. However, these deep-seated social norms are reinforced by legal provisions that mandate female-specific benefits and obligations on employers, which make it more costly for private employers to hire female workers relative to male workers.

Some of the social norms limiting female participation in the private sector include the fact that women's work in a large number of occupations is deemed socially unacceptable. For instance, four of the five most prevalent occupations for men in the Egyptian private sector are either connected to manual construction work or to driving motor vehicles. All are virtually closed to women. The fact that over 90 percent of nonagricultural wage employment is either outside fixed establishments or inside establishments of fewer than ten workers further reduces the social acceptability of such employment. Second, private employers complain of the high turnover among young female workers, who tend to leave their jobs once they get married or have children, which results in the loss of the specific human capital employers invest in these workers through on-the-job training. Third, employers complain that women, because of their household responsibilities, are less willing to work long hours and are more likely to have high rates of absenteeism. Finally, some researchers argue that employers give preference to men over women and are willing to pay them higher wages out of a perception that women are not the primary wage earners and do not need to support their families (Moghadam, 1995c; Joekes, 1985).

Existing labor legislation reinforces the bias against female workers by imposing on employers female-specific benefits related to paid and unpaid maternity leaves and, in some cases, childcare provisions. Although these are essential rights and protections that female workers should have, the fact that their cost is borne by employers rather than covered through the social security system provides strong disincentives to private employers for hiring female workers when male labor is plentiful. The proposed new labor law reduces the number of times a woman can obtain maternity benefits from three to two, but at the same time increases paid maternity leave each time from fifty to ninety days, and increases unpaid leave from one to two years in enterprises employing fifty or more workers. These extensions in female-specific employer mandates are likely to exacerbate the existing reluctance of employers to hire female workers.

These reasons why private employers prefer male workers are not unique to Egypt. Employers in many parts of the world share these views. Employers in labor-intensive, export-oriented manufacturing, however, are a notable exception to this pattern. Researchers across the world have found a strong link between women's employment in the private sector and the importance of export-led industrialization (see Moghadam, 1995c; Cagatay and Berik, 1990; Standing, 1989). In Morocco and Tunisia, where these industries are important, the shares of female workers in factories producing for export markets are particularly high, and so are the rates of female participation in the private sector (UNIDO, 1993: 35–41). Researchers have also found that the proportion of female workers across firms is positively related to the extent to which the product is oriented toward foreign markets (Joekes, 1982). In a survey of employers in the Moroccan clothing industry, Joekes (1985) found that the majority of employers preferred female workers. This was partly because women were as productive as men in similar jobs but cheaper to employ (cited in Moghadam, 1995c: 34). Thus, when subjected to international competitive pressures, employers appear more likely to overcome traditional perceptions about women workers and more willing to hire them.

I have opted to describe the constraints limiting women's employment in the private sector as barriers rather than preferences, even though preferences and barriers are, to some extent, mutually determined. For instance, women's preference for shorter hours, because of their household responsibilities, can turn into a barrier when employers use it to screen out female applicants. Women's need to interrupt their working careers to have children can be construed in a similar light. Clearly, young female new entrants have a strong preference for public-sector jobs because of their more equitable pay scales, relatively short hours, and the job security they provide.

However, this is not the reason why females are not joining the private sector in larger numbers. The low female wage rates in the private sector demonstrate that at least some female workers are willing to work in this sector for very low wages and that the problem is therefore not one of high reservation wage. The problem appears to be the widespread perceptions among private employers that the non-wage costs of hiring female workers are large due to high turnover, absenteeism, unwillingness to work long hours, and costly female-specific legal protections. These perceptions may be based in part on the realities employers observe, and in part on entrenched preconceived notions about gender differences. The point is not that employers are acting irrationally or indulging in discrimination out of choice, but that they are resisting having to bear the costs associated with women's reproductive role when male labor is plentiful.

From a public policy point of view, ways must be found to shift some of the costs of reproduction away from employers and individual women themselves to society as a whole, through publicly supported childcare and maternity benefits that are covered by the social insurance system. This shift is clearly not feasible in the short run, and may be quite costly from a fiscal point of view. In the short run, the objective of public policy should be to set up a policy environment in which new employment opportunities can be created in the private sector in spheres that have traditionally been considered female-specific. International experience has shown that export-led, labor-intensive industries are a good source of such opportunities.

Earnings and Their Determinants:
Benefits of Education and Experience?

Since public-sector salaries are often set through formal wage-setting rules based on seniority and educational credentials, while private salaries are more likely to be determined by market forces, wage formation should be examined separately for the public and private sectors. Analysis of the determinants of earnings for salaried workers, using the EIHS of 1997, shows that education has a stronger impact on earnings in the public sector than in the private sector. When education is included in terms of years of schooling, the rate of return to one year of schooling is 5.5 percent per year for public-sector workers and 4.4 percent per year for private-sector salaried workers. When data are disaggregated by educational level, however, a somewhat different picture emerges. There is a significant increase in earnings resulting from the completion of preparatory education in both the public and the private sector, with the bigger change occurring in the former. The rate of return to one year of schooling up to that level is 5 percent per year in the public sector and 3.7 percent per year in the private sector. There is very little change in earnings between the preparatory and technical secondary levels, and only a small change between the secondary and the nonuniversity postsecondary level. University education is fairly lucrative in both the public and the private sector. It produces rates of return to schooling of 8–9 percent per year of education above the secondary level.

Similar results were obtained from the October 1988 LFSS, but because the sample for that survey was larger, it was possible also to disaggregate data by gender. The results reveal that at the secondary level, rates of return to schooling are higher in the public than in the private sector, and higher for males than for females in both sectors (Assaad, 1997a). In fact, the October 1988 LFSS data show that for the largest category of female wageworkers, namely those who hold technical secondary degrees and work in white-collar occupations, rates of return to schooling are negative. At the university level, there is greater parity in the rate of return to schooling in the public and private sectors and between males and females.

According to analyses using EIHS 1997 data, work experience counts for more in the private sector in the early years, but there is more curvature in the wage experience profile of private-sector workers. At low levels of experience, one year of experience results in a 2.6 percent increase in wages in the public sector and a 4 percent increase in wages in the private sector. Similar results are obtained across the two sectors for male workers from the October 1988 LFSS data. However, the results do not appear to hold for female workers in the 1988 data, which reveal that experience counts for less in the private sector than in the public sector (Assaad, 1997a).

Thus the analysis of earnings for salaried workers reveals that rates of return to schooling are lower in the private sector, confirming the lower value that private-sector employers place on education. This is especially true for technical secondary education, for which there is practically no educational premium. In contrast, university education appears to be valued in the private sector for both males and females. The low premium placed on technical secondary education in the private sector is the result of an oversupply of workers with those credentials. Young people have striven to achieve technical secondary credentials over the past thirty years as a way to obtain access to public-sector jobs through the graduate employment guarantee scheme. Now that these jobs are not forthcoming, youth are crowding into the private sector, which has little use for the skills they have to offer and is therefore unwilling to pay them any more than someone with only a preparatory education.

Self-Employment

Given the limits of wage employment in the private sector, especially for women, and poor prospects for any increase in public-sector employment, does self-employment offer a realistic alternative? Self-employment is increasingly seen by Egyptian policymakers as a potential solution to the problem of unemployment among graduates. Numerous programs try to promote the establishment of small business and microbusiness through loans and technical assistance. It is therefore interesting to see what recent data reveal about the structure and determinants of self-employment in Egypt.

According to the EIHS of 1997, 15 percent of male workers and 12 percent of female workers were self-employed outside farming in 1997. Male self-employed workers are concentrated in trade, 28.3 percent, and manufacturing, 27.6 percent, as compared to 7.2 percent and 19.5 percent in these two industries for all male workers. Female self-employed workers outside farming are also concentrated in the two industries, but much more so in trade, 55.1 percent, than in manufacturing, 24.4 percent (see Table 5.7).

The same survey shows that self-employment among males tends to be associated with low levels of education, but a significant proportion of self-employed males have a technical secondary education, 18.9 percent. Among females, the vast majority of the self-employed either have no formal schooling, 60 percent, or incomplete primary schooling, 14 percent. Thus self-employment appears to be an option that male graduates are willing and able to take up, but for female graduates who have the greatest problems with unemployment, it seems to be very rare. The male graduates who become self-employed are likely to have industrial vocational degrees. Female graduates, who mostly have white-collar skills, don't seem to have this option.

I conclude from this analysis that policies to promote self-employment among graduates through subsidized credit and technical assistance are going against the grain of existing practices. They seem somewhat more appropriate for males with technical secondary education, who tend to have manual skills, but are of limited value either for university-educated males or for all females graduates. Since over 60 percent of all graduates entering the labor market every year, or about 380,000 individuals, have technical secondary credentials, there is an urgent need to make the skills they obtain in vocational secondary schools more relevant to the needs of private-sector employers.

Conclusion

The main feature of the Egyptian labor market at present is the absence of viable alternatives for educated young females entering the labor force, now that the public-sector employment option has been closed. Compared to their less educated counterparts, females with secondary school degrees are much more likely to participate in the labor force. In fact, the main goal of acquiring this educational credential in the past thirty years was to join the ranks of government workers, and in turn the ranks of the middle class. The challenge now is to meet this increasing supply of labor with new sources of labor demand in the private sector.

For a variety of reasons, the Egyptian private sector appears to be highly inhospitable to the increasing number of educated females entering the labor market every year. Their male counterparts appear to be increasingly able to find work in the private sector. Many of the jobs they are taking were previously not deemed education-appropriate, but in the absence of the public-sector employment option are now being taken up. Self-employment seems to be a viable option only for male technical secondary school graduates, who are more likely to have manual skills.

The obstacles faced by young women in obtaining private-sector jobs are due to a complex set of social factors related to their need to harmonize wage employment with what is still perceived as their primary responsibility, namely to start a family, bear children, and undertake most of the domestic work of a household. In those occupations that are considered socially acceptable to both men and women, employers generally prefer men because of a widespread perception that men are likely to remain in their jobs longer, are more willing to work long hours, have fewer legal provisions regulating their employment, and have lower absenteeism rates—in short, because their attachment to the labor force is more solid and they do not have to share their time between their work and their families to the same extent as female workers. Women are therefore relegated to a few gender-typed occupations, where overcrowding results in depressed wages. The problem is particularly acute for technical secondary school graduates (60 percent of all graduates), and to a lesser extent, for graduates of postsecondary higher institutes (10 percent of graduates). This category of graduates experiences unemployment rates in the range of 50–60 percent, which are extremely high by any standard. Among those under thirty years of age, unemployment rates can reach 70 percent.

Egypt is not unique in this respect, but is experiencing the problem more acutely than other countries for two reasons. First, the opportunity of accessing public-sector employment in the past has raised the demand for certain types of education and concomitantly the demand for wage employment outside the home for educated women. Second, suitable employment opportunities have not materialized for women in the private sector because of the limited extent of labor-intensive, export-oriented manufacturing industries, which have been the most important source of demand for educated female labor in many parts of the developing world. The development of these industries has been limited for the most part by structural factors, such as the protective trade regime, the importance of resource transfers from abroad, and the concomitant appreciation of the exchange rate. In combination with substantial social barriers to entry of female workers in much of the private sector, these factors have resulted in excessively high open unemployment rates for educated females.

The employment inadequacy facing uneducated workers does not show up as open unemployment. These workers typically do not appear in any significant numbers among the ranks of the unemployed because they simply cannot afford to remain without work for extended periods of time while searching for an appropriate job. Visible underemployment is one way of uncovering employment inadequacy among these workers. According to the EIHS of 1997, 9 percent of males and 6 percent of females appeared to be visibly underemployed, in the sense of working fewer than forty hours per week and being available for additional work. Most of these are poorly educated, typically working as casual workers in rural areas or as farmers. Admittedly, visible underemployment does not capture full-time employment at very low levels of productivity and earnings, which is another measure of employment inadequacy that is relevant for the poor.

It is even more difficult to ascertain the employment prospects of females with less than a secondary education because most of them are simply classified as being outside the labor force. Only 12 percent of these females, most of whom have no education at all, are economically active. Those who are economically active are generally working in farming, in self-employment (mostly in trade), or as casual workers. Most of those in farming and about half of the self-employed are working part-time and are not available for additional work because most of their time is presumably occupied by their heavy domestic responsibilities.

Increasing employment opportunities for females in the private sector will be a slow and long-term process. It will require a combination of policies in many areas, including a reduction of the disincentive to employers to hire women, reforms in the skills development system, and structural reforms to encourage export-oriented manufacturing. Since social norms about the suitability of various jobs to women will change only slowly, short-term objectives should aim at increasing opportunities in traditionally female spheres, such as garment and textile manufacturing, pharmaceuticals, food processing, and electronics assembly. The growth of such activities can be fostered by policy reforms that aim to reduce biases against exports, particularly manufactured exports.

To reduce the nonwage costs of employing females, female-specific mandates on employers, such as lengthy paid and unpaid maternity leaves and provisions for employer-paid childcare, should be reduced to a minimum in labor legislation. Moreover, active labor-market policies to facilitate the insertion of formally educated but low-skilled job seekers into the labor market should also be considered. These may include programs to reduce the cost to employers of newly hired inexperienced workers while they are receiving on-the-job training. These training subsidies would be particularly important for young women because they are perceived by employers to have high labor turnover and therefore to be unworthy of the initial investment. Other active labor-market policies to facilitate the insertion of youth that have proved effective in other countries include job-search assistance and certain types of targeted training.

Notes

1. "Graduates" denotes individuals who have completed a secondary or higher education: those with general and technical secondary school degrees, those with postsecondary higher education, and those with university and graduate degrees.

2. Such comparisons should be made with caution due to significant differences in data-collection methodologies between the two surveys. The greatest differences, however, are in the measurement of women's labor force participation in agricultural and informal activities. These differences should not affect the labor force status of educated females, since few of them engage in such activities.

3. The results of the latest published CAPMAS Labor Force Survey (May 1995) confirm this pattern. It reports a female unemployment rate of 23.6 percent compared to a male rate of 7.2 percent. Much of the fluctuation in the female rate among different sources can be attributed to differences in the numerator of the unemployment rate—the estimate of the female labor force—rather than to estimates of the number of unemployed.

4. This analysis considers only visible underemployment, which is defined as fewer hours of work than a certain norm and a desire to work more. It does not consider invisible underemployment, which is defined as employment at a lower level of productivity or wage than a certain norm.

5. Occupations are defined here at the three-digit level of the Standard Arabic Occupational Classification.

Laurie A. Brand

6

Jordan: Women and the Struggle for Political Opening

What contribution do women's organizations make to processes of political opening, or liberalization? And what is the relative impact of domestic versus international or global influences? The demonstration effect of openings in one country on others and the impact of "liberal" ideas on more authoritarian political systems have received considerable scholarly attention; however, little of the mainstream literature on "political transition" has taken an interest in the role of women, women's organizations, and women's issues in these political processes. A vast literature has developed on the role of so-called civil society organizations in underpinning or fighting for democratization around the world, some of which suggests that women's movements may be expected to be in the forefront of a push against the limits of authoritarian regimes. The argument is made that, because they assert such basic claims as individual dignity and equality, women's organizations are not easily assailed by the state. There is also a contention that because they do not generally seek the reallocation of resources, they are less likely to be seen as a threat and are less susceptible to co-optation.[1] In a similar vein, based on feminist literature arguing that women's nurturing role orients them toward peace and conflict resolution, one might presume that women would be among the first to support regimes demonstrating respect for human rights, and would be likely to manage their own organizations according to particapatory, rather than authoritarian, principles.[2]

An examination of women's experiences with and in democratic transitions in Eastern Europe, and redemocratizations in Latin America, reveals that such literatures and claims may not take us

143

very far in understanding women's possibilities and fates during periods of liberalization or democratization.[3] In the former socialist countries, state-sponsored women's organizations established under the communist regimes were largely discredited, along with the idea of women's role in the public sphere, as a result of the transitions. And although women were certainly among the opposition to the communist governments, in no case were they organized *as women* against the regimes. The reemergence of organized women's groups has been slow and has enjoyed only limited appeal. In Latin America the situation was quite different, as in a number of countries women played active and visible roles *as women* in pushing for the transitions. This was the case with the gradual "decompression" in Brazil and with the Madres de la Plaza in Argentina. As a result of both their oppositional roles and their visibility, the successor regimes were forced, or saw it to be in their interests, to respond to women's demands as a part of the liberalization process.[4]

The argument to be made and illustrated below is that while the impetus to liberalize may owe in part to external pressures or influences, the role of women and women's organizations during the most recent period of political opening was overwhelmingly shaped by two domestic factors: the nature and extent of women's organizing prior to the beginning of the liberalization, and the nature of that organizing's relationship to the state. While women's groups are characterized by certain vulnerabilities that may well be particular to them, the case of Jordan will be used to demonstrate that women's organizations are likely to be just as constrained and shaped by existing social and political structures and practices as are institutions run by men. The continual imperative to address their special vulnerabilities may well make many of the efforts of women's groups more heroic on some scales than those of their male counterparts, but these efforts do not seem or promise to constitute a conscience or a special category with more likelihood to serve as a basis for greater opening or civility of practice than their counterparts in other sectors.

The discussion that follows will first examine the nature of the Jordanian state and then present a brief history of the women's movement prior to the most extensive political liberalization in the kingdom's history, that of 1989–1994. The main body of this chapter will then address the experiences of three women's organizations in the post-1989 period, to draw lessons about women's relations with the state and the degree to which they are affected by domestic versus external forces. The chapter concludes with the lessons that emerge from this experience.

The Jordanian State

Jordan is a monarchy in which the king both reigns and rules. The kingdom has long had a functioning parliament, comprising both an upper (appointed) and a lower (elected) house; but with only brief exceptions prior to 1989, the parliament has had little more than a rubber stamp function. Political parties were outlawed in 1957, martial law was imposed, and political oppositional activity of any sort was forced underground. On the economic front, the kingdom has long relied on strategic rents, paid in turn by Great Britain, the United States, and the Arab Gulf states, in exchange for the buffer or security role that Amman has played in the region. These rents, combined with state policy toward their use, produced oversized civilian and state bureaucracies as well as an economy dependent upon regular infusions of aid from abroad, rather than domestic productive activity, to finance expansion.

In the realm of so-called civil society, only professional organizations such as unions of doctors, engineers, lawyers, and the like succeeded, despite state interference, in maintaining an independent and at times vibrant existence during the martial law regime. Women's activity was particularly vulnerable to state and societal coercion because of women's heavier burdens in the home (and hence the greater opportunity cost associated with engaging in activities outside the home) and because people associated political activity with jail, and jail with the loss of a woman's honor.

The role of family, clan, and tribal ties is also basic to understanding society and politics in the kingdom, for these structures underpin a conservative society. For many women, considerations of family honor (which is understood to reside first and foremost in women) mean that women's mobility outside the home is restricted to varying degrees, with the most acceptable reasons for such movements being those associated with securing family needs, whether this means household errands or perhaps paid labor. Beyond such considerations, which region or tribe one is from—whether man or woman—has direct implications for many aspects of daily activity, from bureaucratic and judicial procedures to government policy and appointments. For example, such factors may well make the difference in being admitted to a particular university faculty, receiving a fellowship, or securing state employment. At the national level, prime ministers and cabinet members are also generally chosen because of the family or region from which they hail, and the cabinet is regularly shuffled as a means by which the king cultivates patronage and preempts alternative centers of power from developing.

Turning to the question of political liberalization, Jordan has experienced three identifiable periods of "opening." The first, 1954–1957, came shortly after Hussein's assumption of the throne and was precipitated by the general political ferment in the region as well as the direct impact of the 1948 Palestine War and the consequent influx of large numbers of Palestinian refugees (as well as the subsequent annexation of the West Bank) into the kingdom. The second opening came in the wake of the 1967 war, as the regime, discredited by the swift and humiliating defeat inflicted by Israel, was forced to rein in its security forces. The third period, the impact of which on women will be more thoroughly explored in this chapter, came in the wake of economic riots in 1989 and lasted until summer 1994. At that point the liberalization stalled and has been periodically turned back, in some cases—although not in the case of women—with a vengeance. As this periodization indicates, a high vulnerability to external influences characterized Jordanian politics well before the penetrative forces currently associated with globalization began to attract scholarly attention. Jordan's location and economic situation led to an early, dependent incorporation into the regional oil and war economy—shaped heavily by Western penetration and involvement.

A Brief History of the Women's Movement

Although the amirate was founded in 1921, one cannot speak meaningfully of organized women's initiatives until the mid-1940s, and even then such efforts were limited, generally involving meetings and seminars aimed at raising awareness of child health and welfare issues. Thus the activity was aimed at making women better mothers and at rearing the next generation, not at substantially changing or improving women's socioeconomic status or legal position. The establishment of the Arab Women's Federation (AWF; Ittihad al-

Mar'ah al-'Arabiyyah) on June 17, 1954, marked a qualitative change in the type of women's organization found in Jordan. Among the AWF's goals were fighting illiteracy, raising women's socioeconomic level, preparing women to exercise their full rights as citizens, and developing bonds of friendship between Arab women and women around the world to improve the situation at home and to strengthen peace.[5] Branches of the AWF quickly spread beyond Amman to Irbid, Zarqa, Karak, and Salt, and membership grew to thousands of women.

Among the AWF's early demands were changes in the personal status, labor, and electoral laws.[6] With support from the political parties and professional associations, in early November 1954 the AWF presented its first memorandum to the prime minister requesting a change in the electoral law to give women the right to run for office and to vote in municipal and parliamentary elections. The government took the matter under advisement, and the legal committee in the parliament recommended that an amendment be discussed. However, when the proposed changes were published, they stipulated that only educated women be given the vote, something that caused great outrage, since any illiterate male had the right to vote for—and sit in—parliament. The women continued to send memos each time there was a cabinet reshuffle, and finally the government agreed to reexamine the electoral law. Unfortunately, other events at the national level conspired against the federation and its goals, as a coup attempt in early April 1957 led to a political crackdown that counted the AWF among its casualties.

Any sort of organizing activity of an even remotely political nature was frozen until after the Arabs' defeat in the June 1967 war, when attention turned to the question of Palestine and the newly occupied West Bank and Gaza Strip. At this point, those interested in political activity, men or women, began to gravitate to the constituent factions of the Palestinian resistance movement. The renewed possibility of political organizing was a direct result of the 1967 war, which had discredited the Jordanian regime, its military, and the security services. The Palestinian guerrilla organizations began to take advantage of the consequent political opening to expand their operations.

Their popularity brought new recruits, among them young women. In addition, the General Union of Palestinian Women, a popular organization that was part of the Palestine Liberalization

Organization (PLO), which had been forbidden to open an official branch in Jordan prior to the 1967 war, also took advantage of the opportunity to offer such facilities as literacy classes, first aid and civil defense instruction, embroidery workshops, and sewing courses in the kingdom. However, although the women were working in the framework of a political organization, very few were integrated into the decisionmaking frameworks of the resistance organizations. As a result, much of their work ended up resembling that of a women's auxiliary group (Brand, 1988: 199–200), although the very act of leaving the house to go to the office of a resistance organization was a major step of liberation for many young women.

In September 1970 major fighting broke out between the Jordanian army and the Palestinian resistance. By July 1971 the remnants of the resistance had been driven from the country, and its institutional infrastructure, including that of the women, had been destroyed or closed down. A multifaceted backlash followed. On a communal level, suspicion and enmity between Transjordanians and Jordanians of Palestinian origin soared. On another level, there was a reaction against what had been viewed as the greater social freedom exercised by resistance members—both men and women. But the response targeted women and involved new "protective" measures in the form of a resurgence of "weapons of virtue" and concern with family *sharaf* (honor) as primarily based in the chastity and modesty of its female members. This was part of a revival of "traditional" values and practices, most certainly encouraged by the regime. A hesitation or reluctance to raise women's issues was a natural result in the renewed atmosphere of repression that characterized the martial law regime (Tall, 1985: 58).

For several years, activist women had limited options: they could work either with one of the underground parties or with the charitable society of their choice. The first sign of renewed movement, but certainly not in the context of a political opening, came in a March 5, 1974, letter from the king regarding the franchise for women. The king's letter, which included a royal decree finally amending the election law to give women the vote, came against the backdrop of preparations for the UN Decade for Women, scheduled to begin in 1975. At about the same time, a group of women, many of whom had been active in the AWF, met in anticipation of the UN conference to form a preparatory committee to celebrate women's year in the name of what they called the National Women's Grouping in Jordan. In addition to their work on the upcoming UN meeting, one of their most important goals was to reestablish a women's federation in the kingdom. As a result of intense activity, on August 13, 1974, the Society of the Women's Federation in Jordan (WFJ) was licensed by the Ministry of the Interior.[7]

The goals of the WFJ were familiar: to raise women's educational and socioeconomic level; to support women's exercise of their full rights as citizens, workers, and heads of households; to strengthen bonds of friendship and cooperation with Arab and international women's organizations; to represent women in Jordan in international Arab and women's conferences; to support Arab solidarity in the economic, cultural, educational, and social fields; and to support women's effective participation in building the Arab homeland (Tall, 1985: 131–132). In the six years of the WFJ's activity, its membership grew from 100 to some 3,000, with 1,500 in the capital (Tall, 1985: 134; Mu'adh, 1986: 61).[8] Its leadership included both Palestinian and Transjordanian women from a broad range of political affiliations. The federation operated training and literacy centers, and sponsored support services for children, including nurseries. Among its regular programs were weekly seminars, lectures, story or poetry readings, trips, fundraising dinners, and annual charity bazaars to sell the products of the various training centers.

In the political realm the WFJ demanded the right to participate in discussions of the labor law, the right to attend seminars and conferences to offer better presentations on women, and the adoption of international and Arab resolutions opposing discrimination against women. While the federation played an active role domestically and internationally, with the parliament inactive there was no opportunity to mobilize women to exercise their newly granted right to vote or run for election (Tall, 1985: 141–142).

In 1980 a meeting was held so that Jordan's official delegation to the upcoming UN Decade for Women meeting in Copenhagen, headed by newly appointed Minister of Social Development In'am al-Mufti, the first female minister in Jordan's history, could make a presentation about its activities. It was at this meeting that the idea of establishing another women's organization was vetted with the presentation of a paper titled "The Ministry of Social Development—Women's Organizing," which spoke of the need to establish specific federations (for rural women, professional women, etc.). A "General Federation of Jordanian Women" was one of the unions to which the paper referred (Tall, 1985: 162–163).

However, since none of these organizations existed in fact, a new idea was put forward: to combine the existing women's social societies and agencies with a number of prominent individual women activists as the base of the new general federation. The women present at this meeting, none of whom were WFJ members, were then invited to a meeting on September 5, 1981, at which the bylaws of the new federation were proposed. All those who came were considered members by virtue of their attendance, and their attendance was understood to imply their acceptance of this new formula (Tall, 1985: 164). The General Federation of Jordanian Women (GFJW) was considered operative from that date.

[handwritten margin note: GFJW established to replace existing womens orgs including WFJ which was ordered to close]

What was the purpose of this government initiative? Beginning about the time of Mufti's appointment, the state authorities had begun to harass WFJ delegates to Arab and international conferences, claiming that the federation took positions antagonistic to the kingdom (Mu'adh, 1986: 64). Rumors began to circulate that the Ministry of the Interior intended to close the WFJ, and finally, on December 18, 1981, the WFJ received a letter from the ministry, dated October 26, 1981, ordering its closure. After discussions between the women and the minister of the interior subsequent to the arrival of the closure letter, the minister scaled down his objections to the WFJ, stating that the problem was in its name, which was similar to that of the new union. The WFJ responded by changing its name to Al-Rabitah al-Nisa'iyyah f-il-Urdunn, the Women's League in Jordan, in order to continue its work (Tall, 1985: 157).

In the meantime, however, the WFJ activists had also decided to fight the order, and two prominent lawyers took their case on a pro bono basis. The High Court of Justice did look into the case and in fact ruled against the Ministry of the Interior. Not surprisingly, however, in the battle of bureaucratic wills during a period of martial law, the ministry succeeded in blocking the implementation of the court's ruling.[9] The name change, therefore, did not save the federation: the activity of the former WFJ was frozen, and the state-sponsored GFJW was left as the only umbrella women's organization in the country. It remained so until after the beginning of the 1989 liberalization.

For the social, political, and economic reasons noted earlier, civil society in the traditional Western sense was able to carve out only a very small sphere in Jordan. At the same time, the societal restrictions on women's movement and activity outside the home placed further constraints on women's participation in the institutions that were permitted to operate. Women's participation in charitable societies was generally tolerated, although at times some charities encountered obstacles when trying to obtain registration. The lesson of the pre-1989 period seems to be that what the state and the men who run it think of as "women's work" is viewed as apolitical and nonthreatening. Indeed, not only does such work reinforce women's existing roles and activities, but it also encourages a status quo rather than a transformational strategy, which is certainly more acceptable to the upper echelons of the state and society, both men and women.

On the other hand, women's activity that implied the potential development of kingdomwide structures outside a governmental framework was much more problematic. The success of the AWF may be attributed to the political organizing space that the period of relatively greater freedom (1954–1957) had allowed. The same may be said of the activities of the unofficial branch of the General Union of Palestinian Women, which operated openly throughout the country between 1967 and 1970. When the political crackdowns came, ending these periods, the women's unions met the same fate as other non-state-sponsored actors (with the exception of the professional associations): closure or the freezing of activity. In both cases, women's organizations took advantage of political openings, but did not or were not in a position to push for anything more. The fate of the WFJ was particularly closely tied to regime preferences: it was established to provide Jordan a representative for an approaching UN conference and was closed down—apparently—when its activist program was judged to have exceeded the bounds of what was deemed acceptable by the state. The leadership clearly did feel that participation by a Jordanian delegation in the UN meeting related to women was important, but probably largely for the sake of appearances. At this stage there is little indication that external forces or ideas were having any practical impact on domestic policymaking. The whole episode suggests a state apparatus involved in demobilization of women or obstruction of their organizing efforts when such efforts move into realms viewed as politically problematic.

Women's Organizations During Liberalization

The most recent period of political liberalization began in early summer 1989, triggered by April riots protesting the lifting of subsidies on petroleum products; the latter was part of the government's implementation of the agreement it had signed earlier that year with the International Monetary Fund (IMF). Economic pressures on the kingdom had been building as the regional oil economy slipped into recession. The economic downturn, in large part a result of the Iran-Iraq war, affected both the level of expatriate remittances Jordan received, as well as the levels of foreign aid offered by the oil-producing states. A disastrous export credit program with Iraq only increased the kingdom's woes and drew down its gold reserves. In late summer 1988, the dinar had lost nearly half its value, and by January 1989 it was clear that Jordan could no longer service its external debt. As part of the liberalization that followed, the press began to feel the loosening of the reins of censorship, members of outlawed political parties were able to resurface with impunity, and parliamentary elections, the first in twenty-two years, were announced for November 1989. The campaign period was quite lively, and the outcome—the taking of more than one-third of parliamentary seats by Islamist candidates of various stripes—was a surprise to many, especially the state authorities. After a new prime minister was appointed, the increasing relaxation of limits on expression became clear, political exiles began returning home, and those dismissed from civil service jobs because of political activities deemed unacceptable in the pre-1989 period began to be restored to their jobs.

The General Federation of Jordanian Women

As the GFJW, along with other organizations, began to emerge from the martial law period, a complex controversy arose that illustrates a number of the key elements and problems at work as the kingdom moved away from its martial law past. The trigger was the approach of long-overdue elections for the federation's seventeen-member executive committee. Prior to the elections, Minister of Social Affairs 'Abd al-Majid Shraydeh, identified as an independent Islamist, dismissed the existing executive and appointed a temporary committee to oversee the elections, scheduled for August. This caused a huge row, as GFJW members claimed that the minister had no right to make such a decision.[10] The dismissed members of the executive proceeded to take Shraydeh to court.

The controversy then expanded as the result of a legal/administrative development. During the term of the then–recently ousted executive, a new set of bylaws had been drawn up that allowed for an enormous increase in the federation's membership by adding the possibility of individual membership through a new category of "local committees," which could be established by any group of thirty women.[11] The union's executive committee opened the way to such individual membership on February 11, 1990.

The women who initially took greatest advantage of this change reportedly were the members of Rand, the Democratic Women's League, associated with the Democratic Front for the Liberation of Palestine (DFLP). Yet while the leftist women may have been the first to take advantage of this change, beginning in March, women who "looked like they belonged to the Islamic sisterhood," according to one GFJW member, began to show up regularly at the GFJW headquarters. They came in large numbers to pay their membership registration fees.[12]

The uproar that ensued indicated that the changed bylaws were at best complicated and at worst open to contradictory interpretations. Some contended that the problem originated with the initial drafters of the changed bylaws, although observers also seemed to agree that it was Shraydeh's subsequent interpretation of what became the infamous Article 12—which regulated voting representation—that was the problem because it gave unfair representation to Islamist women. For their part, the Islamist women claimed that it was only when Shraydeh's interpretation did not meet the liking of the other women that they cried foul. The story from the other side was that the decry against the minister came earlier: that the original executive was dissolved not because its term had expired (more than a year earlier), but because it had refused ministry interference in the union's internal affairs.[13]

It was clear from the beginning that this was in part a power struggle between Islamist women and others over control of the union. Leftist women argue that, given the political opening at the national level and the union's move to expand membership, they had hoped to forge a national coalition, including centrist and Islamist women. They claim that the Islamist women rejected the coalition idea and instead sought to win complete control of the union at a time when a number of Islamist members of a revitalized parliament were calling for women's return to the home.[14] The Islamist women, on the other hand, portrayed their efforts as aimed at thwarting an attempt by a coalition of nonrepresentative leftists and elite women to take control of the union.[15] Given the political climate at the time—the newness of the liberalization experiment and the Islamist victories in the November 1989 parliamentary elections—the secular women's fears and the Islamist women's sense of rising fortunes probably ruled out any possibility of compromise even before the fact.

When elections for the executive committee of the Amman chapter were finally held in mid-July 1990, it was—to the surprise of many—not the Islamist women, but a nine-member national bloc, that won. The leftist (many from Rand) and centrist (progovernment) women had managed to construct an alliance that swept the elections, as a record 228 out of 238 representatives of organizations and individuals had turned out to vote. But however important this victory, the real test—the vote for the national executive committee—still lay ahead.[16]

Shraydeh set a date of August 3 for this next vote. On July 18 a seven-member women's delegation met with the speaker of parliament to protest Shraydeh's decision, to ask that proportional representation be guaranteed, and to request a delay in the elections for the national executive.[17] The most convincing evidence they gave for their demands was that 4,500 women of the various clubs and societies were, according to the minister's interpretation of Article 12, represented by five women, while 1,250 individual members were represented by sixty women. At the same time, the Ministry of Social Affairs denied the eighty-five (non-Islamist) representatives of the Irbid district's 1,385 individual members the right to participate in the elections, saying that they had not fulfilled the conditions of membership in time, although federation officials denied the charge.[18] Outside those circles directly involved, several members of parliament openly voiced their support for the women and called on the ministry to reconsider.

Despite the uproar, Shraydeh insisted that the elections be held on time, and as a result the non-Islamist women in the capital, as well as the representatives from the governorates, boycotted, leading attendance at the session to include only the sixty Islamist representatives of local committees from the capital. There were protests and even physical altercations outside the voting hall.[19] To no one's surprise, the boycott led to the victory of the Islamist list, headed by Mahdiyyah Zumaylah. The non-Islamist women decried the outcome. First, they argued, the ministry had proceeded with the elections despite the boycott, and the nominating and voting processes had been conducted by a show of hands, not by secret ballot, as the bylaws required. Second, the boycott by the representatives of the governorates meant that the federation had ceased to be a national union. As a result, the non-Islamist women decided to take the Ministry of Social Affairs to court.[20] By this time, however, attention had turned to the Iraqi invasion of Kuwait, and consideration of all other issues was postponed.

While the non-Islamist women awaited the outcome of their court case, a January 1991 cabinet shuffle brought a new minister to social affairs: Yusuf al-'Athm, a Muslim Brother. Later that month the non-Islamist women won their appeal to the higher court to have the 1990 election results reconsidered. But at this stage, just as Shraydeh's presence had made a difference, so now did 'Athm's: rather than implementing the court's decision, he insisted that the existing bylaws were problematic and that they should be reviewed. In early May the court ruled the 1990 election results void and illegal, but 'Athm refused to implement the decision.[21]

However, only a few weeks later, the prime minister and his four-member cabinet were dismissed and the Brotherhood's presence in the ministry came to an end. The new minister of social affairs, 'Awni Bashir, was none other than the son of former GFJW head Haifa Bashir, who had been president of the union when the problematic articles were introduced into the bylaws. After only a month in office he assembled a seventeen-member committee of women of various political affiliations and gave them sixty days to prepare for new elections. On October 18, 1991, new elections for the GFJW general congress were held, with elections for the nine-member executive committee to follow. The Islamic Action Committees, Islamic Voluntary Societies, and independents decided to boycott these elections.

Not surprisingly, a group of non-Islamist women, led by Haifa Abu Ghazalah, a longtime employee of the Ministry of Education, won the elections. Abu Ghazalah had been the choice of the outgoing president (and also, reportedly, of higher powers in the kingdom). The other women who were elected with her were more politicized, like those who had been elected to the Amman council in

1990.[22] But the story does not end here. As a result of what was viewed as yet another unrepresentative outcome as well as the lingering dispute over the bylaws, lawyer and GFJW member Na'ila Rashdan filed a suit charging that the new election results should also be overturned: a major segment of women (the Islamists) had boycotted, and one particular trend, that of the leftist women, whom Rashdan claimed in no way represented average Jordanian women, had taken control.[23]

The saga dragged on until August 1992, when the higher court abolished the regulations regarding individual membership and declared the GFJW executive board illegal. The court ruled that all members had to belong to social organizations registered with the Ministry of Social Affairs.[24] In the end, the elections were repeated and Abu Ghazalah won again, in part because of her position as incumbent president and in part because of support she received from above. However, given the termination of the committee form of membership, the leftists who had been voted in with her in 1991 were no longer union members. The outcome was an executive committee more akin to the pre-1989 structure: a coordinating committee among organizations with no common program. As a result, the final settling of the election and the issues of leadership and membership did not lead to a reenergized union.

This brief post-1989 history of the GFJW is explained in part by political rivalries among various women (particularly the non-Islamists versus the Islamists), but also by the changing composition of subsequent Jordanian governments and particularly by the political inclination of the successive ministers of social development. It is clearly a story rooted in and produced by domestic politics. The introduction of the new membership category underlines the fact that until 1989 there was no real interest in individual members, something that is quite telling about the GFJW's role and reach. The executive appears to have sought to change the bylaws to check its growing irrelevance and perhaps also to curb or co-opt the more politically activist women as the liberalization began. What they did not expect, however, was the surge in organized Islamist interest in the GFJW. In the end the strategy backfired, as it led to instability in the leadership and a stagnation of activity on the ground.

The failure of subsequent ministers to resolve the issue owed to their own political inclinations as well as to the determination, alternatively, by women on both sides of the divide not to accept the status quo. Had Jordan not been in a period of liberalization, it is possible that the issue would simply have been dismissed, that the state would have imposed a new leadership immediately, or that the federation's activity would have been effectively frozen. Thus the liberalization itself opened the way for a certain amount of contestation and infighting. However, the state's failure to act decisively to resolve the issue in the context of close ministry responsibility for the GFJW indicates both bureaucratic malaise and a continuing lack of interest in seeing women develop effective institutions to articulate their interests. In the end, the state's ambivalence toward the federation resulted not only in its being taken over by a leadership that appeared to have little commitment to serious activity, but also in its being superseded by new women's groups, one the reincarnation of the WFJ and the other led directly from one wing of the palace.

The Jordanian Women's Union

One clear positive development owing to the political liberalization was the reemergence of the WFJ, under the name of the Jordanian Women's Union (JWU). As in its previous life, its members were generally of a leftist or pan-Arab persuasion, tending toward a more political, if not always feminist, analysis of women's problems in Jordan and therefore less interested in traditional forms of charitable social work. The JWU ranks benefited from both the malaise in the GFJW as well as the annulment of its individual membership category. Once it became clear that the GFJW would remain a grouping of societies and not a real women's union, the leftist women who had tried to work within the federation turned their attention to working within the JWU.[25] By 1994 the union counted 3,800 members in the capital alone, in addition to branches and centers in Irbid, Zarqa, Madaba, and Ramtha.[26]

Between 1993 and 1995, the union implemented a number of basic reforms, moving toward greater decentralization, establishment of new branches, more democratic forms of interaction, and guarantees for more effective participation of the branches. Two sets of activities were particularly notable. The first aimed at changing a variety of laws to promote greater equality between the sexes, and the second concerned family relations and domestic violence. To address the first set of concerns, the union assembled a committee to look into proposals for changes in the labor law to enforce equality between men and women, and to accommodate the needs of working mothers.[27] In September 1995 the union initiated a campaign to press lawmakers to amend or overturn a series of other discriminatory laws. The first target was the passport law, which the JWU sought to change so that women would no longer need to obtain their husband's or guardian's permission to obtain a passport. The plan at the time was that every four months the union would focus on a different law that it felt needed amending. Further changes were to be lobbied for in the nationality law, the penal code (regarding abortion), the civil status law (to restrict polygamy and arbitrary divorce), the labor law, the pension law, and the like.[28]

The second thrust of the JWU's work was to raise awareness of family problems, particularly violence against women. In the fall of 1995 the union announced that it planned to offer its premises as a place where divorced parents could visit with their children, to provide an alternative to the existing practice of meetings at police stations. It also launched an initiative to provide free court representation to women, along with the legal advice it had been providing for some time. By early 1995 the JWU had opened three legal advice centers, one in each of the two refugee camps of Al-Wihdat and Al-Baq'a, and the third at the union office in Jebel Husayn. It also established a violence hotline (opened in August 1995 and formally inaugurated in March 1996) and a center that employs counselors who meet with women to advise them of their rights and options.

The JWU's development illustrates a number of the trends noted in the discussion of the GFJW. First, it is clear that the liberalization opened the door to the energizing of this, the one real women's nongovernmental organization (NGO) concerned with national political and social issues affecting women. Second, some of the issues the JWU has addressed—domestic violence, abortion, changing the nationality law—were generally not discussed openly before the liberalization. At the same time, however, the possibilities for expanding the union were limited in part because of competition with the GFJW, but more recently owing to the role and activities of Princess Basma (see below). The JWU was also affected during this period by the growing prominence of its president, Asma Khadr, elected in 1994. Khadr, a lawyer with experience in the human rights field, brought to the presidency a new energy and profile, but also was described by some as having fallen victim to the *za'ama* syndrome (extensive attention and power concentrated in/on the leader). The union became less and less identified as a women's union and more and more frequently identified as Khadr's union. Such a development does not distinguish the JWU from other civil society organizations in Jordan, but that is precisely the point. Contrary to what some of the literature suggests about forms of women's organizing and interacting, there seems to be nothing to distinguish JWU or GFJW internal interaction from that of their male-dominated counterparts. For this reason and those already offered, neither organization's experience offers much support (or hope) that women's organizations will play a vanguard role in political liberalizations. The following section underscores many of the same lessons.

Princess Basma and the Jordanian National Committee for Women

Until her involvement in 1992 as the patron of efforts to draft a National Strategy for Women, Princess Basma, the (late) king's sister, had a low profile in the public life of the kingdom. She was perhaps best known for her honorary chairmanship of the Queen 'Alia Fund for Social Development (QAF), established in 1977 (renamed the Jordanian Hashemite Fund for Human Development in spring 1999), which aims to develop self-sufficiency, especially among women and particularly in rural areas.

According to the official account of the institutional evolution, in September 1991 a delegation from the UN Fund for Population suggested the establishment of a national committee on women to work to integrate women more fully into development.[29] As a result, in January 1992 Minister of Planning Ziyad Fariz and Prime Minister Zayd bin Shakir requested that the princess chair such a committee and choose its members. In March 1992 the princess established the Jordanian National Committee for Women (JNCW), a policy forum on women's issues intended to work to improve women's social status, increase their involvement in development, upgrade their legal status, and improve their political participation. The JNCW was located within the QAF (officially an NGO) and comprised the ministers of planning, labor, education, and social affairs ex officio, as well as representatives of the civil service bureau, the private sector, the GFJW, and women in the public, private, and academic sectors. One of the first tasks set out for the committee was to produce a national strategy for Jordanian women. To that end, the U.S. Agency for International Development (USAID) was contacted and a Women in Development (WID) team that it assembled played an important role in early discussions and proposals for a National Strategy for Women and for an action plan for the JNCW. The USAID team submitted its draft proposal in June 1992.

In 1993 a series of four seminars was held by the JNCW, the first for planners and policymakers and the other three for concerned women in the northern, central, and southern parts of the country to ensure grassroots participation in drafting the National Strategy for Women. Although an attempt was made to include suggestions made at these various meetings, the process was carefully orchestrated from above. For example, at one of these meetings, held in May 1993, it was the ministers who presented papers and who were most clearly directing the intellectual or policy content of the meeting. In this session numerous women expressed concern regarding the intentions of the JNCW, particularly on the question of what role it would allow for existing women's NGOs.[30]

At the final session, a national conference on June 29, 1993, presided over by Crown Prince Hasan, the strategy and recommendations that had been assembled during the meetings in the governorates were distributed, and attendees were divided into two groups: one to discuss political/legal issues and the other to discuss educational and economic issues. When the two groups returned to a plenary, the presence of the crown prince introduced a formality that made further changes impossible. All the participants were aware that they could not leave that day without having produced a document. Some women objected, saying that the draft could serve as a basis for future work, but should not yet be accepted in its entirety. However, at that point a member of parliament (generally described as a leftist) suggested that whoever was in agreement with the document should stand. Not to stand was not really an option, as it would have been construed as a direct challenge to the princess and the crown prince. The document was adopted.[31]

The National Strategy for Women was then passed along to the cabinet, which approved it on October 30, 1993, and called upon all relevant bodies to take the steps necessary to implement it. As a result, one of the key initiatives in the political domain, begun in 1994, was the appointment of ninety-nine women, recommended by the princess, to municipal and village councils throughout the country. (Such appointments could not have taken place, however, had the government not already mandated the dissolution of the legally elect-ed councils as part of its attempt to curb the power of the Islamists.)[32] The appointments were then approved by cabinet deci-sions. The women selected for these posts were chosen from existing or recently established women's committees, which were established in the twelve governorates following the adoption of the National Strategy for Women to promote its goals and to form pressure groups to lobby on women's issues, in addition to their responsibilities in community development in cooperation with QAF centers. These committees were formed with the cooperation of the governorates and the Ministry of the Interior, and operate under the umbrella of the JNCW. Government facilities of various sorts, especially schools, have been put at their disposal, and a large number of memberships have been solicited among teachers.

The appointment of the ninety-nine women to municipal posts was intended to provide them training in government service and local issues, to break the women's and the communities' psychologi-cal barriers to seeing women in such posts, and therefore to enhance their chances for running in and winning municipal elections. Following the appointments a number of training workshops were conducted, and the JNCW distributed flyers encouraging women to register to vote. In the end, twelve women ran in the 1995 municipal elections: one was elected mayor, in the Ajlun district, and nine oth-ers were elected to council slots. Ten, including the woman who won the mayorship, had been members of Princess Basma's women's committees.

But the princess apparently had larger organizational goals as well. On December 29, 1995, in a major step, representatives of these women's committees assembled in Amman for a conference to found a new, kingdomwide women's organization, the Jordanian National Women's Forum (JNWF; Tajammu' Lijan al-Mar'ah al-Watani al-Urdunni). The ostensible reason for establishing this forum was to provide the national institutional framework to push forward the kingdom's National Strategy for Women following the Beijing conference.[33] This structure was also intended to formally link all the local committees. Although it was billed as an NGO and a grassroots effort, with Princess Basma as its head, with logistical and financial support coming from the governorates and ministries, and with its mission the implementation of the government's National Strategy for Women, this was at very least a quasi-governmental organization.

In the press coverage of the event, none of the traditional faces from the "women's movement" appeared and none was mentioned. Only passing reference was made to the past role of the GFJW in the general framework of the JNWF's intention to continue to work with other women's organizations.[34] The founding of the forum was completely unexpected and literally everyone involved in women's issues—from employees of UN agencies to women activists of various stripes—was taken by surprise. The GFJW and JWU were particularly alarmed and requested meetings with the princess to clarify the nature of their relationship to the new JNWF. The princess reportedly reassured them that the relationship would be one of cooperation, not domination or exclusion, but they apparently were not fully convinced. Whether out of a desire to clean house by discharging those who had been prominent but most active in parties and expensive trips, or out of a growing desire simply to establish under her own leadership a formal, national women's organization, the princess had clearly made her move to take control and begin a new era.[35]

Once again the Jordanian state had established a women's federation, this time with very broad reach that could seek to marginalize civil society activity. But by this time the political opening initiated in 1989 had already begun to close. Indeed, one could argue that the establishment of the JNWF was a clear indicator or manifestation of precisely that closing.

The Closing

The political closing, which began to be felt in a sustained way in the spring of 1994, owed overwhelmingly to developments in the Arab-Israeli theater. The Oslo Accords between the Israelis and Palestinians had been signed the previous September, and it became clear that predictions of an impending Jordanian-Israeli settlement were soon to prove true. The state, concerned about expressions of popular opposition to any coming accord and under renewed, if indirect, pressures, first targeted the press. The bounds of freedom of expression further narrowed with the July 1994 signing of the "Washington Declaration," ending the state of belligerency between Jordan and Israel. This declaration, to which PLO chairman Yasir Arafat reacted with displeasure, exacerbated existing tensions between Jordan's Palestinian and Transjordanian citizens, thus providing the regime with an additional reason to clamp down (see Brand, 1999: 54–67).

While the period since 1994 has witnessed various struggles for greater freedoms and state attempts to resist them, the outlines have remained much the same since the closing began. Regime fears of expressions of domestic opposition to the kingdom's peace treaty have alternated with regime concerns over popular discontent with its Iraq policy (particularly 1994–1998), and occasional explosions of a more economic nature in various parts of the south, such as Karak and Ma'an. Then came King Hussein's illness, the change in succession, and a process of consolidation by the new monarch that broached little in the way of challenge. The renewed intifada in the occupied West Bank and Gaza is only the most recent in the seemingly unending series of regional security challenges that has led the regime to resist a broader, meaningful reopening of the range of expressional and organizational freedoms. Women's organizations have suffered from this closing since 1994 to the extent that they have sought to make their voices heard on the contentious questions of Palestine and Iraq. However, as noted above, their freedom of maneuver and possibilities for expansion had already been gradually narrowed by the state's effective appropriation of many of their issues prior to 1994.

Conclusion

There is no question that organizing for and among women increased during the 1989–1994 period. The attempts to reinvigorate the GFJW and to energize a reconstructed WFJ in the form of the JWU are two clear examples. So is the nature of the issues on which the WFJ chose to focus: domestic violence and changes in discriminatory laws. Such issues were not addressed in the preliberalization period. Further evidence of progress was the growing emphasis on women's involvement in local and national politics: no matter whence the initiative, Jordanian society is gradually becoming accustomed to seeing women holding political office. This may be most important at the municipal level, where close interaction or observation of women candidates may lead to a change in attitudes that the presence of a female member of parliament in the capital of Amman cannot.

Moreover, the increasing involvement of women in politics has included most of the political spectrum. The importance of the female vote to the successes of Islamist candidates in both the 1989 and the 1993 elections has been widely acknowledged. The story of the struggle for control of the GFJW was another important episode for Islamist women, even if it ultimately ended in failure. Subsequently, however, Islamist women with an interest in politics have become members of the Islamic Action Front, which at the end of 1995 transformed its women's committee into a more powerful "women's section."

While these developments unfolded in an international context of increasing emphasis on and interest in women's political participation, the experiences of the GFJW and the WFJ demonstrate that some developments were overwhelmingly the product of domestic-level forces. However, the hand of globalization, in the guise of the role of a range of international organizations and NGOs, is evident in the activities initiated by Princess Basma, and in other accompanying developments, such as the many workshops, seminars, and conferences devoted either entirely, or at least in part, to women's issues. While in many cases these were extensions of the activities of existing programs, many others were largely or completely funded or encouraged by foreign NGOs or aid agencies. Without such support, the activities could not have been launched or would have been far more modest.

The problem here is that the princess's (and to a less prominent extent, Queen Noor's) involvement in women's issues also led to a growing monopolization of external donor funds by the royal NGOs, the QAF, and the Noor al-Hussein Foundation (NHF). Unlike other Jordanian organizations with an NGO designation, these royal NGOs (or RONGOs) are not subject to the Laws of Charitable and Voluntary Societies (1966), and they cannot be interfered with in the same way (by having elections monitored or results overturned, for example).[36] They do not need permission from the Ministry of Social Affairs to hold fundraising events or to submit funding proposals to foreign donors (something all other NGOs are required to do), nor are they required to fulfill the same financial reporting requirements as the designated NGOs. In sum, they enjoy all the benefits attending their self-designated (and generally unquestioned) NGO status, while they are subject to none of the controls.

Thus, while this chapter has discussed a number of examples of state interference in women's organizations—either by freezing their activities or by establishing alternatives to existing unions—in the most recent liberalization period (1989–1994), I would argue that the most serious development was the emerging role of Princess Basma, for it represents the most extensive effort to date on the part of a member of the political elite and by extension, the regime, to channel women's activism. And it is precisely these efforts that have been heavily supported by international funders. Basma's initiatives, along with a number of high-level appointments by the late King Hussein and others, might lead one to conclude that these are in fact examples of an embryonic Hashemite state feminism.[37] While state feminism in many other countries has brought myriad benefits to women, it is always at a cost: generally, excessive association of those gains with the regime (which can lead to backlash at the time of regime change, examples of which abound in Eastern Europe); or clear delimiting of the nature and extent of the reforms likely to be proposed. Hence, while one would be hard-pressed to fault Basma for the content of many of the initiatives she has launched or sponsored, such royal sponsorship comes at the price of forced marginalization of authentic civil society activity.

In sum, what appears to have developed during the liberalization as well as during the period of "reclosing" since 1994 is a gradual renegotiation of the boundaries for addressing issues related to women. In their semiofficial and official organizations dealing with women, the powers that be have been careful to stress that change will be introduced, but only if it is within the framework of society's religious and cultural traditions.

Women's organizations did take advantage of the political liberalization. But the Jordanian state, never comfortable with more *political* manifestations of civil society activity, has managed, whether through design, luck, or a combination of the two, to reinsinuate itself into the women's sector. Part of the reason for its success—the domestic explanation—owes precisely to the weakness of civil society institutions. However, part of the state's success also lies in the enthusiasm of the international donor community to fund anything that calls itself an NGO, especially if it deals with women.

Some royal initiatives have led to important changes in relatively noncontroversial laws to women's benefit. But it is clear that there is no necessary connection, and little connection in fact, between these efforts and increasing meaningful *participation* in the political system. That must await the next round of liberalization. One can only hope the wait will not be too long.

Notes

This chapter draws on research originally conducted for my book *Women, the State, and Political Liberalization: The Moroccan, Jordanian, and Tunisian Cases* (New York: Columbia University Press, 1998). For support that made this research possible, I am grateful to the University of Southern California's School of International Relations and Center for International Studies, USIA/American Center for Oriental Research, and the Social Science Research Council.

1. See, for example, introduction to Norton, 1995: 12.

2. Of course, this body of work is roundly criticized by other feminists for its tendency to essentialize women. For a concise summary of main lines of argument in the gender and international relations literatures, see Tessler and Warriner, 1997.

3. See, for example, Moghadam, 1993; Funk and Mueller, 1993; Rai, Pilkington, and Phizacklea, 1992; Jaquette, 1994; Radcliff and Westwood, 1993; Waylen, 1994.

4. For a fuller discussion of the generalizations that emerge from these experiences, see introduction and conclusion to Brand, 1998.

5. Tall, 1985: 126. This work is the only book-length study of Jordanian women.

6. Haifa Jamal, "Juhud Ittihad al-Mar'ah al-Urdunniyyah fi Sabil Tatwir al-Tashri'at al-Khassah b-il-Mar'ah," unpublished paper presented at the first conference of the JWU, June 13–15, 1995, p. 6.

7. The name is significant: the Women's Federation in Jordan rather than the Jordanian Women's Federation, or some similar formulation. It allowed for both Transjordanian and Palestinian women to participate without feeling that they were compromising their communal identities. There was a conscious effort at this point—when the memories of 1970 were still quite strong—to bring together women from both communities to work in a common framework.

8. While Mu'adh cites the same total numbers, she attributes only 800 members to the capital. In most respects, however, her presentation follows that of Tall (1985) extremely closely.

9. It is interesting that in her long newspaper article on the history of the women's movement, "Muhattat Mudi'ah fi Tarikh Masirat al-Mar'ah al-Urdunniyyah," *Al-Dustur*, June 29, 1993, Emily Bisharat, the first president of the AWF and of the WFJ, simply notes that the union was closed. No comment or explanation is offered.

10. *Jordan Times*, July 10, 1990.

11. Author interview with Majida al-Masri, member of the union's executive committee and Rand, Amman, June 9, 1996. The cynicism in the

evaluation is mine; Masri saw the GFJW's attempts at revitalization as of a strategy to prevent the union from descending into irrelevance.

12. *Jordan Times,* June 20, 1990.

13. According to Shraydeh's interpretation of the new provisions, each social institution, club, and society (no matter how large its membership) was to be represented in the regional councils by two members, while each group of fifty individual members was to be represented by three chosen delegates. The result, according to some, was that individual members were overrepresented (since societies generally had more than fifty members), even though they had had very little involvement in the federation's activities up to that time. Ousted members of the executive claimed that Shraydeh had interpreted Article 12 "according to his whim." Shraydeh argued that the ministry had requested federation members to find an acceptable formula for interpreting Article 12 for the provincial committees. When such a gathering failed to produce an agreement, he called for a meeting of delegates to discuss the issue. When differences persisted, the delegates to this meeting agreed to leave the matter of determining a binding ruling to the ministry, after consultation with legal specialists on the interpretation. The former union leadership and their associates were then surprised when the ruling went against them. See *Jordan Times,* July 10, 1990, and July 31, 1990, as well as the commentary by Na'ila Rashdan in *Al-Ra'y,* February 20, 1993.

14. This was the evaluation of Majida al-Masri in my interview with her, Amman, June 9, 1996.

15. This was the evaluation of Na'ila Rashdan, who was close to the Islamist camp. Author interview with Senator Rashdan, who was active with the GFJW during the period, Amman, August 6, 1994.

16. *Jordan Times,* July 21, 1990.

17. *Jordan Times,* July 20, 1990.

18. On the ministry's claim of unfulfilled membership conditions, see *Jordan Times,* August 31, 1990.

19. *Jordan Times,* August 4, 1990.

20. Haifa Malhas in *Al-Ra'i,* August 4, 1990.

21. *Jordan Times,* July 25–26, 1991.

22. *Jordan Times,* October 20, 1991.

23. Author interview with Na'ila Rashdan, Amman, May 22, 1996.

24. *The Star,* August 27, 1992.

25. Author interview with Na'ila Rashdan, Amman, May 22, 1996.

26. Interview with Asma Khadr in *The Star,* March 24, 1994.

27. *Jordan Times,* January 8, 1994.

28. *Jordan Times,* September 25, 1995.

29. See "Draft Project Proposal: Support to JNCW for Implementation of the Political Domain of the National Strategy for Women in Jordan," submitted to the National Democratic Institute, January 1996, and USAID, "Proposed National Strategy and Action Plan for the National Women's Committee," June 30, 1992. I am skeptical of many details about the source of initiatives (one source indicated that a women's committee had in fact

been in existence since the prime ministership of Tahir al-Masri [June–November 1991], although it did not meet until bin Shakir's second premiership, in spring 1992). The logic or coherence of the projects appears only in hindsight observation of their emergence and development.

30. I attended this meeting as an observer.

31. Confidential author interview with a woman who attended the session.

32. By this time, thanks to their opposition to Jordan's participation in peace talks with Israel, the Islamists had become personae non gratae with the regime. Numerous policies, both subtle and overt, were undertaken by the authorities to limit the Islamists' influence on both a national and a local level. The dismissal of these municipal councils was one such policy.

33. *Jordan Times,* July 16, 1995; *Al-Aswaq,* November 26, 1995.

34. *Al-Dustur,* March 1, 1996.

35. *Al-Dustur,* December 30, 1995.

36. Author interview with 'Abla 'Amawi of the UNDP, formerly with the Noor al-Hussein Foundation, Amman, March 18, 1996. 'Amawi did not coin or use the term "RONGOs."

37. The late King Hussein appointed several women to the senate as part of the liberalization: former minister of information Layla Sharaf, lawyer Na'ila Rashdan, Minister of Planning Rima Khalaf, and businesswoman Subeiha Ma'ani. Postliberalization prime ministers have appointed women to the posts of minister of social affairs, minister of trade and industry, and minister of planning. In addition, for a brief period in 1993, Umayma Dahhan served Prime Minister 'Abd al-Salam al-Majali as a special adviser on women. And in 1996, Prime Minister 'Abd al-Karim Kabariti appointed the first woman judge in the kingdom.

Emma C. Murphy 7

Women in Tunisia: Between State Feminism and Economic Reform

Any study of the rights, status, and achievements of women in contemporary Tunisia will inevitably place the state at the heart of its analysis. As Mounira Charrad (1996: 221–228) has pointed out, the processes of state formation and consolidation have been key variables in the evolution of the status of women in the North African countries. Indeed, in the Tunisian case, the state has been the chief agent of change, not only in introducing some enviably progressive legislation, but also in seeking to alter the productive and reproductive roles of women to an extent that justifies use of the term "state feminism."

This enthusiastic championing of women has not been without its limitations, however. This chapter locates the development of that state feminism within a broader construct of a corporatist political system. Under the country's first president, Habib Bourguiba, a political system was established wherein interest groups were mobilized in support of a specific regime. The requirements of these interest groups were negotiated with the state through the mechanisms and institution of a single political party, and were continually balanced against other corporate interests and demands made upon the state.

The replacement of Bourguiba by Zine el-Abidine Ben Ali in 1987 brought both economic and political change. At the political level, Ben Ali promised significant liberalization and even democratization. Despite some promising early moves in this direction, the threat posed by a rapidly growing Islamist movement to the stability of the regime gave the president both the incentive and the excuse to reverse any meaningful liberalization. While token institutions of democracy, such as a multiplicity of parties and relatively free elec-

169

tions, have become features of the political system, the reality is a monopolistic (if much revived and restructured) dominant party, a strong and increasingly authoritarian presidency, and a subjugated civil society. Economic policy under Ben Ali has taken the form of vigorously pursued economic liberalization. Tunisia has consequently become a regional star performer in the eyes of the international financial institutions, and while much undoubtedly remains to be done, there has been a significant retraction of the state from certain arenas of economic activity.

The combination of these regime policies has had a significant impact upon women, and while Ben Ali has pointedly pursued the same objectives of female advancement as his predecessors, at least in terms of legislation and public show, the changes have not all been good. The consolidation of the authority of the state over the associations and organizations of interest groups has tied the fortunes of women still further to the benevolence of the regime. Yet the diminution of the mediating function of the dominant party has reduced the associations' ability to negotiate. Interests are increasingly determined, defined, and addressed from the top down, as independent organization or expression of interests becomes increasingly more difficult.

Given the implications of economic reforms for women, some of which are beneficial and some of which most definitely are not, women have also been affected by liberalization in that sphere. The government has attempted to redress resulting imbalances through a combination of institutional and welfarist mechanisms, including the National Solidarity Fund, with varying degrees of success.

Finally, women have been on the front line in the debate between the regime and the Islamists. Both sides claim to have something to offer women: the regime offers tolerance and secular empowerment; the Islamists offer the reassurance of cultural authenticity and traditionally-defined gender roles. Equally, both inadvertently represent a threat to women. The regime is pursuing economic policies that surrender women to the market, turning them into units of cheap labor and thrusting them into culturally unfamiliar public scenarios. Islamists, by contrast, show only reluctant commitment to established legislation and would undoubtedly rescind many of the privileges currently available to women if they were to gain power. While the regime currently seems to hold the upper hand, it has yet to resolve the outstanding dilemmas and contradictions of its own policies toward and affecting women. However much largesse it is inclined to hand down to women from its bureaucratic heights, it has made little inroad into countering the social conservatism upon which political Islam feeds.

Tahar Haddad: Father of Reform

In the traditional Tunisian society of the early part of the twentieth century, the position of Tunisian women was little different from that of Arab women elsewhere in the Middle East. Urban women lived their lives almost completely in the private domain, cloistered in domestic roles that gave them social value and status only as wives and mothers. They were regulated by the authority of first father, then husband, and constantly in fear of either polygamous marriages or unilateral repudiation. In the words of Henri de Montéty (1993: 9), "Women were so far removed from public life that it was considered impolite to speak about them between men." In rural areas, women played a greater role in providing the agricultural sustenance of the household, although their status was little different and their dependence on their menfolk equally complete.

Female education or even literacy was confined to only a few wealthy and progressive families, and segregation of the sexes (when possible) was a fiercely protected social convention. Women were inculcated with the requirement that they be passive and obedient and acknowledge at all times their inferiority. Concepts of honor and shame were similar to those found elsewhere in the Islamic Arab world, and Islamic obligations that require women to be treated with respect were not enforced, if ever fulfilled.

At the beginning of the twentieth century, a Tunisian Islamic reformist, Tahar Haddad, made a plea on behalf of women. Islam, he said, was fundamentally a religion of equality and justice, and it required that women be treated accordingly. Progress was not antithetical to Islam—indeed the opposite was true—and progress required that women, too, should be educated and have legitimate rights. In his book, *Our Women in the Sharia and Society,* Haddad (1978) called unambiguously for women to be protected from early or enforced marriages and to have the rights to work and to freely dispose of their possessions, all of which was in accordance with the teachings of the Quran. Although removed from his teaching post at the Zitouna University for expressing his views, Tahar Haddad is revered in Tunisia today as the father of family and social emancipation. Islam in Tunisia is considered to be of a tolerant, liberal, and progressive form largely because of his early influence.

Rights for Women Under Bourguiba

The second figure to have a major influence on the position of women in Tunisia was the country's first president, Habib Bourguiba. When he came to power as head of state in 1957, Bourguiba was already deeply committed to improving the status and rights of women. He had witnessed firsthand the humiliation and impoverishment of his divorced grandmother and had seen the burden that his own birth placed on his mother, who was forty when he was born. He considered that women's organizations had played a substantial role in the liberation struggle and that family life required a partnership between husband and wife rather than the enforced slavery of women.[1] More important, perhaps, Bourguiba was dedicated to a vision of a nationalist, secularist, and socialist society in which all citizens participated—a requisite of which was to enable women to become active in the public sphere (Durrani, 1976).

As prime minister, in 1956 he had steered a radical Code of Personal Status through the constituent assembly. This code has been the bedrock of the emancipation of women in Tunisia ever since. It determined that family structures should henceforth be based on the legal equality of the sexes. Women were considered for the first time to have a right to dignity and individual integrity. In particular, a series of measures brought about the abolition of polygamy, the institution of legal divorce (prohibiting the custom of repudiation and enabling women to initiate divorce), the introduction of a legal age of marriage for women (seventeen) subject to the woman's consent, the granting of rights of guardianship to the mother in the event of the father's death, and the institution of obligatory inheritance legacies for the children of a daughter should the daughter die before her father. Perhaps most important, women were given the right to work and to be educated, giving them the opportunity for economic independence.

Bourguiba claimed that, far from being incompatible with Islam, the Code of Personal Status applied the notion of *ijtihad,* or interpretation of the sharia (sacred law), in this instance, in a daring and modern way. The code ended the double standards of the more traditional interpretation (what is good for men is not good for women) and, in the eyes of Tunisian progressives, adapted Islamic law to the conditions of modern life without departing from Islamic values. The essence of the code was to establish the social and moral equality of women within the family, after which the way would be open for women to move out of the domestic confines and into public life, as productive members of civil society.

In 1957, for the first time in Tunisian history, women were able to vote in municipal elections and thereafter in national elections (Moore, 1965: 56). The Tunisian constitution of June 1, 1959, states that women are full citizens with complete legal equality and civic duties, with the full right to exercise their political, economic, and social rights. All men and women over the age of twenty have the right to vote (under the electoral code), and women can stand for all public offices open to men.

Bourguiba encouraged the formation of the National Union of Tunisian Women (UNFT; formally constituted in 1961) to pursue the task of female emancipation by organizing women and girls and educating them in their rights. The UNFT was of course a means of mobilizing women in support of the Neo-Destour—Bourguiba's political party—and it had its origins in the women's national organization (the Union of Muslim Women), which Bourguiba had encouraged before independence as a tactical necessity for the expression of interests, without allowing them to challenge the party.[2]

In the 1959 National Assembly elections, the UNFT mobilized women in support of the Neo-Destour's National Front and its president was herself elected to the National Assembly. The UNFT acted as a channel for women to be elected onto the lists of candidates for the Neo-Destour in local and national elections. By 1960 the UNFT boasted over 40,000 members. In spite of his commitment to women's emancipation, Bourguiba restricted the expression of women's interests to this organization. It was in line with his corporatist model of government to do so, and linked the achievement of legal and social reforms for women to their continuing support for his regime. Under the umbrella of the UNFT, however, various professional women's organizations were allowed to develop, including those for women managers, researchers, and magistrates. Bourguiba did not attempt to confine women's rights to the civil sphere, or to restrict women's social role to the household. His regime made fundamental advances in recognizing women's rights with regard to property and employment on the one hand (moving women toward productive and financial independence) and reproductive rights on the other.

A 1956 amendment to the Code of Obligations and Contracts recognized a woman's rights to sign contracts and to buy, sell, and enjoy the use of her own property. The Law of November 4, 1958, guaranteed the right to education for children of both sexes without discrimination based on race, religion, or society. The Law of June 3, 1968, establishing the status of the civil service (Article 11, 1983 amendment), and the general collective convention (March 10, 1973), stipulate that men and women have equal rights to employment, tenure, and remuneration.

In terms of health and reproductive rights, the 1959 constitution gave women the right to health, and in particular reproductive health. The Law of January 9, 1961, authorized the import and sale of contraceptives, and the Laws of July 6, 1965, and of September 26, 1973, gave women the right to choose abortion. Law 81-7 of February 18, 1981, gave divorced women rights to compensation, improved custody rights, and improved inheritance rights. Law 83-112 of December 1983 gave women the right to two months of maternity leave on full pay and postnatal leave on half pay for up to four months. The labor code gives women a further one hour per day off work for breast-feeding. Enterprises with at least fifty women must provide a baby-nursing room, and under public service statutes women may opt for early retirement on preferential terms if they have three or more children.

Bourguiba also ratified most international conventions concerning women's rights, including the 1959 Convention on Combating Discrimination in the Workplace, the 1967 Convention on the Political Rights of Women, the 1985 Convention on Eradication of All Forms of Discrimination Against Women, and the 1968 Convention on the Economic, Social, and Cultural Rights of Women. Ratification of this last convention effectively nullified those articles of the Code of Personal Status or Code of Obligations and Contracts that mitigate against women's rights, such as a husband's right to veto his wife's acting as a wet nurse, his right to restrict her choice of profession, or his part in guaranteeing the bond of a contract entered into by his wife.

In penal law, too, women were considered to be equal to men. Penal Law 62-22 of May 22, 1962, determined that in a case of adultery (punishable by five years of imprisonment and a fine), adulterous husbands were as liable under the law as adulterous wives (who had been singled out for punishment under previous legal codes). Rape was recognized as a punishable crime and in 1985 the penalty for rape with violence and armed threat became death (as opposed to hard labor).[3]

Contextualizing Bourguiba's Support for Women's Rights

By the time that Bourguiba was removed from office in a constitutional coup, Tunisia had possibly the most progressive legal code for the protection and emancipation of women in the third world, and certainly in the Arab world. Yet there were important constraints on women that need to be recognized. First, the struggle to define and achieve women's rights took place at all times within the framework of either Bourguiba's Neo-Destourian (and later Parti Socialiste Destourien) party or the institutions of the state itself. Indeed, the campaign was initiated from the top rather than as a response to pressures from below, as Bourguiba sought to adjust social and economic relationships to fit his model of a modernizing political society (Charrad, 1996: 226). He was able to draw upon Tunisia's historical legacy of liberal Islam, administrative centralization, and kinship communities weakened by colonial rule, meeting little real resistance to his Code of Personal Status. The process of early state formation required that potential resistance from tribal-based competitors should be undermined and the reformatting of social units was an effective way of doing this. Thus, through the code and through subsequent legislation, the state transferred the balance of weight from the tribal or kin-based unit to the smaller unit of immediate family.

Mobilizing and emancipating women served a further purpose of generating support for the regime from a previously largely passive section of the population. In effect, Bourguiba created a new constituency that owed its very capacity for action to him and his party. The organization of this new political community was established along vertically differentiated lines: the UNFT lobbied for women within a broader corporatist framework in which its interests were mediated through the party and the state. The state thus became the bestower of those rights that it deemed to be in the broader interests of society, and women's organizations did not develop with confrontational agendas that challenged the state's perspective. There was thus no independent feminist movement but rather an elite group of middle-class women who belonged primarily to the Neo-Destourian party or who were state functionaries charged with articulating and negotiating for the interests of women.

A final point to make is that Bourguiba's approach to the emancipation of women went a great deal further than that of many of his radical Arab contemporaries. His was not simply a formal (legal and ideological) commitment, but included a desire to free women from the burdens of their reproductive role. Thus his regime conformed to the state feminism of Scandinavian welfarist governments that sought to "remove the structural basis of gender inequality by making reproduction a public—not a private—concern" (Hatem, 1996: 172).

The incorporation of legislation concerned with contraception, abortion, and guardianship rights into primary legal codes, as well as the government's policies to make appropriate services available and to itself become a major employer of women, all demonstrated that the state was concerned with the social and economic, as well as civil, rights of women. The downside of state feminism is that any improvement in the economic and political options available to women is tied to the state's willingness and ability to enforce that availability. Top-down changes do not alter the fundamental social structures that create discrimination, underrepresentation, and subordination, and as soon as the state weakens or withdraws, those structures can reassert themselves. Indeed, even when the state appears to be actively advancing women's interests, those same social structures can shape that advance and undermine it from within.

Improving the Legal Status of Women Under Ben Ali

On November 7, 1987, Zine al-Abidine Ben Ali seized power in Tunisia in a constitutional coup. Bourguiba had for several years been suffering from increasing senility, and while he retained a place in the hearts of most Tunisians as their great national hero of the past, his removal was greeted with some relief. It was hoped that Ben Ali would make significant and early moves to liberalize the political system and counter the growing threat of instability posed by the regime's confrontation with the forces of political Islam and its economic problems of debt and excessive state intervention.

Initial signs were good. During his first year in office, Ben Ali made significant concessions to democracy, liberalizing the media, releasing political prisoners, reducing the arbitrary powers of the police, and amending the constitution to allow for multiparty democracy (within limits) and a reduced term of office for the president. In September 1988 women's organizations were included (along with now legal political parties and other national organizations) in negotiations, initiated by Ben Ali, that resulted in the drafting of the National Pact in November 1988. The National Pact reaffirmed the importance of *ijtihad* in the development of a modern society and the importance of retaining a rational orientation toward achieving the full emancipation of women. The pact stated: "The principle of equality is no less important than the principle of liberty: that is equality among citizens, without discrimination between men and women" (Government of Tunisia, 1988).

Accordingly, all new political parties were required by the Law on Political Parties of May 1988 to adhere to the principle of equality between the sexes. On August 6, 1988, following changes in the Law of Association (August 2, 1988), Ben Ali broke with Bourguiba's policy of restricting political representation of women to the UNFT. A number of new women's organizations immediately sprang up, many with the active and financial support of the government. They included organizations established under the umbrella of other political entities, such as the National Chamber of Women Heads of Businesses (CNFCE; established on June 29, 1990, as a part of UTICA—the Tunisian Union of Industry, Trade, and Crafts), and the National Federation of Women Farmers (FNA; established on December 21, 1990, as a constituent member of the Tunisian Union for Agriculture and Fishing). Other organizations were established to promote the study of women and to provide information that could be used in determining government policy. These included the Association of Tunisian Women for Research and Development (AFTURD), the Commission on Women and Work (a new structure of the UGTT—the Tunisian General Labor Union), and later the Center for Studies, Documentation, and Information on Women (CREDIF).

In some cases, new organizations were established to directly promote women with regard to broader areas of government policy, including the Association for the Promotion of Women's Economic Projects (APROFE), established in June 1990 to improve women's involvement in investment and employment, with financial and technical aid in start-up projects. Finally, new organizations and associations sprang up to promote women's cultural interests. These had previously been represented by nonpolitical clubs such as the Women's Sporting Club (ASF; 1955), the Club des Anciennes Élèves du Lycée de Jeunes Filles de Montfleury (1978), and the Association des Anciennes du Lycée de la Rue du Pacha (1986). These were now joined by new organizations such as the Club Faouzia Kallel (July 1988) and the Club Alyssa (1990), which were open to a broader membership and promised a gradual erosion of the elitism previously characteristic of women's organizations.

This apparent pluralization of women's organizations is not as innocuous as it seems. While it has undoubtedly led to a broadening of women's participation, the example of the Tunisian Democratic Women's Association (AFD) gives a salutary warning. Under the revised Law of Associations, this organization received formal recognition and support from the Ministry of Culture. It had originally developed as a feminist organization based at the Tahar Haddad cultural center in the heart of Tunis's old medina. Formal recognition ended the independence of the association and thus brought the old state-formulated constraints into play. Even so, the AFD remains a forum not only for debate over practical measures to advance women's interests, but also for the development of feminist intellectual thought.

In general, one can view the fragmentation of the representation of women's interests as having still maintained the corporatist relationship between the state and interest groups, since the new associations exist not to challenge government policy but to contribute to it through institutional structures. Furthermore, their membership, while widening to include upwardly mobile and aspiring sections of the female population, is not yet representative of the broad generality of women.

Ben Ali has also wrought change at the governmental level. In 1992 he designated a new ministerial post, that of minister of women's and family affairs, and a new position of adviser to the president on women's affairs. In preparation for the Eighth National

Plan (1992–1996), a national advisory committee on the role of women in development was created (June 1991) as well as CREDIF, the aforementioned research center. A further national commission was given the task of promoting legislation and legal texts in favor of women, resulting in 1993 in a series of amendments to the Code of Personal Status. These amendments replaced existing clauses that insisted a woman should respect and obey her husband with a provision making husbands equally responsible for household management. Domestic violence became punishable, mothers were given the right to veto marriages of daughters still considered minors, and a fund was established to provide alimony for divorced women and their children (Ministère de la Femme et de la Famille, 1993).

The Code of Nationality was also amended to allow Tunisian women married to nonnationals to pass their Tunisian nationality to their children.[4] The effect of these amendments was to make women equal to men under the law in all but two respects. The concept of *ijtihad* could not allow for a liberal interpretation of two clear quranic instructions: first, that daughters can only inherit a portion of a parent's estate equal to half that given to a son; and second, that guardianship of a child should, in the case of divorce, pass to a husband. In both instances, however, the law made as great an allowance for the woman as possible, with, for example, divorced women being given the right to equal involvement in the conduct of their children's affairs. Moreover, measures adopted in August 1997 enhanced the alimony and child support provisions available to divorced women.

Ben Ali also made a concerted and much publicized attempt to increase the participation of women in the higher levels of government and the civil service. In August 1992 six women were appointed to top-level ministry positions, and the position within the Rassemblement Constitutionnel Démocratique of permanent secretary for women's affairs was created. The government supported the choice of Tunisia as the headquarters of the Center of Training and Research for Arab Women.[5] And as a prelude to World Women's Year, the government created a national commission to prepare a report on what had been achieved in women's affairs in Tunisia, which it presented to the president on September 15, 1994, with great media attention. Media attention was also directed to the fact that the UNFT was awarded the UNESCO prize for the eradication of illiteracy in September 1994, and to the advent of Tunisian Cultural Day, which was held in Beijing to coincide with the NGO Conference on Women.

All of this would seem to indicate an admirable enthusiasm on the part of President Ben Ali and his regime for the promotion of women's interests. Whether such enthusiasm and such demonstrations of commitments to formal advances in the status of women have actually resulted in tangible improvements in the political, economic, and social quality of life for women is another matter.

Women in Tunisian Life in the 1990s

In 1994 there were 4,053,900 women in Tunisia, making up 49.31 percent of the total population and 23 percent of the national workforce, with an unemployment rate of 22 percent, as opposed to a rate of 13 percent among men (CREDIF, 1995: 23).[6] Some 26 percent of working women were employed in agriculture (of whom 40 percent were casual laborers), 53.7 percent of working women were employed in the industrial and textile sector (of whom 28 percent were casual laborers), and nearly 20 percent of working women were employed in the service sector. In agriculture, women made up over 42 percent of the labor force, a number that is increasing as more men seek employment in the towns, leaving family landholdings in the care of women. Of these women, 12 percent were farm managers. Women were well represented in those sectors traditionally familiar as women's space, like education and health. They composed 42 percent of all teaching personnel, 22 percent of practicing physicians, and 50 percent of other paramedical staff. Women also accounted for 23 percent of all judges.[7]

In the business sector, more than 13 percent of businesses registered in the Greater Tunis area were managed by women by the late 1990s, while the number of women heads of businesses rose from 1,000 in 1991 to nearly 1,500 in 1995. Among women journalists, 21 percent held decisionmaking positions, and on at least three occasions, a woman chaired the Association of Tunisian Journalists.

Law 91-65 of July 1991 gave added stress to the importance of educating girls. In 1975 only 38.6 percent of elementary school pupils were girls; in 1997 that figure was 46 percent. Also in 1997, 99 percent of six-year-old girls were enrolled in first grade, while women accounted for 43.7 percent of those attending institutes of higher education.[8] The range of subjects studied at higher levels by girls has also diversified in recent years such that they are now strongly represented in the sciences and information technology. The government has also made strides in improving rural access to higher education and skills education, as well as to general vocational education. Despite this, illiteracy is still a severe problem in Tunisia, particularly among women. In 1992, 37.2 percent of the total population was illiterate, compared to a rate of 48.3 percent among women (CREDIF, 1995). The Eighth Development Plan targeted rural women for programs to reduce national illiteracy.[9]

In employment, women were disproportionately represented in the nurturing (teaching, health) and supportive occupations, rather than managerial and decisionmaking jobs. The discrimination against women is more pronounced in rural areas, although the government claims that promoting the interests of rural women is a target of the current Development Plan (Agrebi, 1992).

Women were still disappointingly underrepresented in political life and in the civil service. They made up 21 percent of the civil service in 1989 (22 percent in 1993). Of these women, 42.5 percent held clerical posts, 31.9 percent held supervisory roles, and just 23.5 percent held managerial posts. Even the government admits that it is still quite rare for women to rise within managerial ranks to the decisionmaking levels (CREDIF, 1995: 51). Just twenty women held senior ministry positions in 1997.[10]

Within the ruling party, women made up 20 percent of the membership, 11 percent of the central committee, and 11 percent of presidential and ministerial appointments.[11] In 1995, 6.7 percent of the National Assembly, 16.5 percent of municipal council members, and one cabinet member were women (CREDIF, 1995). While individuals have gained status in the Ministry of Women's and Family Affairs, women do not achieve high ranks in more traditionally male-dominated ministries, such as the Ministries of the State and Interior, Justice, National Economy, Finance, or Foreign Affairs. Furthermore, the linking of women with family affairs, both institutionally as in the ministries named above and in events such as the annual awarding of the Presidential Family prize (which assumes the primacy of such a linkage), sustains a domesticated image of women even at the highest levels of government.

A final area where one may evaluate real progress in advancing women's interests is family planning. Tunis is home to the headquarters of the International Planned Parenthood Federation, which has gone to great lengths to assert the compatibility of Islam and family planning. A family planning program has been running in Tunisia since 1967, under the auspices of the Office National de la Famille et de la Population.[12] The issue of women's rights is accompanied here by the government's need to reduce population growth rates to manageable levels, but the end result has still been a marked improvement in women's control and rights over their own bodies.[13]

The average age of Tunisian women to marry had risen to nearly 24 by 1991, from 20 in 1970 and 21.7 in 1980 (CREDIF, 1995: 51). The proportion of sexually active women using contraceptives rose from 34.1 percent in 1978 to 59.3 percent in 1994, while the average number of children per woman fell from 7.2 in 1966 to 3.4 in 1995. Life expectancy rose from 51 years in 1966 to 71 years in 1992, while maternal mortality rates fell from 140 to 30 per hundred thousand live births between 1971 and 1994. Tunisian women in the 1990s were increasingly able to participate in the workforce and to take control over their own bodies (International Planned Parenthood Federation, 1995).

Discrimination Remains

In spite of institutional support for their interests and needs, Tunisian women still face practical social and economic discrimination. While the law has advanced, mentalities have proved slower to change. Women are increasingly obliged for economic reasons to pursue outside salaried work, not least because Tunisians have developed the material consumption habits of a developed country. As extended families break down within the urban areas, working women are under growing pressure to fulfill both working and household roles, with men still not taking an equal share of the domestic burden.[14] In 1993 the results of a survey on the impact of gender on the political orientations of young Tunisians found that "the home environment socializes females to accept the unequal status of males and females, and to be reconciled to a lower status for women" (Suleiman, 1993).

This attitude is ameliorated by the educational experience in Tunisia, but evidently the social bias against women remains. A survey in 1993 found that in 79 percent of households, women were still taking sole responsibility for domestic tasks.[15] In an interview with the *International Herald Tribune* in 1997, the president of the UNFT stated:

> It has been forty years since a man could separate from his wife by saying "I divorce you" three times, and it has long been illegal to arrange a marriage without a woman's consent. But it is still very difficult to convince many families to let their daughters leave home to attend university in another town.[16]

Women are still excluded from some areas of public social life. Cafes are still predominantly an exclusively male environment, and women face an unnerving degree of both verbal and physical harassment when they walk or use public transport. In the arts, women are still subject to prejudice against females performing in public, and the professions of actress and singer still carry social stigma. Women find it virtually impossible to live alone, separate from their families. They certainly cannot live with a male partner, unless married, without being subject to both verbal and sometimes physical abuse. In rural areas, women are still subject to the virtually unchallengeable authority of their fathers, brothers, and husbands. In 1993, 62 percent of women still were married to partners chosen by their families (as opposed to 49 percent of men).[17]

The Impact of Ben Ali's Wider Reforms

The above summary of the government's approach toward women, the policies taken, and the status achieved needs to be placed into the context of Ben Ali's wider economic and political reforms. There is no shortage of material highlighting the potential negative consequences of economic liberalization programs for women, which may be summarized as follows:

1. Structural adjustment policies contain an inherent gender bias that assumes that women bear primary responsibility for the socialization of offspring. When the state withdraws some public services or when social services are cut back, women's social reproduction time is overstretched.

2. In the public sector, women are often concentrated in the lower clerical and administrative ranks, and are the first to be laid off

when wage-bill cuts are implemented. This is also true of privatized state industries and small- and medium-sized private companies.

3. Because women are concentrated in the lower rungs of employment, they are disproportionately vulnerable to the impact of imposed "labor-market flexibility," or the introduction of temporary, unprotected jobs. The growth of the informal sector carries with it new opportunities for female employment, but usually on disadvantageous terms for the laborers (Sen and Grown, 1987: 50–77).

4. As wages fall behind price increases, poverty rises, with women—as household managers—bearing the brunt, especially those who support families alone.

There is also a line of argument that asserts the beneficial impact of economic liberalization for women, claiming that any new jobs created are likely to originate in those export-oriented manufacturing industries that prefer women employees (notably because they are cheap and less protected). Whatever the relative economic status of such jobs, they still provide new opportunities for women to gain wage labor, economic independence, and access to the public sphere. Others claim that the expansion of services and tourism can serve to break down traditional cultural values that proscribe against women, allowing them to compete on an equal basis that is impossible with blue-collar forms of employment.[18]

Either way, analysts have concluded that structural adjustment and economic liberalization programs are not gender neutral. Christina Gladwin (1993: 88) has pointed out that the onus is consequently on governments and their funders to ensure that complementary policies are introduced to mitigate against those side effects of economic reform that discriminate most against the interests of women.[19]

In the case of Tunisia the evidence so far would suggest that, while economic liberalization is working against the economic interests of many women, the state is making significant attempts to support women through various welfarist and employment-oriented programs. The view is frequently expressed by representatives of women's organizations (almost invariably off the record) that women have suffered most from the austerity measures of the government. Although it is difficult to find empirical evidence of this, women certainly increased as a percentage of the unemployed in the early years of economic reform—from 18.5 percent in 1984 to 28.4 percent in 1989—and showed an increasing chance of being unemployed longer than men.[20]

Women also fell as a proportion of the workforce from 21.7 percent in 1984 to 19.5 percent in 1989, although this period precedes the growth of textile and other manufacturing industries, which, however slow, is likely to have provided significant new opportunities for women. Although investment in tourism is creating a marked expansion of that sector, women make up less than 6 percent of those employed, a figure that is not growing with the expansion of the sector. Where economic opportunities remain open, and despite legal requirements for equal pay in Tunisia, women are still subject to discriminatory pay practices.

Some representatives of women's organizations in Tunisia believe strongly that as men find themselves increasingly under pressure and threat of loss of employment, a social reaction will make female employment less acceptable. The traditional role of the male breadwinner will then be given new life. They point out that women are caught in a cultural dilemma. The increased economic hardship and the exaggeration of horizontal socioeconomic stratification create among the lower-middle classes and working (both urban and rural) classes—including women—a resentment that equates economic liberalization with the enforced importation of alien cultural values (not least a consumption culture in which they are unable to participate). The reaction to this is to retreat into the indigenous culture and try, through its reassertion, to regain a lost sense of dignity and control over life. This reaction leads to what is called the "housewifization" of women and their exclusion from opportunities for economic emancipation. In other words, in trying to gain cultural emancipation, women lose their economic freedom. Alternatively, the El Amouri Institute has argued that economic reforms that prioritize the market over traditional, solidarity-based production lead women into new forms of employment (such as producing food for sale outside the household), which remain unrecognized and which double their workload without increasing their personal control over their income. Husbands still receive the income and it is they who figure in national income statistics when wives are employed in the informal sector. Thus a woman's workload increases but her status does not (El Amouri Institute, 1993).

Poverty and Government Programs

The government has demonstrated an awareness of the problems out-
lined above, and has sought to provide women with safety nets in the
form of both improved legislation and specific programs of provision. Even so, during the Seventh Development Plan (1987–1991),
6.7 percent of the population were living under the official poverty
line. While this represented a decline in absolute numbers, the rate of
decline had decelerated, as unemployment, subsidy removal, and
inflation were not offset by social transfers. The government had
introduced a program for assistance to needy families in 1986, and
the number of families benefiting from the program increased from
65,000 in that year to 101,000 in 1992 (inflation during that time
rose by an annual average of 7.5 percent, while real wages fell by 1.5
percent a year). In 1992 a new mechanism, the National Solidarity
(or 26-26) Fund (NSF) was established to channel funds into less
developed regions or "shadow areas." Women's organizations such
as the Tunisian Mothers' Association have been given the task of
assisting the government in designing and promoting some of the
NSF's projects in order to specifically reach poorer women. A number of other development and assistance funds were created to help
alleviate poverty, improve access to employment, and establish "integrated social provision." In total, the government increased social
expenditure as a percentage of gross domestic product from 17 percent in 1987 to 19 percent in 1994, amounting to 60 percent of annual budgets. Women benefited from much of this provision, both
directly and indirectly, with female literacy and employment being
specifically targeted by the state.

A major problem for those women who perceive economic liberalization as a threat to their interests is the lack of channels to
express discontent with government policy. Since the organizations
that represent women's interests are all affiliated either to the ruling
party in some way, or to the trade unions that are co-opted into the
government structures, or even directly funded and controlled by the
Ministry of Culture or the Ministry of Women and Family Affairs,
there is no effective independent organization through which women
can challenge the favored economic strategy of the government.
Existing organizations can feed complaints into the system, but they
are met with government claims that the legal environment for
women is continually improving and that safety net funds and wel-

fare payments are adequate to offset the negative impact of liberalization policies. In short, women may not challenge economic liberalization as a policy, but only negotiate for a larger share of reduced
government expenditure.

Thus we may say that the problems associated with state feminism persist. While women may benefit from the direct sponsorship
by the government, they are increasingly vulnerable to its withdrawal
from certain economic arenas. They must themselves find ways of
reconciling the role assigned to them by the state with the combination of other roles demanded by society and the market. Added to
this dilemma is the fact that women's organizations have developed
predominantly through this government sponsorship. Since independence, women have been given rights determined on their behalf,
rather than having to struggle against any gender-discriminating
ethos of the political system. They have not developed, therefore,
either a culture of, or mechanisms for, feminist political struggle.
Their consciousness as an interest group remains that of a co-opted
elite rather than a mass protest or liberation movement. (Thus, for
example, the director of CREDIF stated in a discussion in 1996 that
it was not her organization's role to lead a struggle of women against
anything, least of all men. Rather, the center acted to provide a forum
for gender cooperation and constructive collaboration.) This means
that when their socioeconomic interests are truly challenged, as by
the policy of economic liberalization, women have neither the mechanisms nor the ideology to sustain a counterattack. They simply
attempt to negotiate better terms for themselves relative to other
interest groups within the system.

The response to such an approach will invariably dismiss the rel-
evance of Western-style feminism to an Arab Islamic country trying
to reconcile the demands of economic modernization with a rejection
of the accompanying alien cultural norms, provoking consideration
of assertions of false consciousness versus orientalism.

The Impact of Political Change upon Women

Women are, of course, only half of any society. As such, they suffer
with men when a regime reduces its overall commitment to political
and civil liberty and the protection of human rights. While it is
beyond the scope of this chapter to discuss all the failings of Ben

Ali's regime in this realm, it must be said that early hopes for democratic pluralism and political liberalism have withered in the past few
years. Tunisia has also come under fire from organizations such as
Amnesty International for its increasing disregard for human rights.
Abuses have ranged from arrests, torture, and disappearances to
clampdowns on the press, manipulation of the court system, and
restrictions on human rights activists. Women have been given special attention if they are related to members of the Islamist movement:

> Women relatives have been summoned to the Ministry of the
> Interior or police stations, detained and subjected to cruel or
> degrading treatment. Those who wear an Islamic hijab have suf-
> fered particular harassment. Women who wear the hijab have not
> been allowed to visit detainees and have been told to remove the
> hijab; sometimes the veil is said to have been torn off by the prison
> guards. Veiled women are refused work in government offices and
> schools; sometimes they are refused medical treatment. (Amnesty
> International, 1994)

Ironically, political Islam itself is a large part of the problem, at
least in terms of the Tunisian experience as it provides a justification
for the regime's political intolerance and growing authoritarianism.
Yet at the same time, resurgent political Islam in Tunisia is perhaps
the greatest challenge to women's rights as they are understood in the
West. The battle to retain a distinct cultural identity in the face of
encroaching Westernization has been at the heart of the recent
upsurge in support for conservative Islamist forces in the Arab world.
   In Tunisia, the 1970s witnessed the stirrings of Islamic forces
that had been previously forced into social retreat by Bourguiba's
policies of secularization. The Islamists can be divided into three
camps: the Da'wa, the MIT (later renamed Nahda), and the
Progressive Islamists (Magnuson, 1991). The Da'wa is perhaps the
most strict in its attitude toward segregation of the sexes, the wearing
of Islamic dress and so forth, but since it is more concerned with
individual piety than with the public domain, it poses little challenge
to the established order. By contrast, Nahda concentrates on the
renewal of Islamic society—on the reassertion of Islam in the public
sphere. From its formal establishment as the MTI in 1981 until now,
Nahda has developed its position away from previously more doctri-
naire and socially conservative attitudes, toward a more liberal

emphasis on democratic freedoms and social intercourse between the sexes, manipulating positive symbols in Tunisian life to improve its public image. The progressive Islamists are more concerned with Islamic thought and the correction of the conceptual mind-set and intellectual orientation of Muslims. They focus on broad issues rather than particular judgments and believe that Islamic behavior between the sexes is a matter of Islamic character of the individuals rather than an issue of enforcing segregation. They stand against polygamy and do not demand that women wear the hijab.

Of the three groups, Nahda has undoubtedly had the strongest impact on Tunisian society in recent years. The ideological mentor of Nahda is Rachid Ghannouchi, who has been at pains to emphasize that Islamic forces in Tunisia are neither radical nor reactionary, but centrists who can reconcile flexibility and realism with adherence to Islamic principles.[21] Ghannouchi has moved Tunisian Islamist discourse away from primarily religious and moral issues toward a broader attack on imperialism and social injustice. In doing so, he articulates "many widespread grievances in a religious idiom" (Munson, 1986).

Tunisian political Islam is by no means antithetical to economic or technological modernization, but it does express the anomie and alienation that result from rapid social modernization based on essentially imported social values. Ghannouchi represents the desire to find a culturally authentic path to social modernization, one that stresses Islam as the cultural linchpin for Arab society. Under the present government, religion is an individual's right rather than the basis for social organization. Nahda argues that by marginalizing Islam in this way, by depriving it of its proper place in dynamizing society, Tunisia is condemned to a multidimensional malaise—as if the wrong engine had been put into a car.

Thus Ghannouchi's approach to the role and status of women does not seek to return to the absolute repression of the past. Indeed, he has said that for women that past represented

> a lack of awareness and insensitivity toward the oppression, degra-
> dation, abasement, restrictions of their horizons and roles in the
> life of society that women have endured during the long centuries
> of decline. Women's personality was obliterated and she was trans-
> formed into an object of pleasure—in the name of religion—until
> the Western invasion came to sweep away our values in its destruc-
> tive currents and brought with it the illusory values of freedom and

190   *Emma C. Murphy*

equality. . . . [I]t was natural that the revolution against these
abhorrent circumstances should begin outside of Islam because it
had been inculcated in the minds of women that for them Islam
meant only the veil, seclusion within the house, fulfilling the
desires of men, lack of freedom. (Ghannouchi, 1988: 24)

In his view, a truly Islamic society would not resemble this cor-
rupt and degenerate version of Islam that existed previously.
However, nor would it envisage the freedoms available to women
today. The freedom of a woman to work outside the home, to dress as
she pleases, and to act as an individual are in his eyes only a different
form of enslavement, to capitalist, media, and political institutions:

What the Muslim women needs now is a liberation movement to
restore to herself and to her innate nature as a guardian of the heritage of mankind and a companion of man in the jihad to liberate
herself and him from the forces of exploitation and oppression in
the world and to liberate herself from all control and submission
except to God. (Ghannouchi, 1988: 24)

Nahda argues unmistakably that women properly belong in the
home, raising children and safeguarding the family. Nahda does distinguish between what is permissible and what is preferable, being
careful to specify that it is the conditions of employment and the
effect of absent mothers that are objectionable, not the simple fact of
employment itself. While Nahda does not actively oppose working
women, it envisages a society that would restrict, rather than expand,
opportunities for women to work outside the home (S. Waltz, 1986:
669).

Ghannouchi defends the right of women to belong to policymaking bodies of the Nahda and by extension to have a political role in
Tunisian life. How this would fit in practice with the notion of
women having a home-based role in society is difficult to see. He has
modified his opinion of the Code of Personal Status; for a long time
he asserted that it was part of a campaign of enforced and alienating
Westernization. Today he claims that it is "a body of choices and
decisions which are part of different schools of Islamic thought"
(Ghannouchi, 1988: 24), an example of *ijtihad,* and on the whole a
positive element.

In general, the Islamic movement's attitude toward women seems
to have increasingly taken account of the fact that too many reversals
in the rights so far given to women by the state will be unpopular

with at least half of any potential constituency. This is in line with the acceptance of democratic elections as a route to power. The movement claims that it offers women an identity and a safe place in the modernized world, enabling them to reject the materialistic and object-oriented status given to women by Western cultural norms. While it asserts that women must reject the notion of feminist "rights" within that Western paradigm, it claims to offer them a more authentic and culturally familiar set of rights that will be protected by true adherence to the tenets of Islam. In practice, however, it is clear that without formal institutionalized acknowledgment of these rights, the status of women would under an Islamic government would most likely revert to the submissive and subservient one of the past.

The Islamic paradigm does have appeal to both men and women. Its message is one that offers women a solution to the contradictions of a society that demands that they not only be the guardians of family honor and purity, but also participate in a modern, technologically advanced, and socially liberal environment: "The appeal of Islamism for many young women, in a world where social and sexual behavior have become unpredictable, is as basic as it can be and easily masks any costs in terms of personal economic or political prosperity" (S. Waltz, 1986: 669). For men, it offers a reassertion of the traditional breadwinning role (pushing women back into the home will provide new jobs for men) and a dignity that has been removed by the confusion of rapid transformation of people into economic units, by the process of rapid urbanization (which confuses one's perception of one's place in society), and by appearing to offer cultural harmony with the economic order.

The government is obviously aware of the appeal of Islamism across the sexes. It includes the women's associations and the creation of new legislation in favor of women among its assets in the struggle against the political challenge represented by Nahda. The women's associations act as a channel for the socioeconomic grievances of women to be articulated and contained. While they are dominated in their management levels by educated, urban, middle-class women, they have been directed to address the issues facing women across the urban-rural and socioeconomic divides, increasing the awareness of women over what they risk losing, as well as the benefits brought to them by the regime. Legislation gives women rights and opportunities that the regime hopes they will be loathe to give up, or to surrender to an Islamic regime. Thus, incorporating women

into the regime and accommodating their interests within government policy and legislation have become tools of the regime in a
wider political struggle against the Islamist challenge.

Conclusion

Tunisians are justifiably proud of the advances they have made
toward the emancipation of women. The relatively moderate line that
Nahda has been forced to take on the issue is testament to a general
unwillingness to reverse what is seen to have been a progressive and
constructive process of social modernization. Simultaneously, however, there are still substantial problems of discrimination in both
public and private spheres. Progressive government legislation has
not eradicated discrimination in political and economic spheres. Nor
has it succeeded in transforming social values and norms at a comparable pace. When economic pressures are felt at the level of family
and locale, women's vulnerability inevitably places them on the front
line of change. The state, which has given itself the role of their
defender, must balance its benevolence without demands being made
upon it, and the absence of autonomous mechanisms through which
women can voice their grievances leads to alienation, frustration, and
in some cases greater vulnerability.

Tunisian women must still do daily battle with traditional norms
and social demands. But the simple fact that Tunisian women figure
so highly on the national political agenda, for whatever reason, offers
them opportunities to continue to both develop their own definitions
of their needs and interests, and to campaign actively in their pursuit.
Meanwhile, the restrictions placed on their organization and the
expression of their demands are part of a wider struggle for democracy that is being waged throughout the developing world.

Notes

1. For more details of Bourguiba's personal approach to women's
emancipation, see Hopwood, 1992.

2. Ibid., p. 160.

3. While I recognize the progressive aspects of these laws, I do not in
any way support criminalization of personal behavior or the use of the death
penalty.

4. There have been complaints that although this law exists, it is not actually being put into practice.

5. This was supported by the Arab Gulf Programme, the Arab Council for Childhood and Development, the UN Population Fund, the International Union of Family Planning, and the UN Development Programme.

6. On population and workforce statistics, see "Tunisia: An Active Role for Women in Tunisian Society," *International Herald Tribune,* July 11, 1997, p. 3.

7. www.tunisiaonline.com/women/wom.html, March 5, 1998.

8. "Tunisia: An Active Role for Women in Tunisian Society," *International Herald Tribune,* July 11, 1997, p. 3.

9. For more information on disparities between girls and boys education and male and female employment, see Birks, Papps, and Sinclair, n.d.

10. www.tunisiaonline.com/women/wom.html, March 5, 1998.

11. Ibid., p. 13.

12. For more information on the development of a family planning strategy in Tunisia, see Thorne and Montague, 1976.

13. Abortion is legal in Tunisia if a couple already has three children, if the mother's health is at risk, or if deformation or serious illness compromises the health of the fetus. A woman does not need her husband's permission to have an abortion.

14. In 1993, 69 percent of families were nuclear, as opposed to 31 percent extended.

15. MAFF and UN International Children's Emergency Fund (UNICEF), *Enquête sur la famille,* 1993.

16. "Tunisia: An Active Role for Women in Tunisian Society," *International Herald Tribune,* July 11, 1997, p. 3.

17. Ibid.

18. These arguments are summarized in Moghadam, 1995c.

19. Valentine Moghadam balanced this argument at a conference at the University of Coventry in March 1996. She asserted that the universalization of norms of pay and conditions for women, which takes place as part of the globalization process, may well mitigate against the negative effects of economic liberalization and bring real bonuses for women in the long term.

20. See Institut National de la Statistique, *Enquête nationale population emploi, 1989* (Tunis: Ministère du Plan et du Développement Régional, 1989).

21. See, for example, Ghannouchi, n.d.

Sudanese Women in National Service, Militias, and the Home

In tracing the causes, nature, and impact of the rise of radical/political Islamic sentiment in northern Sudan, which reached a crescendo in the 1980s and its culmination in 1989 with the Islamist overthrow of the elected government in Sudan, I have been exploring dual, interconnected processes: (1) the economic restructuring of Sudan in response to pressures from international monetary organizations and global capitalism, and (2) the invention of the "authentic" Sudanese citizen as "modern Muslim," and the ways in which women are central to this construction.[1]

I argue here that economic pressures, resulting in restructuring, among other things, have thrown women into new or reinvented roles that directly involve them in tending the Islamic nation (*umma*). Some of these new roles within the gender division of labor have to some extent transgressed conventional roles. Many women are serving in the paramilitary National Service and militias (e.g., the Popular Defense Force). Simultaneously, women are summoned to upgrade more conventional roles—to rebuild family economies for less reliance on imports, and to reproduce the next generation of devoted and "authentic" Muslims. I argue also that the seeming discovery by women of the roots of their oppression in "Arab custom and patriarchy" (i.e., not Islam), has encouraged them to seek out "authentic" (i.e., original) Islam for their rights and emancipation.

Many of the social rearrangements that we can observe in contemporary northern Sudan are the effects of twentieth-century ruptures of land, labor, and capital. Changes in class structure, class realignments, forced male labor outmigration, and consequent changes in the gender division of labor within Sudan are all processes

195

set in motion by the imperatives of international capital and its agencies. The Sudanese response was initially gradual and then swift in the form of an Islamist-undergirded military coup d'état. What followed was a mobilization of the northern population to build an Islamic nation, including a prevailing upon women to "tend the nation."

Part of the success of the Islamic state is a result of the mobilization of public consciousness about citizenship in an Islamic nation. That this citizenship is gendered according to economic formula is the main theme of this chapter. I am interested in the shift in identity construction of the woman citizen—mother, Muslim, militia woman, and National Service volunteer—an expanded essentialism that has been sharpened since the regime has been under attack militarily and in international critiques.

Theoretical Framework

"Sudan" as a concept and as a contiguous, official political entity was constructed by colonials. Hardly anything altered that artificial structure for most of the twentieth century. Now, against a backdrop of radical/political Islam, there are a number of potentially transformative processes taking place. Not only is Sudan's revolution one of the most active and seemingly successful Islamic movements in the world, but the National Islamic Front (NIF), the initial organization behind the military regime, and its successor, the National Congress (NC), have attempted to transform national identity.[2] The state's strategy includes the invention of the "new Muslim woman," an important segment of the reinvention of national identity as "Muslim," as it is disaggregated from "Arab" in a striking departure from the vigorous putative claims to Arab genealogy that have characterized much of northern Sudanese identity. The two categories (Arab and Muslim) were historically conflated, but are now being treated as discrete. A second process is the legitimizing of the Islamic state through a process of "authenticating" the economy (establishing or expanding Islamic banks, insurance companies, and other economic institutions that have an "Islamic character") as well as the culture. Women are key to that authentication.

Islamist and non-Islamist women are both embracing and rejecting one of the main mechanisms men in power are using to create and maintain hegemony: positioning women to serve the culture, not only as the carriers of culture, but also as the carriers of morality. This means fashioning women through the media, the schools, the legal apparatus, and community organizations to develop an authentic Sudanese culture and economy based on an original interpretation of Islam. As Islamist women leaders and elites have fashioned it for themselves, this is to be an Islam separate from, though connected to, "Arab" culture.

Within the framework of state economic restructuring caused by international pressure, I have tried to account for (1) the particular nature of the Sudanese state's reconstruction of citizenship and identity, (2) the state's manipulation of religious ideology, (3) the reinvention of cultural identities to conform to state ideology, and (4) the centrality of gender in this process, especially the division of labor. One manifestation of the combination of these processes is the building of a force of mujahidin, a holy army, supported by the citizenry of the Islamic nation, which has involved recruiting both men and women and adjusting gender constructs accordingly.

These processes are of course dynamic, reflecting the changing interests of international capital and the collaborating bourgeoisie. This is a gendered process, not only with consideration for the impact on women and gender arrangements, but also for the importance of women and men as self-interested gendered actors in the process.[3]

History and Political Economy

In a brief chapter it is not possible to elucidate some of the complexities of Sudan's colonial history and its ties to international capital as these relate to gender and the contemporary restructuring of the economy. Nonetheless, in considering capitalism and class formation, one would need to consider the ways in which, through various colonial regimes, Sudan was drawn into the global system of capital exchange, leading to a situation in which twentieth-century colonial and postcolonial developers have used a growth-pole strategy: the concentration of investment in a favored region to create centers of growth. The rationale has been that there would be a spread to peripheral areas. In Sudan, as in most other areas with pronounced core-hinterland disparities, this has hardly occurred. Although a middle class of peasants has emerged in the Gezira and elsewhere, they are involved in commodity production: agricultural labor further serving capital accumulation.[4]

The Dynamics of Postindependence Politics

Every Sudanese party or political/religious interest group has had to contend with significant social and economic issues: the civil war, the drought, the chronically bad and worsening economic situation, the interference of international capital, and the restless and ambitious military.

The Islamist military government that has held power since 1989 carried out some draconian acts: it immediately dissolved a democratically elected People's Assembly, suspended the constitution, and outlawed all political parties, unions, and professional associations. Sharia was imposed even on non-Muslims (nearly one-third of the country's population). Rights of due process were suspended or ignored, hundreds languished in jails, executions were common, and torture and disappearances were reported by Amnesty International and other human rights watch groups. Middle-class civil servants, including large numbers of university faculty, were sacked. In general, opposition elements were eliminated, and thousands of activists (including even some of the more conservative sectarians), intellectuals, and leftists went into exile.

The country is in economic disarray.[5] The capital is overextended in social services and has become poverty-ridden, unhealthy, and dangerous. Migrants—especially southerners and westerners—pour into Greater Khartoum only to have their shantytowns demolished by the government and themselves driven out into the desert. As local militias carry out genocidal attacks, thousands of southern and western Sudanese starve.

In this atmosphere women's freedom of movement and association were sharply curtailed and the women's rights agenda was co-opted by the Islamic revolution. Juxtaposed with rhetoric about women's rights under Islam are such statements as the one made in November 1991 that "henceforth all Sudanese women will wear long black dresses to their ankles and a black veil covering their head and face . . . those who disobey to be instantly punished by whipping."[6]

Such are the tensions of gender politics in Sudan, a society where a weak state has been buffeted by competing oppositional groups, where the processes of state feminism have been discontinuous, and where we see a resurgence of the warrior tradition and a remasculinization of the society.[7] This remasculinization is a corollary to the (re)positioning of women as bulwarks for the (re)building of "authentic" culture.

State Ideology: Gender, Labor, and Class

Clearly, at least for particular classes of women, a crisis has been developing in Sudan for some time. In recent decades, capital-intensive economic schemes, the appearance of multinational corporations and agencies, uneven regional development, labor migration, ethnic power realignments, and developments in cultural imperialism have all preceded sociopolitical and economic crises, which in turn have profoundly impacted gender arrangements.[8]

A crisis for many middle-class and professional women has been the rise to power of Islamists in the 1970s, whose proponents' ideological expressions promote a romantic image of women that effectively fulfills the gender ideology of the middle-class Islamist movement. This essentialist representation requires the redomestication of women, the reconstruction of the moral fabric of society, and the assignment of women as agents of that reconstruction. Furthermore, the romanticizing of reproduction can pressure some categories of women to leave the labor force or maneuver them into "appropriate" jobs. Yet the problem is attenuated (and unsettled) by the fact that the ruling party also uses the claim of "equal participation" for women. One cannot deny the larger number of women participating in national political events than in the past. Nor can one deny the extent of the development of state feminism in the form of government-sponsored conferences, various commissions, and forms of governmental support.

Although the forces that brought the NIF to power had been accumulating for some time, recent phenomena associated with international capital intensified the buildup. In the 1970s, for example, the unemployment rate rose and salaries did not keep up with inflation, enormously increasing male labor outmigration. At first, because the outmigration comprised the working class or minor civil servants, gender arrangements did not tilt in such a way as to threaten the prevailing gender ideology. Soon the migrants were intellectuals and middle- to senior-level personnel. This "brain drain" coincided with pressure by the World Bank and the International Monetary

Fund to prune the overburdened civil service, and the labor force felt the impact. A number of reports verified the impact of this labor out-migration (Sanyal, Yaici, and Mallasi, 1987).[9] When women began to move into some of these better jobs, formerly held by men and per-ceived to be their domain, the effect was to tilt the gender ideology.[10]

With more and more sectors of the economy being brought under international capital, most rural families, by necessity, were expected to produce for the cash economy. Consequently, women and children were forced into heavy, more capital-intensive agricultural activi-ties—at the expense of domestic crops. Aping the West, development planners have assumed men to be heads of households and the central breadwinners. Improvements are usually aimed at men: improved seed, credit, and marketing facilities, and agricultural extension services. At the same time, with male labor outmigration rates growing, women and wives increasingly become single heads of households, managing and supporting the family, caught between their continuing roles as family food-producers and domestic repro-ducers, and the pressures on them to engage fully in the market econ-omy. No amount of science or technology, as we currently under-stand them, will resolve this dilemma. It was clearly a dilemma for the new Islamist regime, which has responded by substituting Islamic versions of capitalism, worsening Sudan's already poor situ-ation.

By 1983 the Nimieri military regime was in grave difficulty. Many factors provoked the World Bank and the International Monetary Fund to put pressure on the state to prune the civil service and raise food prices: the spiraling national debt, an increasingly suc-cessful insurrection in the south, the formation and development of the National Front (a coalition of political opposition groups), a three-month-long judges' strike in 1983, and the doctors' strike in early 1984. All of these events led to various desperate moves on the part of dictator Jaafar Nimieri. Judges and doctors were powerful professional groups, the Sudanese Doctors' Union being one of the most prestigious organizations in the country. The strikes led to the declaration of a state of emergency.[11] In suppressing these rebellions, Nimieri resorted to increasingly harsh measures, including the noto-rious "September Laws," severe interpretations and enforcement of sharia (sacred law). Nimieri aimed to distract people from the struc-tural adjustment that was soon to dominate the national economy.

Gender and the Social Forces of Greater Khartoum

Just as these economic processes are gendered, so are they focused in Sudan's urban areas, especially in Greater Khartoum, where most of the population lives. Now the strain on the capital is even greater as a result of the influx of thousands of refugees from civil wars—those of Sudan as well as those of neighboring countries. We see only population estimates now; it would be dangerous for the government to acknowledge the demographics in print, as the numbers in the burgeoning shantytowns would then require a reassessment of services needed. Counting the fringes might also necessitate recognizing the decline of Arab/Nubian numerical domination.

The country's most skilled and formally educated people, as well as a large proportion of its wealth, are concentrated in Greater Khartoum. In addition, one finds extreme centralization in the political and administrative spheres. Greater Khartoum seats the central government and the judiciary, is the headquarters of most political parties, and is the repository of the majority of people active in national, ethnic, religious sectarian, and gender politics.

In social services, Greater Khartoum ranks highest in the urban hierarchy. It is the most important educational center; similarly, there is a marked concentration of medical services. The townspeople in the formal workforce obtain their living essentially in one of three places: government, commerce, or industry. There is a hierarchical class structure in this center of enlightenment.

Greater Khartoum's burgeoning subaltern population is among the poorest in the world. These urban slum-dwellers and foragers, a large proportion of whom are women and children, who in any way possible eke out an income (rather than being "paid"), have become some of the most resourceful people I have ever encountered. Yet the poverty is staggering and the social consequences are great. Greater Khartoum's residents have learned to depend on the state, yet know that they cannot. Basic utilities and social services cannot even be supplied to the middle and upper classes, who spend increasingly less time inside the country.

Greater Khartoum's dire condition reflects the poor health of both the nation and the people who hold it together. Older residents worry that the city is falling apart. They see displaced populations taking over. "Many . . . bemoan the massive westernization of their culture, the disembodying signs of illicit sex, drugs, and alcohol" (Simone, 1990: 166). Anything, the secular might argue, would be better than this fragmenting culture—even Islam. What holds the city together are loose urban networks (e.g., illicit distribution systems, illicit services, non-Islamic ritual practices) that neither the Islamists nor any other political groups choose to notice; when they do, it is usually in an attempt to eradicate rather than help them.

Women establish and control most of these loosely knit networks, hold many of the illicit jobs (e.g., prostitutes and brewers), and participate in a number of non-Islamic practices (e.g., the Zar).[12] They are ingenious planners and everyday visionaries. Sudanese feminists and Islamists often rely on the financial and political agendas of their party or the state for their feminist and womanist projects. But most women of Khartoum do not, and cannot, rely on or look to agencies or organizations for their survival as women, nor for their religious expression. They are too busy foraging, holding the family economy on their backs as the government increasingly cuts back on help. They are asked to pick up the slack of what the government cannot provide, to maintain a totally self-sufficient household with reference to imported goods, to return to some of the craft and domestic skills of the past, and to inculcate in their children the ideals of the Islamic state. All this with considerable obstacles put in their paths.

Subject to Debate: Women, Labor, and the Islamists

Before the consolidation of Islamist power in 1989, formal and informal national and local debates were taking place about gender, law, and labor—spheres in which the interests of Islamist men and non-Islamist women, in particular, sometimes conflicted. The Islamist process was not only gendered, but also clearly a product of the middle class, one highly engaged in commerce and other "worldly" pursuits. The relationship in Sudan of Islam, commercialism, consumerism, and urban-middle-class occupations has its roots in the nineteenth century.[13]

This relationship between Islam, the middle class, and capitalist activity is certainly on the rise today. That is, Islamism as an ideology reflects class interests. Islamic "fundamentalism," at least in the form of the Ikhwan (Muslim Brotherhood) and the NIF in Sudan, and now including the Islamism of the ruling party, has mainly recruited from the urban professional middle class. The state is developing a sophisticated rationalization and articulation of Islam and commerce. Women are definitely important in the building of the infrastructure of the new Islamist middle class, but not in the important ways that professional and middle-class women were involved in a more secular environment.

In the three decades after independence and before the Islamist takeover, legal and constitutional apparatus seemed to support the idea of women being active in the workforce. Nonetheless, women's entry into the paid workforce was less a matter of volition than a result of the dire economic conditions that compelled most women to seek work. Still, the tension between the demands of women's material lives and the Islamist ideological prescriptions was palpable by the late 1980s. Subtle legal means had already been discouraging women from some areas of work, and by the early 1980s religion was being brought to bear on the creation of the woman citizen— even in the documents of the "secular" Union of Sudanese Women (of Nimieri's Sudan Socialist Union). Although this organization with its co-opted name was an arm of the state, it had many progressive and feminist members and was the main women's organization during a time when the leftist Sudanese Women's Union was banned. A 1980 summary of the working plans of the Union of Sudanese Women articulates the proper role of women and moral checks on their behavior (Sudan Socialist Union, 1980: 5). In the area of planning and research, the summary declares the organization's agenda to be "*scientific* research on certain topics . . . women and *Islam; Islamic laws* for women" (Sudan Socialist Union, 1980: 13, italics added). Thus women's labor was being highly scrutinized and manipulated by the 1980s. In the hands of the young, recently urbanized middle class, Islamism has emerged as a capitalist enterprise, replete with ideological prescriptions about women's labor (i.e., rationales for limiting women's access to a number of jobs).

As discussed above, Sudan's economic situation had reached crisis proportions by the 1980s. The government was extracting surplus, and inflation was increasing; only the upper middle classes were doing more than surviving. The unemployment rate rose and salaries could not match inflation.[14] Another factor affecting male workers was the pressure that international lending agencies were applying on the Sudanese government to reduce Sudan's overdeveloped civil service. This resulted in even fewer jobs. Men left to find jobs and earn more money. Marjorie Hall and Bakhita Amin Ismail remark: "The dearth of trained personnel, especially with the emigration of many Sudanese [men] to the oil-rich Arab States, acts in women's favour and enables them to rise rapidly . . . to positions of *great authority*" (Hall and Ismail, 1981: 251, italics added).

It took a while for the population to realize that women were taking over jobs vacated by the absent men. At first the gender arrangements were not affected in ways that threatened the prevailing gender ideology, and thus men, because the outmigration of male labor was of an expendable class. But soon the exodus was of intellectuals and middle- to senior-level personnel who left behind jobs perceived by Islamists and others to be the preserves of men, which were then being filled by women.[15]

Islamists interpreted this demographic upheaval as a threat to their class interests and began to agitate. An example was the national debate, called by conservatives, about whether too many women were being allowed to study medicine. They pointed to the dramatic increase in women entering the Faculty of Medicine at the University of Khartoum. But the fact remained that over 80 percent of male medical graduates were leaving for more lucrative positions in the Gulf states.[16] Faced with that reality, political conservatives, underpinned by Ikhwan and later NIF ideology, mainly took the position that women doctors were needed, but should be directed into "appropriate" fields of medicine. Among the fields deemed inappropriate for women, surgery and obstetrics were seen as too strenuous for them. Obstetrics was further thought inappropriate for women because they might be called away from their family duties at any time, day or night. Leaving their homes for work late at night is not considered respectable or safe for women, no matter what the work. Despite objections, women began to invade these two fields—not incidentally the most lucrative in Sudanese medicine. As one woman obstetrician remarked, "They expect us to believe their logic about why these particular fields were singled out as inappropriate for women when we know the underlying question is who will have economic power! They must think we are fools!"[17]

The general alarm that traveled through the urban population of middle-class professional women was justified, especially if one observed the number of well-known, impeccably credentialed women doctors who might potentially be deprived of senior positions in certain areas of medicine. With some stealth, the Ministry of Health attempted to channel women into mother-and-child health clinics, public-health positions, and more significantly, into the least prestigious field, general medicine.[18] Islamist women doctors, who have been organizing and recruiting extensively within the field of general medicine, act as apologists for this discriminatory policy.[19]

In their attempts to offset local and international criticisms that there has been a generalized demotion of women from more prestigious jobs, Islamists have been clever in their strategies. For example, Islamist women professionals have tried to allay the fears of non-Islamist women in their self-representation as being active and successful and as not suffering any losses due to the formation of the Islamic state. Furthermore, the changes have been gradual: women in lucrative positions are being replaced in small, nearly imperceptible increments intended to extend over a long period. However, even though women may not have been directly fired from their posts, the Islamist ethos concerning their usefulness has been changing. Women with lucrative jobs are no longer seen by state and individual male Islamists as making a major contribution to society, but are seen as competitors. One Islamist man explained it to me very carefully:

> It is not that we forbid women to work. If she must work, then perhaps it is to the husband or to other male members of her family where we should look for any criticism. We only blame her if she goes to work as a frivolous act and does not behave appropriately in the workplace. For example, she must dress according to the respect she wants. We *want* to respect her.[20]

Islam and sharia contain provisions for women to work outside the home, but such provisions are conditional: women's jobs should threaten neither the power structure nor the intact family, and should be "appropriate"—that is, their jobs should be extensions of their domestic labor and reflect the "essence" of woman, which consists in upholding the special qualities of the Muslim woman.

What about the working class? The state can tolerate having unskilled and noneducated women in the workforce, but these workers, although needing to work, generally cannot afford to have their children cared for. Furthermore, jobs in the informal economic sector held by low-income women (e.g., vendors of local brew, sex-industry workers, and some entertainers) are under attack as being offensive to Islam.[21] Prostitutes have been purged from the streets and jailed by police and paramilitary Islamic guards, and brothels and beer halls closed. Still, the jobs themselves have not been eliminated. Does that tell us that the jobs are needed by society? These jobs are basically held only by women, yet women are being told by the Islamists that they cannot hold them. Necessary but not appropriate is the labor message given a large number of Sudanese women workers; appropriate but not necessary is a companion message.

Gender, Identity, and the State: The Formation and Expansion of the "New Muslim Woman"

Designating appropriate work for women, in both the public and the domestic arena, is at the heart of the movement to authenticate the Islamic revolution. The state makes claims about the equality of women and denies discriminatory policies and practices. Islamist activists, both men and women, point to the active political role of women in the movement. Even though women are central to the movement in many ways, there are limitations. Cultural nationalists, from whom most contemporary Islamists have sprung, have historically opposed women's emancipation in the Western sense, arguing that it was an imitation of the West that would weaken the basic Islamic unit, the family.

Islam is the apex of the new Sudanese culture, placed there by the newly educated urban middle class. This class attaches profound importance to the family, and romanticizes women's primary role in the rejection of Western culture. Islamist men—using law, education, and media—position women within the culture to serve the movement and to represent rejection of Western culture. Women become the embodiment of oppositional culture. This approach creates a new trend in the gender division of labor whereby women are active in the workforce, but only under conditions that fulfill the requirements of the party/state and of the *umma*. Islamist women, at least the activists, are complicit in this process.

Because of economic and military imperatives, however, the Islamic state has had to expand its notion of the "new Muslim woman" and keep it flexible. The needs of the expanding state have become militarized, and women are now being reshaped to fulfill both specific and androgynous roles: mothers, members of militias, students, social reproducers of Islamic values, political organizers, and citizens. The state's modernist agenda has entailed the encouragement of institutions generally considered secular, although these are shaped in an "Islamic way." Now most important among these are the military and paramilitary.

Meanwhile the debate on women's rights has been totally co-opted by Islamist leaders and Islamist women's auxiliaries. These factions explain their goals in the language of liberals, such as helping working women, fighting gender discrimination in employment, extending maternity leave, offering free transportation for women workers, organizing women in the informal sector, and the like— even sometimes co-opting the discourse of the left. Most of the rhetoric, however, is dressed in familiar essentialist language.

Tending the nation began to be a prime agenda item for women in the 1980s. Islamic welfare work was certainly a dominant function of the women's organizations registered under the Ministry of Social Welfare, and virtually all of these twenty-some organizations aimed to educate women about Islam; create nurseries; work on child-rearing, health, and nutrition; build awareness of Islam and the nation; "eradicate bad customs," build an image of the "ideal Muslim woman," and teach Islamic citizenship.[22]

For the most part, by the late 1980s image invention had been co-opted by Islamist voices, especially the voices of politically active women. In the mid-1980s the most visible Islamist woman activist was Suad al-Fatih al-Badawi, an NIF member and one of only two women representatives in the People's Assembly. She took great effort to sound forward-looking, stating, for example, that "I do not believe in separatist roles [for men and women] in the construction of the nation. Men and women complete and perfect each other. . . . It was an obligation for women [to make] the representation of women *authentic* and *real*" (Badawi, 1986: 10; italics added).

Nonetheless, what should devout Muslim women do about an idea they reported to me as fact: that men oppress women through various patriarchal customs? A strategy had to be worked out whereby Islam could be seen as a method for rescuing women from oppression. To do that, it would be more effective to demonize some aspect of the population. The strategy was not to totalize men, but to target a category of men. It began to make sense to point the finger at "Arabs," meaning "Arab men."

Male oppression of women stood in the way of Islamist women's agenda—at least the educated, politically savvy elite. For example, Wisel al-Mahdi, the spouse of Hasan al-Turabi, former leader of the National Islamic Front and later the Popular Congress (PC), asserted that it is Arab customs and traditions, not Islam, that have been oppressing women. At the same time, women have to be able to maintain their difference from men, for example, through their emotionality, sentimental nature, and their "femininity."[23]

The question of "feminism" is often posed to Sudan's elite Islamist women because of their seemingly militant pro-women stance. Suad al-Fatih al-Badawi, at an International Women's Forum in Khartoum, 1996, was both evasive and adamant. To quote Margot Badran:

> Souad Al-Fatih spoke of women's need to communicate with the wider world. When asked if feminism might function as a common language, she gave a firm no. When asked if what had been going on at the Khartoum Forum could be called a kind of Islamic feminism, she gave another no, and added that, "Islam would push feminism into a corner." She added, ". . . men historically have been more advanced. Women must be brought to the same level." (Badran, 1996a: 12)

As if sensing that her words had begun to ring feminist, she abruptly shifted gears: "We have *taqwa*—piety. If we understand *taqwa* we will never have feminism in Islam" (Badran, 1996a, 12). Nonetheless, what cannot be mistaken is the appropriation of the feminist rhetoric with regard to women's rights and oppressive Arab customs. Such tones and stances are characteristic of Suad al-Fatih al-Badawi's public statements, whether delivered prior to the Islamic revolution of 1989, or after the UN Women's Conference in Beijing (1995). That women could have it both ways seemed a useful Islamist strategy: so long as they dress respectably and act appropriately, they could work and have a career, and yet still be a dutiful wife and mother, the crux of the family. That such a life was only possible for those who could afford servants was rarely ever mentioned.

As one might expect in a developing Islamic state, there are a number of inconsistencies and paradoxes when one contrasts state requirements for maintaining gender ideology and labor needs. One was able to observe some of the same contradictions within the former NIF between the availability of human resources and the imperatives of the organizational strategies of such a small group. That is, despite some ideological prohibitions, in a number of ways women were truly the nexus of the NIF in the 1980s. They were among the active organizers in the schools, where women constitute the majority of teachers, in neighborhood medical clinics, in NIF nursery schools in the mosques, as consumer/producers, and in the recruitment into the militias. This is still true of women active within the ruling party, the PC. Islamism has strong appeal especially to women at the universities. Women are active in the student unions, in the recruitment of students into the government militias. To symbolize their citizenship in the new Islamic nation, many university women have been wearing the hijab for over a decade.[24]

For their part in socializing the young with Islamic values, Islamist women have received a great deal of praise and attention. The resuscitation of the complementarity approach to gender is serving the party/state in its ability to have a flexible labor pool, that is, to move women in and out of the workforce and in and out of appropriate and inappropriate jobs in the name of helpmates, but also in the image of woman as creator of life and nurturer of the society. The government boasts that women serve the society in all capacities: in the home, in schools, in the workforce, and in the Popular Defense Forces (the main government militia). The nature and arrangement of women's work, however, serve class interests.

The reconstruction of gender ideology was apparent at a 1996 conference in Khartoum, where Suad al-Fatih al-Badawi was elected president of the newly formed International Islamic Union of Women. She led the *sahwa Islamiya* (Islamic awakening) of women toward the development of an Islamic global gender network and proselytization. Egyptian writer Safinaz Kazim, in a plenary address, maintained that Muslim women have two identities—one androgynous, the other specific:

> Pointing to an androgenous [*sic*] Muslim lays stress on the community of Muslims and their equality and common purpose. But, to convene an all women's forum was to address women separately. Women's specificity was heralded and indeed overtook the rhetoric of the androgenous Muslim. The project of the organizers was to politicize women and mobilize their public energies toward helping achieve the establishment of Islamist states. But, at the same time women must be reminded that their first and highest duties were as wives and mothers, and their primary arena the home. The co-mingling of the rhetoric of the *ungendered Muslim* with the rhetoric of women's specificity juxtaposed the rhetoric of equality (of the androgenous Muslim) with the rhetoric of equity (the complementarity of the two sexes). In *time of need* the androgenous

> Muslim (woman) must be activated; in "ordinary circumstances"
> (when women are not needed politically) they must be repatriated
> to the sanctity of the home. (Badran, 1996b: 12, italics added)

Kazim's "time of need" is clearly economic and military. Since the
1990s, women (and men) have been recruited into the Popular
Defense Forces. Until 1998, however, the local and national militias
were called upon mainly for a show of force, commitment to the
Islamic regime, and public service work. By the late 1990s, young
women in hijab, with khaki camouflage and carrying guns, had
become a familiar sight. At an August 1995 workshop in Beijing, one
of the young women of the mujahidin offered photo displays of all-
women militias training for the defense of the nation. She articulated
a battle cry that could only raise a smile on the faces of liberal or radical feminists in the United States:

> We will defend our new Islam, our Nation. Women are more quali-
> fied to do this. We know more things than men do and we can do
> more things. Look at me. I am liberated under my Islam. I am
> ready to fight to the death. I have received military training. I know
> how to use a gun, and I am educated and know the reasons for
> *using* a gun.[25]

Conclusion

The Islamic state is constantly involved in military struggle with the
east and the south (including the Nuba Mountains). The result has been
to force young people to leave school and join the struggle (the universities, all thirteen of them, were closed for a time so that hastily trained
male students could be moved to the front). Women militia members,
however, are fulfilling the jobs that are extensions of their domestic
labor: nursing, preparing food for the soldiers, communications, raising
the next generation of soldiers, and the like. They are the Greek chorus.

But will this "military service" instill ideas of emancipation in
the minds of militia women and others serving the state? In fact, to
problematize the question, most of the Islamist women I have talked
with consider themselves "emancipated" already. We have not yet
had any women martyrs to buoy the image of the woman warrior.
But an element that will be very important to women after the war(s)
is that they have been absolutely necessary in the war effort.

For many women there are no contradictions in their performance of gender-designated "domestic" tasks (which are being constantly redefined) while wearing a hijab and camouflage, carrying a gun, and defending the nation. Yet we hear so little discussion of the economic and labor sacrifices women are making, or of the enormous burden on them of the war, economic restructuring, and the building of the *umma*.

One of the ironies of contemporary Sudanese political economy is that the New Sudanese Movement (as the Islamist movement was referred to generally when not specifically referring to the National Islamic Front) can be seen as a countermovement at the same time that the nation is participating more fully in international capitalism. The modernism that constructs the "ideal" or "authentic" Muslim woman is simultaneously an economic modernization that defies the kind of stereotypic classification that would deem this movement "fundamentalist" or "atavistic."

Notes

In writing this chapter, I have relied on data from several segments of my fieldwork in northern Sudan, extending from 1961 to 1988, and on recent dialogues I have had with exile communities in Addis Ababa, Ethiopia, Asmara, Eritrea, and Cairo, Egypt (1994–1998), especially with regard to the National Democratic Alliance (NDA) based in Asmara. I have also relied on Internet sources. The examination of the National Islamic Front (NIF; successor to the Ikhwan, or Muslim Brotherhood), is partially based on research in Khartoum in 1988. Some of this field data was published in Hale, 1996b, and Hale, 1996a: 177–200. The 1988 fieldwork was partially funded by a grant from the UCLA Center for the Study of Women and the G. E. von Grunebaum Center for Near Eastern Studies. Subsequent trips have been funded by UCLA's African Studies Center, the Center for the Study of Women, and International Studies and Overseas Programs.

1. I do not attempt to define "authentic." Sudanese used the word to refer to a culture that emanates from "true Islam." I grew to realize that "true Islam" was as much an invention of culture as a return to something (as is connoted by "fundamentalism" and denoted by "atavism").

2. Shortly after coming to power, the ruling party was named the National Congress. In 2000 there was a split in the leadership ranks of the ruling party. Hasan al-Turabi, leader of the former NIF, was arrested and his party removed from power. His faction was renamed the Popular National Congress (PNC). The ruling party, led by Hasan al-Beshir and backed by the army, continued as the National Congress. It is too soon to draw fine ideological or practical distinctions between these two factions.

3. I am using "gender arrangements" to refer most particularly to the gender division of labor, but also to domestic arrangements in general, for

example, how the family is structured, family ideology (including reproduction), and specifically the relationship of men and women in terms of status and power. The term also refers to production, reproduction, and social reproduction.

4. Fatima Mahmoud (1984: 2) offers a useful politico-economic history of Sudan, using the analysis of Samir Amin (1977: 333):

> He traces the pre-mercantilist period back to the era of the Sultanate, when long-distance trade existed with Egypt and to the East. According to Amin, Sudan was integrated in the capitalist market during the Turko-Egyptian colonial period, when Sudanese nomads participated in trade by acting as middlemen for Turkish, Syrian, and European merchants. They then moved to agriculture on lands given to them by the Turko-Egyptian system. These agricultural undertakings were largely commercial. At this stage, although new farming methods were introduced, the relations of production were still based on the use of serfs and slaves. Wage labour was not known.

See also Barnett, 1975 (esp. p. 203); Collins, 1976 (esp. p. 10); Niblock, 1987; O'Neill, 1988: 25–59; and McLoughlin, 1962: 377. For an argument about the role the Sudanese capitalist class plays in Sudanese politics, see Mahmoud, 1984, in which it is argued that the Sudanese bourgeoisie has no progressive role to play in the development of Sudan because of its alliance with colonialism. For an analysis of regional disparities, see Roden, 1974: 498.

5. Although oil had been a prospect in southern Sudan for decades, it was not until the late 1990s that the government began exporting oil. The presence of oil in southern Sudan has exacerbated the north-south civil war, but it remains to be seen how much it will affect the national economy.

6. Reported in the *Sudan Democratic Gazette* no. 19 (December 1991): 8. My report on current conditions in Sudan has been gleaned from personal letters, colleagues' firsthand reports, news dispatches and exchanges on the Internet, *AfricaWatch* and *The Nation,* and a number of U.S. and European newspapers.

7. For a discussion of state-sponsored tribal militias, see Salih, 1989: 168–174.

8. For a useful analysis of Sudan's crisis, see Barnett, 1988: 1–17; and O'Neill and O'Brien, 1988 (esp. introd. and chap. 1).

9. See also Galaleldin, 1985: 1–52.

10. See 'Abd al-Gadir, 1984, and Nagar, 1985. This information is also based on 1988 author interviews with Afaf Abu Hasabu, UN program officer; Nahid Toubia, medical doctor, Khartoum; and Fawzia Hamour, Development Studies and Research Centre, University of Khartoum.

11. These events have been well chronicled, especially in a special Sudan issue of *Middle East Journal* 44, no. 4 (1990).

12. The Zar is a self-help, women's solidarity, therapeutic protest cere-

mony, sometimes referred to as a "spirit possession cult." Women congregate to aid the subject in purging herself of troublesome spirits and, in the process, the possessed woman protests her situation.

13. According to Jay Spaulding (1985), commercial capitalism began to replace feudalism in the Nile valley about 1800 and accelerated after the Turko-Egyptian conquest of 1821. Aristocracy gave way to a new middle class consisting mainly of merchants who needed a more sophisticated legal and commercial code, which turned out to be Islam, an urban and commercial religion with a codified legal system.

14. For an analysis, see Ahmed, 1987.

15. See 'Abd al-Gadir, 1984, and Nagar, 1985. Information also based on author interviews with Afaf Abu Hasabu, Nahid Toubia, and Fawzia Hamour (see note 10).

16. Author interview with Nahid Toubia, Khartoum, July 22, 1988. Toubia, a former member of the Council of Surgeons and former head of pediatric surgery, was active in the debate.

17. Author interview with anonymous woman doctor, Khartoum, July 8, 1988.

18. Author interview with Nahid Toubia (see note 15).

19. Agriculture is another important field in Sudanese society that was also being debated, again because women were entering this male bastion in greater numbers. Part of the agriculture debate was captured in *Sudanow* (October 1979–January 1980). In one issue, for example, Omer el-Farouk Hassan Heiba called for the "banning of girls from agricultural education." See "Letters," *Sudanow* (October 1979).

20. Author interview with a male member of the NIF (name withheld by request), Khartoum, July 25, 1988.

21. In written responses to my August 3, 1988, interview questions, Batoul Mukhtar Mohamed Taha, Republican activist niece of executed opposition leader Mahmoud Taha, described her 1983 experience of being in prison with a number of these vendors, portraying them as innocent and economically desperate women who had simply been trying to earn a living. See also her critique in the local press, "Today, No Guardian," *Sudanow* (January–February 1987): 13.

22. I obtained this typed registry in July 1988 from the Ministry of Social Welfare in Khartoum (n.d., probably 1985–1988).

23. Author interview with Wisel el-Mahdi and two other Islamist women, Khartoum, July 12, 1988, at Mahdi's house.

24. In 1988 some 70 percent of women students at the University of Khartoum were wearing the hijab. Author interview with Mohamed Osman, who was doing research at the University of Khartoum on the social and political aspects of the hijab.

25. Informal author interview with a young Sudanese woman in military fatigues (camouflage) and head scarf, who would not give me her name, Beijing, August 1995, at the UN Fourth World Conference on Women.

Mary Ann Tétreault

9

Kuwait: Sex, Violence, and the Politics of Economic Restructuring

The globalization of finance and trade is forcing restructuring—also called structural adjustment—on the economies of nearly every country in the world, and the politics of this restructuring is creating winners and losers across the social and political map of each. Globalization as a process is not a post–Cold War novelty.[1] What seems new is its intensity, the geographic extent and socioeconomic depth of capitalist penetration, and the acceleration of the rate of adjustment demanded by the processes of global capitalism as a constitutive institution of modernity (Giddens, 1990). Perhaps the most interesting and complex engine of global capitalism in the twentieth century is the international petroleum regime. The experiences of oil exporters illustrate the economic restructuring consequent on incorporation in this regime regardless of whether oil prices rise or fall (Tétreault, 1985).

Where costs and benefits are in the process of shifting, pressures from the powerful encourage costs to be displaced disproportionately on members of less powerful groups. In Kuwait, such groups include alien labor, stateless residents locally known as *bidun* (Arabic for "without"—without citizenship), and, among Kuwaiti citizens, women. Kuwaiti women lose out regardless of whether and how restructuring costs are distributed among other groups. Alien labor in the form of low-paid household workers constitutes perhaps the greatest contribution to the standard of living of Kuwaiti women and the chief support for those employed outside the home. Restrictions on the availability and cost of household help add to social pressures intended to keep women out of the workforce (Rahmani, 1996a). If bidun were naturalized and given political rights, this could delay the enfranchisement of Kuwaiti women on the grounds that a sudden more-than-doubling of the politically active population would be destabilizing.[2] At the same time, the exclusion of bidun from citizenship and its material benefits imposes direct costs on their Kuwaiti wives who, being women, cannot transfer their citizenship rights to their spouses and children (Tétreault and al-Mughni, 1995a).

Kuwait's relatively transparent politics provides an unusually candid picture of attempts by various individuals and social groups to seize the lion's share of oil rents in what, until recently, was a contracting economy. This picture is as comprehensible to Kuwaitis as it is to outsiders, making it difficult for the ruling family and wealthy merchants to displace the costs of restructuring onto others without an energetic public struggle. Attempts to impose widespread economic restructuring in Kuwait began during a period of economic strain arising from the costs of postwar reconstruction, and political conflict arising from reactions to reports of embezzlement and fraud by top officials. The political salience of what Kuwaitis term the "theft of public funds" focuses attention on the social effects of differential accumulation and the justice of the means chosen to correct the problem and manage conflicts arising from it.

The recent unexpected rise in oil prices, which has preoccupied citizens and governments in oil-exporting as well as oil-importing countries since early 2000, could change the politics of restructuring in the Gulf states. On the one hand, the immediate need to curb government expenditures has been washed away by the rivers of revenue rolling into the oil exporters' coffers. As a result, some aspects of restructuring have been de-emphasized, although everyday life in Kuwait and elsewhere is not likely to return to the halcyon days of the welfare state. On the other hand, the economic problems plaguing these countries go beyond annual budget totals, centering more on structural problems ranging from regulatory rules and a rapidly expanding Islamist presence in institutions dispensing entitlements to the size and composition of the civil service.[3]

Ideally, radical restructuring undertaken during a period of high state income could minimize political backlash if it were accompanied by onetime side-payments to losers. In the case of Kuwait, however, the side-payments to a large portion of the losers would themselves be structural—not onetime buyouts or buyoffs, but lifetime access to social, economic, and political power. It also is likely to require a review of the colonization of state agencies such as the

Ministry of Education by tribalists and Islamists who use their positions for parochial concerns, such as giving jobs to friends and relations and shaping policy implementation to conform to movement goals. Consequently, control over the status of women and their rights to the entitlements of citizenship becomes a valuable prize in a contest to determine the winners and losers in Kuwait's restructuring game.

The game is not one-sided. Liberal political forces have mobilized strongly and publicly in favor of women's rights since 1999, when the amir himself, Jabir al-Ahmad al-Sabah (r. 1977–), in a surprising move, issued a decree that would have allowed women to vote and run for political office. The decree was promulgated following the amir's dismissal of the parliament in May, and was required by the constitution to be affirmed by the new parliament elected in July. Unfortunately, the body rejected the decree in November and, by a narrow vote, also defeated an identical measure originating in the parliament itself. However, the fight is far from over and the decision of the amir to weigh in, however tepidly, on the side of this highly visible token of social liberalization has increased the anxiety of its opponents, who are losing ground in a conflict they see as key to determining their future power and authority.

Differential Accumulation

It is customary in political *science* to distinguish between the nature of power and wealth. Power is described as a relational variable measuring the capacity to effect desired outcomes in the face of opposition—the ability of A to make B do what A wants regardless of B's own desires. Wealth is measured absolutely—how many dollars, factories, and other valuable objects A or B owns. In political *economy*, the distinction between these two concepts is less clear-cut.[4] Wealth is an integral component of power and therefore is seen at least partly in strategic (relational) terms. In most of these formulations, however, depictions of wealth continue to emphasize its material utility, such as the capacity to buy weapons and pay and equip armies.

Jonathan Nitzan regards the conceptual duality between power and wealth as based on an artificial separation of economics from politics. He invites us to look at economic restructuring as a redistribution of power, domestic and international, much of it measured in money. Winners, those who gain more as the result of restructuring, can use those gains to rise to commanding heights (1998). Concentrating on contemporary national economies, Nitzan argues that individuals, companies, and banks with the closest ties to power-wielders in the government are most likely to benefit from restructuring, even in cases where restructuring leads to a lower average rate of profits. This is because it is the *relative* position of economic contenders that is the measure of their power differential, not absolute rates of profit and accumulations of wealth that distinguish the winners from the losers. Historian David Hackett Fischer finds differential accumulation to be a pattern characteristic of the last stages of the four last global "price revolutions." During all four periods, rapacious redistribution upward was "disastrous not only for the poor who were the principal victims, but for entire social systems" (1996: 257). The world economy is currently undergoing such a period of economic restructuring and Kuwait is not exempt from the process or its consequences. Even in this "best" case, however, the corrosive politics of differential accumulation stimulates violent reactions.

The Engine and Its Drivers

Oil was discovered in Kuwait in 1938 and, following the hiatus imposed by World War II, production capacity expanded rapidly. Kuwait's oil was cheap to produce and could be exported easily from its port. Production levels were determined less as a matter of how much money Kuwait "needed" than how much oil the companies owning its production wanted for their global operations.[5] Consequently, oil production and revenues expanded dramatically, and how Kuwaiti rulers spent their "excess" cash set the stage for today's restructuring battles.

Oil revenues added directly to the power of the ruler and his family, the Al Sabah. Prior to 1896, the Al Sabah was relatively weak compared to the large merchant clans (Rush, 1987); prior to 1938, the ruling family was poorly institutionalized as an instrument of rule (Crystal, 1990). The only Kuwaiti ruler to assume power as the result of a coup, Shaikh Mubarak (r. 1896–1915) departed from a tradition of shared authority to govern Kuwait exactly as he pleased and without the assistance of his family: "The heads of his departments are mostly slaves," wrote the Persian Gulf gazetteer, John Gordon Lorimer. "[H]is near relations are excluded from his counsels; even his sons wield no executive powers" (Crystal, 1990: 62). Mubarak also governed without consulting the merchants, then a novel approach in Kuwait and one continued by his successors. In 1938, following the discovery of oil, the merchants tried to assert some of the authority they had enjoyed before the accession of Mubarak. They elected a parliament and demanded the right to participate in political and financial decisionmaking for the nation. After quashing this movement, then-ruler Ahmad al-Jaber (r. 1921–1950) invited members of his family into the government, both to increase his control over them (his cousin, Abdullah al-Salim, had assisted the merchants during the parliamentary movement) and to strengthen the family's hold over the country and its resources (Crystal, 1990: 62). Most of the ruler's new helpers demanded cash allowances; some took over properties with his consent and then charged high rents to the people living there. Some of this land also was sold to merchants. Jill Crystal notes that corruption was rampant among ruling family members in charge of government departments, just as smuggling was a major source of income to the merchant class (1990: 64).[6]

When Abdullah al-Salim (r. 1950–1965) succeeded his cousin in February 1950, he began his rule in a strong financial position. As a result of the fifty-fifty profit-sharing regime initiated by Venezuela in 1948, he was able to renegotiate the terms of the Kuwait Oil Company (KOC) concession and increase Kuwait's per-barrel revenues. The flow of oil revenues swelled to tidal wave proportions. Much of the public expenditure of this money went toward big development projects, nearly all constructed by British firms. Britain, as Kuwait's "protector" in the region, saw Kuwait's oil income as a British resource, and sought to use its half ownership of KOC and its role as Kuwait's external protector to shore up its declining global power position.

Abdullah al-Salim was determined to win full control of this money. He did so by changing the laws to direct more of the benefits of oil revenues toward Kuwaitis. Foreigners doing business in Kuwait were required to include Kuwaiti partners as majority owners, thereby channeling streams of profits to favored locals, including members of the ruling family. Kuwaitis were awarded dealerships, monopolies, and government contracts that produced additional long-term income streams for favored recipients. Large amounts of money were also transferred directly from the state to landowners through a program called the Land Acquisition Plan (LAP) (Khouja and Sadler, 1979).[7] Under the LAP, the government purchased land at inflated prices, ostensibly for public development projects.

In the struggle among Kuwaiti elites over who would capture the lion's share of Kuwait's oil revenues, members of the ruling family were in a more favored position than the merchants. Al Sabah family members heading government departments, most prominently Fahad al-Salim and Abdullah al-Mubarak, turned them into personal financial empires that sucked money from the state and extorted even more from clients. To counter the power of his "imperial" relations, Abdullah al-Salim spread the wealth to other family members. Meanwhile, Kuwait's economic importance to Britain, which had increased as other parts of the British Empire became independent, prompted the British government to challenge the growing autonomy of Abdullah al-Salim as well as the corruption of key family members with regard to the allocation of oil revenues. Administrators were sent to Kuwait to help the ruler bring his finances under control and, not incidentally, to ensure that more of the money earmarked for development projects actually was spent as intended. The British advisers failed in their attempt to oust Fahad al-Salim from his dominating position, but their contribution to continuing crises in state administration opened some space for Abdullah al-Salim to gradually reorganize the government so that other family members could help him rein in the excesses of the most abusive ones (Crystal, 1990).[8]

Kuwaiti merchants were also-rans in the differential accumulation race to capture oil revenues. Abdullah al-Salim edged the merchants out of politics as his income was now large enough to free him from dependence on their financial support to run the state.[9] His reorganized government included a Supreme Council monopolized by family members. But Kuwaiti merchants were less concerned that their political authority had eroded than that their economic primacy was ending. They invested wartime profits in the postwar boom fueled by oil-industry demands for supplies and services, and development projects initiated by the new Kuwaiti welfare state. But having to compete with insiders from the ruling family meant that merchants found themselves losing ground with respect to the Al Sabah. When a financial crisis in 1953–1954 forced Abdullah al-Salim to borrow money from the merchants to meet his current obligations, it provided an opening for the merchants to exact concessions.

Crystal identifies the resolution of this crisis as the birth of a new social contract in Kuwait (1990: 75). In return for their lending him money and agreeing to stay out of politics, Abdullah al-Salim promised the merchants he would rein in the members of his family who were blocking merchant access to Kuwait's oil wealth. He gave the merchants a substantial share of monopolies and agencies, provided them with capital—for example, by depositing U.S.$1 million dollars at no interest in the fledgling National Bank of Kuwait (NBK), established in 1952 by representatives of five prominent merchant families[10]—and revised the terms of pending development contracts to award a generous portion to merchant-owned firms. Some government operations were privatized, and joint ventures with merchant partners were established in the state-owned oil industry, most notably an oil-tanker company, petrochemicals ventures, and the first developing-country-owned multinational oil firm, the Kuwait National Petroleum Corporation (KNPC) (Tétreault, 1995: chap. 5).

Abdullah al-Salim also embarked on an ambitious program of oil-wealth distribution to the population as a whole. Free public education was expanded rapidly beginning in the 1950s, and parents were first encouraged and then required to educate their daughters as well as their sons. Free healthcare; subsidized food staples, utilities, and housing; and programs providing direct financial support to families improved living standards and life expectancies, while job training programs, some provided by KOC in response to government mandates, gradually increased the national pool of semiskilled and skilled labor (Mughni 1993). Even before the establishment of Kuwait University in 1969, young Kuwaitis could be educated free of charge as far—and as far away—as their abilities could take them. Alongside the children of merchants grew a new "middle" class made up of the bright and ambitious sons and increasingly also the daughters of sailors, shopkeepers, fishermen, and settled tribesmen. Graduates who could not find work in the private sector could go to an expanding public sector in which every citizen who wanted a job could get one. Even the unborn were provided for, via a special Reserve Fund for Future Generations (RFFG), into which 10 percent of state revenues were deposited every year.[11]

The appeal of Egypt's President Gamal Abdul Nasser and other prominent Arab nationalists to the Kuwaiti masses in the 1950s, along with a growing sense of entitlement by Kuwaitis to the benefits provided by the state, encouraged the government to promote a feeling of privilege associated with Kuwaiti citizenship (Longva, 1996). Kuwaitis received job preferences, social allowances, preferential access to social benefits, and salary differentials based solely on citizenship (Crystal, 1990; Longva, 1996; Tétreault, 1995). Benedict Anderson (1991) defines nationalism as identifying with an imagined community. These distinctions in entitlements are embedded in conceptualizations of Kuwaiti citizenship and in Kuwaitis' visions of themselves as a privileged community separate from non-Kuwaiti Arabs as well as from others more clearly "foreign."

Intranational distinctions, such as between tribesmen and townsmen (*badu* and *hadhar*) or Sunni and Shiite Muslims, show how boundaries control the relatively privileged and the specially protected. The connection between privilege and maintaining good relations with the regime kept the relatively favored in line even when they resented their loss of status vis-à-vis their fellows. Ghanim al-Najjar reports that the rise of nouveau riche clients of the ruling family was resented by old-line merchants, who nevertheless went along for fear that they would be excluded from future state largesse if they were to protest.[12] Yet although they appeared to accept as peers men whose fathers had been their servants, they refused to give their daughters to such "new men" or to their sons (Mughni, 1993). Instead, the merchants deployed their daughters in strategic maneuvers to maintain their dominant status in Kuwaiti society. In addition to endogamy, their main strategies were to block the rise of middle-class women to positions of authority, and to use their daughters to stake out key positions in government and the economy that otherwise might have gone to middle-class men.

State-sanctioned and -supported voluntary associations are primary venues of the Kuwaiti public sphere (Mughni, 1993).[13] Voluntary associations also provide alternatives to the family as bases for mobilizing citizens according to their interests and affinities. Although they are as vulnerable as newspapers to government closure when the regime wishes to stifle criticism and dissent, voluntary associations are vital components of Kuwaiti political and social life. Voluntary organizations are theoretically and, to varying extents in practice, at least as democratic as *diwaniyyat,* although in different ways. Diwaniyyat are regular meetings usually held in private homes, whose primary political advantage lies in their status as protected spaces (Tétreault, 1993). The family basis of the diwaniyya, along with the limits imposed by their physical location in the family home, diminish their democratic character as compared to voluntary associations, and bias them toward supporting the social status quo. Yet, as Haya al-Mughni shows, women's voluntary organizations, though nominally in the public sphere, also display pro–status quo attributes, particularly with regard to their suppression of the development of political skills and access by nonelite women (Mughni, 1993).

> Theoretically, Kuwaiti women's associations should be free spaces, public places in the community . . . in which people are able to learn a new self-respect, a deeper and more assertive group identity, public skills, and values of cooperation and civic virtue. . . . [They] are settings between private lives and large-scale institutions where ordinary citizens can act with dignity, independence, and vision. These are, in the main, voluntary forms of association with a relatively open and participatory character. (Evans and Boyte 1992: 17–18)

In such settings, citizens learn leadership skills such as public speaking, financial management, and how to organize public gatherings and carry out complex projects. Leaders become adept at public performance, giving interviews, speaking for their groups, and having their photos and their opinions published in the newspapers. But Kuwaiti women's organizations provide little free space. Leadership positions are retained at the pleasure of the officers. A leader's ability to attract votes in the periodic elections of association officers rests on the influence and extent of her kinship network, together with her willingness to be responsible for the day-to-day organizational chores associated with her position (Mughni 1993: 105). A leader's success depends on promoting ideas and activities that buttress her family's interests and that also do not require major efforts by members outside her kin network.

Kuwaiti women's associations present themselves as advocates for women's interests, but precisely what these interests are and which ones will be pushed forward are matters permeated by class concerns. Consequently, during the 1970s Kuwait's first two women's societies found themselves working at cross-purposes. The Women's Cultural and Social Society (WCSS), formed in 1963, fits the mold described above—a small group of wealthy women who gather for social events and light charity work. A second group, the Arab Women's Development Society (AWDS), was also formed in 1963. Organized by a middle-class woman, Nouria al-Sadani, its initial goals were to modernize Kuwaiti society and raise the status of women, primarily through promoting women's education. As Haya al-Mughni notes, both groups started out working within a male model of female social activism conceived as supporting male interests—that is, not challenging patriarchal familial or social structures (1993).

During the 1970s, however, the AWDS began to promote feminist goals, calling for equal rights for women, including "the unconditional right to contest elections," and for changes in Kuwaiti family law (Mughni 1993: 77). Voting rights for women and a proposal to outlaw polygyny were debated in parliament. At the same time, government restrictions on women's employment were easing and women were becoming more visible in the workforce. The proposal to abolish polygyny drew the most vociferous opposition from outraged parliamentarians, but both measures frightened opponents of gender equality. The AWDS drew even more attention to its gender radicalism when it called conferences in 1974 and 1975 to examine the situation of Kuwaiti working women. These public forums allowed middle-class women to "put forward their grievances" (Mughni 1993: 82). The AWDS also transgressed class boundaries by attracting merchant-class women as members. This earned it the enmity of WCSS members, some of whom supported its issues but nearly all of whom saw the AWDS "as stealing a show which should have been theirs" (Mughni 1993: 84).

The class and programmatic antagonisms between the AWDS and the WCSS provoked a campaign to oust the charismatic Nouria al-Sadani from the AWDS leadership and to reorient Kuwaiti women's groups closer to the status quo. After a few years of intense conflict featuring the formation of a new women's group by Nouria and some of her merchant-class allies, the government closed down the AWDS for alleged financial irregularities and forced Nouria to go into exile (Mughni 1993: 87). Suppression of feminist activity continued with the chartering of Islamic women's groups promoting religious values and traditional female roles. The older merchant-class groups soon became identified as the "progressive" women's organizations, but they remain little more than lukewarm supporters of nonelite women. For example, the Women's Cultural and Social

Society shelters on its premises but does not work directly with or for a group of middle-class women seeking to restore full citizenship rights to Kuwaiti women married to foreigners (Tétreault and al-Mughni, 1995b). During the 1996 parliamentary election campaign, young middle-class women organized events promoting women's rights. Their actions were deplored by leaders of established women's groups, particularly those with male family members running for parliament who were concerned that such "uppity" public behavior would mobilize religious voters against their husbands and fathers.[14]

Another class strategy employing women to shore up the positions of Kuwaiti elites is to use them as "placeholders," occupants of visible positions of authority, some of which also allow them to act as gatekeepers. Ruling family women along with women from the merchant classes occupy these desirable slots. Examples include Shaikha al-Sabah, director of marketing for the Kuwait Petroleum Corporation; Farida al-Khorafy, rector of Kuwait University; Fatima Hussain, originally editor of the daily *Al-Watan* and later the editor of its women's magazine; and Amal Hamid, who serves under the minister of information and effectively runs much of the ministry. Such women are at least as competent as male counterparts holding similar or higher positions, but this begs the question of whether members of Kuwait's new middle class, men and women, could not do as well or better given the opportunity.

The Engine Stalls

The current cycle of restructuring in Kuwait began in the early 1980s. It was triggered by the crash of the Suq al-Manakh, Kuwait's unofficial stock market, in September 1982, and it accelerated after world oil prices collapsed in June 1986. Economic uncertainty was paralleled by military insecurity arising from the first Gulf War (1980–1988). Kuwaitis sitting in their living rooms could hear the rumble of artillery from war zones on the Fao peninsula, and they endured attacks on oil installations and public gathering places by Kuwaiti supporters of the Islamist regime in Iran. In retaliation for Kuwait's assistance to Iraq, Kuwaiti shipping came under attack from Iranian military forces. Criticism of government policies by members of the 1985 parliament, whose issue and ideological concerns spanned a wide range of behavior that included suspicions of financial irregularities by powerful ministers, added to the tension.

In July 1986 the amir dismissed the parliament and suspended provisions of the constitution protecting civil liberties. Closing down parliament gave the government a free hand to deal with the economic crisis. Among the areas under scrutiny for cost-cutting were labor imports, which drained resources through claims for expensive public services, and the civil service, the employer of last resort for Kuwaiti citizens.[15] With the demise of the parliament, the oil minister, Shaikh 'Ali al-Khalifa Al Sabah, halted official reporting on the Kuwaiti industry, even to other ministries, freeing himself from domestic checks and setting the stage for his controversial policy of producing oil over Kuwait's OPEC quota (Tétreault, 1995).[16]

Among the first to feel the pain of restructuring in the mid-1980s were foreign workers, religious and ethnic minorities, and bidun. Among foreigners, Palestinians were especially resented by Kuwaitis. Having come to Kuwait in large numbers following the founding of Israel in 1948 (Ghabra, 1987), well-educated Palestinians occupied key posts in the private and public sectors, and their children were highly visible at Kuwait University, where they were regarded as showoffs and usurpers.[17] Palestinians resented their outsider status and permanently subordinate roles in the economies of Kuwait and other Gulf states, particularly when citizens with inferior training and experience were promoted over themselves.[18]

Among Kuwaiti citizens, middle-class Shia suffered most acutely from the economic downturn. Because of the war and regardless of their wealth, Kuwaitis of Iranian descent, also mostly Shia, were socially ostracized and some faced economic discrimination, particularly young men and women seeking their first jobs.[19] Bidun were targeted by stricter enforcement of laws requiring employees to present evidence of citizenship. Without such evidence, bidun were subject to harassment and, as the squeeze continued and was extended, some bidun with Kuwaiti wives were even fired from their jobs and deported.[20]

Women were independent victims of restructuring. As noted earlier, when gender is a weapon in interclass competition, it does not necessarily provoke rivalry between women and men. In struggles for upward mobility within classes, however, gender often becomes an axis of conflict as new men seek to eliminate able women from every social class—including their own—from the competition. This rivalry begins at school. Traditional child-rearing practices in Kuwait place few demands or behavioral restraints on young boys and male adolescents, but many on their sisters. Girls develop work habits that lead to superior academic performance, a pattern that persists at Kuwait University, where women competing for admission to technical, high-status majors such as medicine and engineering have an edge over men if grades and performance are the primary criteria for selection and retention.[21] Young women's academic achievements are generally considered as having been unjustly acquired. "Girls have to stay at home," said a father of a high-achieving daughter and a son who left the university because of bad grades. "What else can they do but study? It's not fair."[22]

Women already working became targets of intense propaganda efforts to get them to quit their jobs. Working mothers were accused of neglecting their children and contributing to poor Arabic language skills among Kuwaiti youth, allegedly from handing over responsibility for child-rearing to Asian maids—a phenomenon just as visible in families whose mothers did not work outside the home as in those whose mothers did. Delinquency, divorce, rising alcohol consumption, and even disunity in Kuwaiti society as a whole were blamed on women leaving their homes for paid employment (Tétreault and al-Mughni, 1995a). These allegations resonated with the slogans of an ongoing campaign to promote national unity by "Islamizing" the state. Calling directly on patriarchal images and values deeply embedded in local religion and culture, slogans and speeches originating from the highest levels of the regime legitimized what has become a highly focused and generally effective attack on women's human rights by Kuwaiti Islamist leaders.

Islamism finds ready adherents among the angry young men at Kuwait University and in Kuwait's secondary schools. The Islamist agenda in parliament attracts them because its highly publicized initiatives would improve their chances of success at the university and eventually in the job market. These initiatives are couched in terms of tradition and religion; they promise to redraw the parameters of a system widely perceived as biased in favor of women, and bring it into conformity with what most Kuwaitis believe God and nature intended. This image and its translation into advocacy of policies that would erect barriers against women's academic and economic advancement attract large numbers of young men to Islamism.

The political values of young Kuwaiti Islamists are reinforced by their social isolation and their perception that they are victims of injustice (Thakeb and Scott, 1982). Most Kuwaiti Islamists are of recent badu origin. Badu make up an estimated 65 percent of the citizen population. Collectively, badu are the least socially assimilated and economically advantaged segment of the citizenry, and their growing involvement in Kuwaiti political life contributes to what Shafiq al-Ghabra calls "desertization . . . the transfer of the desert's customs, traditions, beliefs, dress codes, and mentality into the city" (1997: 367). Desertization of the National Assembly began following the 1981 election.[23] In the parliament, tribalists and Islamists—categories with significant overlap—join together to push for further Islamization of society, primarily by imposing social and economic restrictions on women.

Several Islamist proposals advanced during the 1992 parliament threaten women's education and job rights. For example, a proposal to ban any Kuwaiti woman from traveling abroad unless escorted by a mahram, a male relation prohibited from marrying her under Islamic law, would constrain professional travel as well as opportunities for education abroad. The central role of Kuwait University as simultaneously a site and an object of contestation puts regulation of faculty and student behavior at the top of Islamist concerns.[24] A proposal to impose gender segregation at all schools and colleges in Kuwait was the most radical among several Islamist initiatives designed to regulate the university. Most failed, but a modified gender-segregation bill was adopted in July 1996. Opponents succeeded in removing the segregation requirement from private schools, but all public postsecondary institutions were ordered to be gender-segregated within five years. This leads to concern about the status of proposals to found new, and much-needed, private universities.

Working women also felt the power of parliamentary Islamists, but here the attack was more subtle. Kuwaiti labor participation rates for both sexes are low due both to the large portion of the population that is underage and to early retirement—Kuwaitis may retire as early as fifty years of age. Despite these limits, women's labor participation has risen rapidly. The proportion of women of all ages in the labor force rose from 2 percent in 1965 to 17 percent in 1997, and the labor force participation rate of Kuwaiti women between the ages of twenty and forty recently has been increasing at a faster rate than that of other age groups (Shah, 1994; NBK, 1997): "In 1989, 50 percent of women aged 20–40 were working and by 1997 their percentage increased to 60 percent" (NBK, 1997: 34). Women's labor force participation is linked to education: "[O]f the 22,373 net new jobs requiring university or professional degrees that were occupied by Kuwaiti workers during the past eight years, 62 percent were filled by females, while Kuwaiti males filled the remaining jobs" (NBK, 1997: 36). The 1992 parliament's gender politics, which also produced a less publicized 1995 law allowing working mothers to retire after fifteen years of service regardless of their age, is aimed precisely at these women. Submitted by Khaled al-'Adwa, a flamboyant Islamist from the tribal area of Ahmadi who spearheaded many antiwoman proposals, the new law adds to the already substantial social pressure on Kuwaiti women to leave the workforce at the peak of their professional capabilities (Rahmani, 1996a).

Kuwaiti liberals became more assertive on issues of women's rights following the amir's initiative, and managed to restore gender equality in retirement policy in 2001. Despite a strong push by Islamists to roll it back, the new law was reaffirmed in January 2002 and may indicate a deflection of the Islamist trend, whether or not it signifies that a new and more liberal trend has taken its place.

Religion, Violence, and the Politics of Restructuring

Islamist movements use religious symbols to mobilize people for political action. In so doing, they tap into emotions so powerful and deeply embedded in the human mind that we cannot comprehend them except through myths, or bring them under our conscious control except through exemplary rituals like the Catholic Mass or the Muslim ram sacrifice.[25] All religions have at their disposal a repertoire of such myths and symbols, whose effects can be benign or malignant.[26] They rationalize powerful negative emotions like anger, fear, insecurity, and dread. Among the ways they do this is by selecting sacrificial victims to offer for the deliverance of the community as a whole—that is, by scapegoating—and by demonizing enemies to explain their power to harm and hurt, and also to mobilize opposition to them.

Symbolic violence and real violence are connected, and religion seems uniquely able to trigger both because it is so intimately connected to primordial human emotions.[27] The introduction of a religious dimension into a political conflict increases the likelihood that the conflict will become violent because religion can also be used to undermine the legitimacy of efforts to bring it to an end. Acts of discrimination embedded in other collective identities—such as ethnicity—that evoke primordial emotions may also set the stage for violence. For example, in Kuwait, violence against Palestinians following liberation was foreshadowed by scapegoating and acts of discrimination (Hunter, 1986; Tétreault, 2000a). Violent language also leads to violence. The attempted assassination of a member of the suspended 1985 parliament, which also occurred during that period, was accompanied by hate campaigns against critics of the regime (Tétreault, 2000a: 87, 93–94, 103).

Crime of all kinds has risen astronomically in Kuwait since liberation. Newspapers are filled with reports of murders, rapes, and vandalism in a country whose inhabitants, on my initial visit there in 1983, were stunned by the news of a recent robbery in the suq (marketplace), the first major crime that had been reported in several years. Since then, domestic terrorism, foreign invasion and occupation, and violent repression by the state of political dissidents (violent for Kuwait) have all raised the threshold of what constitutes an acceptable level of public violence. White-collar crime also appears to have risen, particularly theft and embezzlement. Charges that government officials have stolen public funds evoke reactions confined mostly to platitudes and attempts to muzzle critics by manipulating the justice system. For example, during the 1992 parliament the amir called on the courts to support his position that a law protecting cabinet ministers from being tried in the regular courts, which was passed by fiat during the 1986–1992 parliamentary suspension, could not be voided after parliament resumed. Article 71 of the Kuwaiti constitution explicitly provides for such a procedure. The amir withdrew his appeal a month later, but the government continues to act as though this constitutional provision does not exist (Tétreault, 2000a: 167–169).[28]

Political violence supports criminals in high places by discouraging their exposure by critics and whistle-blowers. Abdullah al-Nibari, a member of five parliaments, including all three postliberation assemblies, has spoken tirelessly for more than a quarter century against mismanagement and theft of public funds by those entrusted with their supervision. Abdullah's independence and insulation from retaliation by the regime were highlighted by two key events: his lone vote against gender segregation in 1996 and his subsequent reelection in spite of that vote. Together they demonstrated his almost unique imperviousness to what has become one of the standard ways of controlling the political opposition in Kuwait, that is, by manipulating religious sentiments. Without such political leverage, Abdullah's staying power as a regime critic was effectively unchallengeable. Shortly after the 1996 election, exposure by the state audit bureau of unauthorized withdrawals from the RFFG, alleged bribery of those charged with investigating ministerial peculations, and refusal of ministry heads to enforce laws and economic regulations against members of the ruling family and their Kuwaiti clients provided new fuel almost daily for Abdullah's fiery speeches in parliament and at the diwaniyyat. On June 6, 1997, he and his wife were shot as they returned to the city after a weekend at their beach house—by a relation of the finance minister and two of his servants.

After his recovery, Abdullah was reelected to his seat in parliament in the unscheduled 1999 election. Meanwhile, the perpetrators were arrested, tried, found guilty, and jailed. However, the complexities of post–September 11 redistributive politics in Kuwait continue to unfold in unexpected ways. Abdullah, an advocate of oil nationalization in the 1970s, has today become an advocate of privatization. In the contemporary context, privatization, although strongly supported by the government, also reflects desires among liberal segments of the opposition to increase transparency in political and economic decisionmaking as well as to rationalize employment and transfer state assets to private hands. Abdullah's support of privatization proposals has allowed his Islamist enemies to attack him for having sold out his principles, a fight that brought Abdullah to tears during a particularly vicious debate on this issue on the floor of the National Assembly in December 2001.[29]

These are just a few of the highly contentious and increasingly fluid political battles over power and status in postliberation Kuwait. Conflict between the government and the political opposition—which includes Islamist as well as liberal deputies—is only one facet of this phenomenon. Conflict within each faction and, outside the parliament, among factions in their respective "traditional" constituencies, has also intensified. For example, the dismissal of the parliament in May 1999 resulted from a confrontation between the government and its supporters, and Islamists and their supporters—categories with significant overlap. The controversy arose over errors in the printing of copies of the Quran, which resulted in the distribution of volumes with misplaced pages, missing verses, and other flaws that the accusers insisted constituted blasphemy. To avoid another showdown that could force the rulers to form a new government in response to a parliamentary attack on a minister, the amir closed down the entire parliament in May 1999 and called for new elections in July.[30] This was the first legal dissolution of the parliament since the Kuwaiti constitution was adopted in 1962. The two previous dismissals of parliament each lasted for several years and their ending was preceded by significant institutional reorganization (Tétreault, 2000a).

Yet prospects for peace between the regime and its critics were not improved by the election results. The size of the opposition increased in the 1999 parliament as compared to the 1996 body, while the proportion of liberals among opposition members also increased. During the two-month parliamentary interregnum, the amir issued some sixty decrees on issues ranging from the annual budget, through restructuring proposals and radical changes in foreign investment policy, to the unexpected measure granting full political rights to Kuwaiti women (Tétreault, 2000c). The women's rights decree absorbed most of the attention devoted to the election in the domestic and foreign press, but the other measures were even more important from the perspective of the regime. I believe the women's rights strategy was used to deflect popular attention from these measures.[31]

The continued imbrication of women's issues in restructuring is revealed in the conflict over whether to have a lower retirement age for women and how the gender-segregation policy at Kuwait University and at private universities, three of which are proposed for inauguration within the next two years, will actually be implemented. These issues highlight the ideological split within the opposition. Liberals and Islamists may join at times in opposition to the regime, but they tend to split over most issues of policy. As we saw in the saga of Abdullah al-Nibari, many parliamentary liberals are neoliberals, people who believe so strongly in globalization that they are willing to risk some of the social costs of the restructuring that accompanies it. Kuwait's neoliberals see economic liberalization not only as an opportunity for Kuwait to rationalize its economy, reduce its costly welfare commitments, and become both more modern and less dependent on oil revenues. They believe that economic liberalization will constrain governmental power and thus strengthen their relative position as members of the state. In contrast, parliamentary Islamists oppose restructuring measures that would impose costs on their constituents, especially those that undercut male authority in the family. They fought unsuccessfully against a 2001 law that limits child support allowances to a maximum of five children per father, while liberals were enthusiastic about this law and another one that, for the first time, entitles Kuwaitis employed in the private sector to receive such allowances as well. Plans for rationalizing civil service employment also split Islamists from liberals. In interviews I conducted in Kuwait in January 2002, even very religious liberals expressed concerns that Islamists and tribalists had so colonized the civil service that the ability of the state to conduct normal business was impaired by worker incompetence and demands for bribes.

By seeking support from liberals to open the economy to foreign investment, shrink subsidies, and tackle some of the labor issues that underlie so much popular discontent, the amir has opened himself to demands to be more politically responsive to his liberal critics. Islamists, particularly tribal representatives who, although they are not formally affiliated with Islamist political groups, see themselves as defenders of religious values and tradition, have been the mainstay of the regime since desertization began. However, they, like most Islamists, oppose restructuring measures. An additional dilemma pushing the regime to shift its constituency base rests on the fact that movement Islamists, those who are members of organized Islamist groups, are also in the forefront of the opposition to high-cost weapons purchases. Many are openly anti-Western. If the amir were to commit himself exclusively to the Islamists, it would put the Kuwaiti government at odds with its principal military protector, the United States.

Their eroding position in parliament and among the population as a whole seems to have goaded some Islamists to extreme public behavior. In October 1999 the chair of Kuwait University's political science department was brought into court by Islamists who charged him with blasphemy. The accused, Ahmad al-Baghdadi, was convicted and immediately sent to jail, where he promptly went on a hunger strike. Islamist leaders saw his conviction as a victory in their religious crusade and some were moved to ratchet up their militancy by attacking the women's rights decree as having been imposed by the United States. However, the danger to Ahmad's health—he has a heart condition—and the vigor with which his colleagues and neighbors responded to his plight, soon moved the amir to have him released from prison and his critics brought in for questioning.[32]

Popular Islamist reaction to restructuring has also been expressed in incidents of violence against women. A long battle initiated by Islamists against two female writers resulted in their conviction for blasphemy in January 2000. One of them, Kuwait University philosophy professor Alia Shuaib, was sentenced to two months of imprisonment. The sentence was overturned on appeal and a fine was substituted, but according to *Christian Science Monitor* reporter Ilene Prusher, "In the court of public opinion . . . the trial continues." Prusher tells of how strangers approach Alia on the street and, after verifying her identity, spit on her. Although she is nominally "free," Alia told Prusher that she believes that if she is to continue to teach and write what she thinks, she will have to do it somewhere other than Kuwait (Prusher, 2000).

A second example occurred shortly after the cases against the two female writers were adjudicated. A female Kuwait University student was whipped and her arm broken by a gang of young male Islamists, allegedly for leaving her home without a veil. Known locally as the "Desert Flogging Group," these youths are part of the entourage of the Kuwaiti Taliban, Sulieman bu Ghaith (Pearl, 2001). They also were reported as having been associated with a spate of violent incidents directed against video shops and persons the group said were immoral. A dozen men were arrested within days of the attack and seven were later tried for the crime.

Two months later, the judge in the case, Abdul-Rahman al-Darmi, acquitted all seven men. He offered ten reasons for his decision. Among them was that the victim's testimony to the police had many inconsistencies, that she failed to identify all her attackers, and that her testimony and that given by a young man alleged to be her boyfriend differed on several points.[33] Although the decision and the reasons given may seem unjust from a civil liberties perspective, they are consistent with decisions and reasons given in other cases in which gender was the primary issue and the court favored outcomes supporting traditional gender roles and behaviors. What is different about this case is the widespread publicity it received and the number of persons who were willing to speak in favor of the young woman, not because they thought that she had behaved properly but rather because they thought her rights had been violated. "She was at fault for her behaviour but she should not have been attacked," student Khloud al-Malabi said (Shaheen, 2000).

The rise in political conflict in Kuwait, including incidents of violence, accompanies a demographic phenomenon that Jack Goldstone (1986) found to be a trigger of revolution in seventeenth-century England: a large rising generation among the old elites for whom preferment is no longer automatic. In Kuwait, such elites include a huge ruling family and the smaller, though larger in the aggregate, families of the Kuwaiti rich. Other potentially violent young men are their apparent opposites, those for whom a lack of opportunity, preparation, or discipline leaves them with no alternative to civil service sinecures if they are to support themselves as adults. The visibility of women in high-status positions fuels these men's misogyny and their willingness to scapegoat women as the cause of their difficulties. As elsewhere in the Middle East, such women appear most directly threatening to young men who compose the first educated generation from poor families but who are neither skilled enough nor well-enough connected to make their eventual economic rise a foregone conclusion (Mernissi, 1991: 160; Tétreault, 1990: 17–18). Such persons make up the largest pool of potential recruits to Islamist movements (Thakeb and Scott, 1982; see also Roy, 1994).

At the same time, globalization and its accompaniment, the accelerating spread of modernity, are simultaneously imposing adjustment burdens on populations and governments and changing elite and popular views with regard to the meaning of human rights. Those rights associated with social liberalization also affect the struggle for wealth and status. They are instrumental in creating new hierarchies of power while they destroy customary protections for individuals and families and the legitimacy of worldviews supporting the old ways. Not surprisingly, as in earlier periods of price revolution and capitalist integration, those marginalized by these processes do not remain supine in the face of imminent ruin.

Conclusion

Kuwait today is experiencing the same sort of social dislocation that Karl Polanyi (1944) described for European countries during periods of intense structural adjustment to the spread and deepening of capitalism. Polanyi saw this "double movement" as having two interdependent parts. One encompasses the self-reinforcing processes that, once initiated, push the spread of markets into every aspect of life. The other consists in the self-defensive reactions of those who are or fear that they are losing ground. As Polanyi and others have documented, the double movement produces more than polite protest. The spread of militant religious and nationalistic movements, rising public and private violence, and official and popular campaigns to identify and punish scapegoats are common strategies adopted by the dispossessed to resist further erosion of their already insecure positions.

Women are implicated in all of these strategies, not only because they are themselves objects of value and symbols of communal identity, but also because their emancipation introduces a new class of competitors for political and economic positions. Yet women also are conveniently "other." In narrowly instrumental terms, women are the class of competitors easiest to drive out of the marketplace or at least to relegate to inferior roles when restructuring intensifies the struggle among men to hold or gain economic ground. In a larger sense, questions about the status of women and who shall control them are always political, not only because such issues are metaphors of state-society relations (Hunt, 1988)—in the sense of whether political relations and family relations should be hierarchical/patriarchal or, to some degree, democratic—but also because women are so frequently implicated in practical strategies for community self-definition and governance. As a result, structural adjustment is never a gender-neutral process. In Kuwait as elsewhere, today as in the past, it presents formidable obstacles to women's hopes for equality and to everyone's hopes for civil peace.

Notes

An earlier version of this chapter was published in *The International Journal of Feminist Studies* 1, no. 2 (September 1999): 237–255.

1. See, for example, Wallerstein, 1973, 1986. See also Wolf, 1982.
2. Ghanim al-Najjar, quoted in Tétreault, 2000a: 218.
3. These are analyzed for Saudi Arabia in Chaudhry, 1997.
4. Compare, for example, K. Waltz, 1979, and Lindblom, 1977.
5. This critique can be found in Mallakh and Atta, 1981.
6. On merchant accumulation, see Khouja and Sadler, 1979.
7. See also Najjar, 1984.
8. Fahad al-Salim's providential 1959 heart attack also contributed to the ability of Abdullah al-Salim to reallocate fiscal power to the state.

9. Alan Rush in *Al Sabah* (1987) points to the dependence of the ruling family on fiscal support from the merchant class as the linchpin of the merchants' social and political authority prior to the era of Mubarak. Kuwaiti rulers who resented being under the thumb of the merchants had sought independent financial resources since the nineteenth century, first in the form of date plantations in Iraq and subventions from foreign governments, and finally in their control of oil revenues. See also Anscombe, 1997.

10. Interviews with Ghanim al-Najjar, Kuwait, spring 1990.

11. RFFG capital was invested overseas in blue-chip securities. By 1983, RFFG income plus earnings on other state investments and deposits exceeded U.S.$6 billion annually, an amount sufficient "to cover more than three-quarters of the country's imports and, roughly, a similar fraction of the government's budgeted expenditures" (Stauffer, 1984: D7–D8). RFFG resources were the primary asset of the Kuwaiti government-in-exile during the Iraqi occupation, and allegations that they were plundered before, during, and afterward have been a staple of Kuwaiti domestic politics since liberation.

12. Author interview with Ghanim al-Najjar, Kuwait, February 1990.

13. See also Tétreault, 2000a; and Ghabra, 1991: 199–215.

14. Author interviews, Kuwait, October 1996; and Tétreault, 1996: 36–39.

15. Author interviews, Kuwait, spring 1990.

16. The Organization of Petroleum-Exporting Countries instituted a production ceiling and allocated quotas to members for the first time in 1982. Widespread cheating made the quota system problematic from the start. The price collapse of 1986 was triggered by overproduction by OPEC and non-OPEC producers.

17. Author interviews, Kuwait, spring 1990.

18. Ibid. and Hunter, 1986: 606. Olivier Roy (2001) looks at the "deracination" of the children of displaced Palestinians as one of the supports for Osama bin Laden's extremist Islamist group.

19. Hunter, 1986: 605; and author interviews, Kuwait, London, and the United States, 1990–1992.

20. Author interviews, Kuwait, 1990–1996.

21. These patterns are also class-based. Upper-class families tend to restrict their male children more than others, and are more likely to send them abroad for university training. At the same time, fewer women than men study abroad regardless of social class. One result is that the population of Kuwait University has been about 60 percent female for some years, and includes large numbers of young women who are highly able, along with average and poor performers. The top performers among young Kuwaiti men of every social class tend to study abroad, leaving the less able in their age cohorts to compete against a pool of women whose intellectual ability and social skills are better than theirs. See Tétreault, 1990: 17–18.

22. Author interview, Kuwait, May 1990. The speaker worked for KNPC. This rationale came up repeatedly in interviews with students, professors, and parents, both before the invasion and after liberation.

23. This is because of the enfranchisement of large numbers of badu, along with a redistricting scheme that reallocated representatives to heavily tribal areas. See Tétreault, 2000a: 108–110.

24. According to Olivier Roy (1994), the focus of Islamist gender politics on educational institutions is characteristic of fundamentalist movements throughout the region, not only in Kuwait.

25. For a discussion of the ram sacrifice and its political significance in Morocco, see Combs-Schilling, 1989. Michael Sells (1996) examines the use of religious and quasi-religious rituals to mobilize Serb nationalists to attack Bosnian Muslims. Both Combs-Schilling and Sells emphasize the sexualization of religious symbols used in this way.

26. The contribution of religious myths to centuries of European anti-Semitism, and the use of religious symbols and stories to mobilize nationalist movements today, for example, in the former Yugoslavia, are subjects of intensive study. For an example of the former, see Langmuir, 1990, and for the latter, Sells, 1996. The present civil war in Algeria as described by novelists such as Aïcha Lemsine echoes the patterns of interwoven politics, sexuality, and religion documented by Gavin Langmuir and Michael Sells in these other cases. Studies of religious justifications of violence in the modern Middle East (though not including Algeria) can be found among the articles in Juergensmeyer, 1992.

27. Connections between "real violence" and "symbolic violence" are explored in the introduction to Juergensmeyer, 1992.

28. Press freedom remains tenuous in cases where either the ruling family or Islam are targets of criticism. A new attempt was made to quash press criticism of the regime when the government threatened to close two newspapers for publishing a false decree that was supposed to have raised the salaries of police and military personnel (see *Deutsche Presse*, February 16, 2000, Gulf 2000 archive). However, the amir intervened and the crisis dissipated. Private citizens also suffer from a lack of freedom of the press. In the fall of 1999, two political scientists were accused of blasphemy by Islamist plaintiffs and one was tried in court and convicted—see U.S. Department of State, 2000.

29. *Arab Times,* December 5, 2001, pp. 1, 7.

30. Only a year earlier, the amir had been forced to reorganize the government in response to an Islamist-led attack on the information minister, who also was a member of the ruling family, on the grounds that he had allowed the sale of allegedly un-Islamic books at a book fair. See Reuters, March 22, 1998, Gulf 2000 archive.

31. *Arab Times,* December 5, 2001, pp. 1, 7.

32. Reuters, October 18, 1999, Gulf 2000 archive; and private communications to the author from Ghanim al-Najjar.

33. Agence France Presse, "Kuwait Nabs Islamist Ring After Attack on Girl," April 9, 2000; Reuters, "Attackers of Unveiled Kuwaiti Woman Arrested," April 9, 2000; and Laila Shaheen, "Debate Rages over Acquittal in Girl's Assault," *Gulf News,* June 15, 2000, all from the Gulf 2000 archive.

Eleanor Abdella Doumato

10

Education in Saudi Arabia: Gender, Jobs, and the Price of Religion

Wherever one looks in Saudi Arabia's capital city, every woman is dressed in the black abaya, whether Christian, foreign Muslim or Saudi, schoolchild, teenager, or elderly. Twenty-five years after the development rush began, the ubiquitous abaya, which in the past was rarely worn by anyone except Saudi women, appears to signal the ultimate triumph of the conservative reaction to globalization. But a second look reveals something else: in upscale neighborhoods, in the comings and goings at private schools, and in shopping malls, women's faces are unveiled, or at least their eyes are fully uncovered. And the abayas are really not abayas at all, but coats of silk that are slightly form-fitted, embroidered, flowing, and almost sensual. Gone is the shapeless shroud that hung from forehead to foot and hobbled the wearer's movements, and gone are the thick folds of black gauze tied across the face. And in these upscale neighborhoods, gone too are the invisible boundary lines that kept women off the streets, away from public conveniences, at home and out of sight. Instead, teenagers in the new abayas rove in packs through the malls; women meet in restaurants, shop in supermarkets, and visit art galleries and public libraries. Women and girls have taken possession of new public spaces that did not exist a generation ago.

What does this public "face" of women tell us about the changes in society and in women's lives after more than twenty years of Saudi Arabia's engagement with the global economy? Does the very existence of the abaya stand as a symbol of Saudi Arabia's unique segregation of women and the staying power of conservatism in the face of the West's cultural onslaught? Or is the modern abaya instead a symbol of the triumph of women's agency and the overwhelming

239

appeal of integration and economic equality between men and
women? As this chapter shows, the abaya, in its ubiquity and in its
new forms, represents the clash and accommodation of conservative
tradition with political power-brokering and new-world cultural and
economic imperatives.

Focusing on the role of mass education as the chief instrument of
infusing a common conservative tradition throughout Saudi Arabia,
this chapter shows how education, the school curricula's representa-
tions of gender, and economic conditions come together in a dynamic
that is both a major stimulus for women to enter the job market and a
major deterrent: a stimulus because education has disrupted the paradigm of women as belonging in the home just by virtue of giving
girls a legitimate destination outside the home, while also imparting
secular knowledge and raising women's expectations about their own
capabilities; a deterrent because the traditional gender paradigm has
been incorporated into the mandatory religious studies curricula to
satisfy Saudi Arabia's powerful and culturally defensive ulama
(Muslim scholars of religion). What was once a cultural understanding about keeping women segregated from men has become a moral
imperative that is more firmly instilled and more thoroughly defused
throughout society. At the same time, household income has dropped
dramatically, the country as a whole suffers from very high unemployment, and with a continuing balance of payments deficit the state
can no longer keep its unproductive citizens happy with oil-rent disbursements. Because of the worsening economic situation, many
women need to work to supplement family income. By negotiating a
path between the pull of conservative Islam and the push of globalization, with its cultural and economic entailments, women fight for
limited public-sector jobs, create new job options for themselves,
and invest in imaginative ways to carve out opportunities in an environment that is unwelcoming to women.

Saudi Arabia's Conservative Tradition

As the country studies in this volume show, women in every part of
the region must deal with some form of conservative gender ideology, but in Saudi Arabia that ideology, in its contemporary incarna-
tion, is far more restrictive.[1] Segregation of unrelated men from
women is held as the highest social value and given the force of law

in every aspect of public life: the schools are segregated, including the universities, and men and women are not to work in the same places. Men, furthermore, are responsible for keeping women separate and control their movements: women are not allowed to drive, or to travel or check into a hotel or undergo surgery in a hospital without written permission from a father or husband, and only in the year 2001 were women allowed to receive an identity card in their own name instead of being registered with the state only as a member of a man's family.

This conservatism about the role of women has its origins in both religion and local customary practice. The Arabian peninsula is home to a religious movement that arose in the eighteenth century and is centered on the idea that the true Muslim community is one that lives in conformity with God's laws, with the life and practice of the prophet Muhammad as the model for emulation. Taking his inspiration from thirteenth-century jurist Ibn Taymiyya, the movement's founder, Muhammad ibn Abd al-Wahhab, argued that the basis for knowing God's laws and for knowing the model for emulation was the Quran and Hadith, read literally, without reference to historical context, without interpretation, and without reference to commentaries after the first three centuries of Islam's judicial heritage. Since the goal is to create the perfect community by ensuring that all members incorporate correct behaviors into the totality of daily life, scholars who know the Quran and Hadith well and have come to a consensus on particular meanings have guidance to offer others. How should one dress? What constitutes modesty? Should the thobe be calf-length or cover the feet? How should a man trim his beard, or cut his hair, greet another Muslim, treat the outsider, wash and brush his teeth, make love to his wife when she's menstruating, or mourn the dead? Should a woman use perfume, speak out loud in the marketplace, pray in the marketplace, or join in the communal prayer for rain? The Wahhabi presumption that scripture provides clear guidance runs afoul of the complexities of interpretation of language and the presence of contradictory passages in the canonized collections of Hadith narrations and quranic verses. However, like all modern fundamentalisms (Marty, 1992), Wahhabism avoids these uncertainties by employing scripture selectively, and by interpreting the meaning of scriptural passages based on what is already thought to be known and presumed to be true, as if the meaning of the text were obvious. In so doing, Wahhabi scholars are as much engaged in scriptural exegesis as the scholars of the past whose interpretative readings Wahhabism denies.

At its inception, what made the interpretative power of the ulama a force in shaping society was the political alliance between religion and state, and the empowerment of the ulama to enforce their version of Islamic law on subject peoples. This alliance was renewed at the opening of the twentieth century by Abd al-Aziz Ibn Sa'ud, who began the process of nation-building among what were disparate tribes and peoples by fusing religious affiliation into identity with an Islamic state, and took on the mantle of the just ruler whose legitimacy comes from his ability to rule according to the sharia. Because the legitimacy of the Muslim ruler depends on his willingness to listen to the advice of the ulama, Ibn Sa'ud maintained a council of religious advisers, and this council has since become part of the state civil service bureaucracy that serves to create the appearance of a working partnership between ulama and state.

This body of official ulama, the Supreme Council of Religious Scholars, is often used to provide religious cover for policy decisions taken by the state, but council members also issue opinions about social issues and lobby to see that their opinions are incorporated into royal decrees. In addition, the senior scholars also set policy for the Committees for the Promotion of Virtue and Prevention of Vice (Al-Hay'at al-Amr bi'l-Ma'ruf wa'l-Nahy 'an al-Munkar), which acts as an enforcement arm for moral offenses, such as drinking or producing alcoholic beverages, rude behavior of boys in public shops, public mixing of men and women, shops not closed during prayer time, men loitering during prayer time, women with their faces uncovered or their abayas too short, and anyone selling women's fashion magazines with suggestive photographs. While the *mutawwa'in* (morality policemen) represent a potent symbol of the Saudi regime's commitment to Islamic governance, they also create a climate of fear and are an intimidating presence, particularly for women who choose a more liberal lifestyle.

Over the period of globalization, the influence of the ulama has spread throughout the kingdom along with the development of a mass media, with the increase in literacy, and most significantly with the spread of public education (Doumato, 1999, 2001). As Mai Yamani has documented, this influence has penetrated so deeply and successfully that the primary identity among Saudi citizens today is with Islam, and with the particular kind of literalist version that the

Saudi ulama promote. This is the case even in regions of the country in which a more liberal Islam was predominant (Yamani, 2000). At the same time, the "woman" issue has assumed a place of unprecedented importance in the definition of Islamic values and Islamic behaviors, mainly because in the rush of development and the infusion of Western culture, there is little else of symbolic value that is so visible, and no other group in society whose behavior can so easily be controlled, and no other challenge to religious values that threatens male identity or affects people's lives so personally (Doumato, 1991). The most effective medium used to reinscribe a "traditional" place for women has been the national education system.

The Politics of Education

For many places, public education has been shown to be a politically driven, efficient method of instilling desirable qualities in citizens. As Timothy Mitchell has shown in *Colonizing Egypt* (1988), the establishment of public schools in Egypt based on European models was consciously designed to inculcate certain attitudes and values in order to produce model citizens for a future model society. Building on Mitchell's work, Gregory Starrett suggests that an educational system should be viewed as more than "a mechanism of diffuse and invisible power, it is also . . . an engine of tension and contradiction." "Students," he says, "are neither the passive pawns of educational organization and ideology, nor are educators their absolute masters" (1998: 24). In Saudi Arabia, there is no doubt that social engineering has been a goal of public education, and that a political agenda lies behind the curricula. However, the individual agency of students, the influence and social standing of their parents, and the economic environment are critical factors in determining outcomes of the educational process.

In Saudi Arabia, the ruling elite at every step have taken the lead in opening educational avenues for women. At the same time, however, the state is tied to its highly conservative Wahhabi ulama and to their most dependable supporters, the people of the central province of Najd, who also tend to be Wahhabi in their worldview—a worldview that doesn't welcome women as actors on the public stage. The regime and its conservative constituencies have served each other well, most notably through the manipulation of the national education curricula, which both use to further their own interests.

For the regime, the public education curriculum has been a means of homogenizing the language and religious orientation of its people, of infusing them with a common identity and sense of nationhood, and overtly instilling allegiance to the ruling family. Education has thus been a critical part of Saudi Arabia's nation-building machinery, employed, in the mode identified by Benedict Anderson (1991: 5–7), to create a community out of the imagination where one did not exist before. For the Najdi constituencies, the curriculum is the chief vehicle of propagating and freezing in place an explicitly Wahhabi character to society while ensuring for themselves a place, both theoretical and real, in state decisionmaking. In postdevelopment Saudi Arabia, therefore, everyone straddles the pull of Wahhabism and the push of globalization, but no group more so than women. The ethos taught in the schools' mandatory religious studies program is heavily invested in "women" as the central emblem of morality and family values to which society as a whole would aspire.

Mass Education:
A Curriculum to Affirm Women's Segregation

The official education policy of the kingdom, written in 1970 and since unchanged, places Islam at the center of the curriculum (Mamlakat al-'Arabiyya al-Su'udiyya, Wizaraat al-Ma'aarif, 1995). Through the 1990s, as globalization put Saudi conservatives ever more on the defensive, the role of religion became even more firmly prioritized: an experimental "modern secondary" program for high schools that would have allowed students to tailor programs to suit their goals and interests, including avoiding religious classes altogether, was fazed out in 1993 (Salloom, 1995: 41). In addition, pass-fail conditions were reordered to make passing religious studies courses the prerequisite for proceeding to the next grade level.

From elementary through middle school, schoolchildren in Saudi Arabia devote so much time to religious studies that there is little time left in the school day for other subjects: nine hours each of Islam and Arabic per week at the elementary level, with three hours for science and five for math, and in middle school, eight hours of religion with six for Arabic, leaving four hours a week each for

English, math, and science. The three-year high school program continues the same emphasis: the first year all students take four hours of religious studies, nine hours of Arabic, four in history and geography together, and six in science. Then students may choose to specialize in math and science, humanities, or religious studies. Whether the student chooses science or humanities, religious studies are still required: four hours a week in the second year and three in the last year. According to statistics for the year 2000 published by the Ministry of Education (Ministry of Education, 2000), more than a quarter of second-year students opted for religious studies and completely ended their acquaintance with math, science, foreign language, social sciences, and history. Since more than a quarter of children never continue beyond elementary school, on top of the significant percentage of high-schoolers concentrating in religion, and a quarter of university students are attending an Islamic university, it is fair to say that the majority of young people educated solely through the Saudi public school system have limited acquaintance with the type of skills that are necessary to compete in a modern economy.

Publicly funded education for girls began only in 1960, seven years after the first schools for boys opened. Because of initial opposition from religious conservatives, girls schools, from kindergarten through teachers college, were placed under the supervision of a board of ulama called the General Presidency for Girls' Education (the General Presidency for Girls' Education was closed down in March 2002 and girls' education was placed under the Ministry of Education). Although the board's official policy limits girls' education to subjects that "suit their nature," the curriculum in the girls schools provides almost the same course of study offered to boys, one exception being that girls study home economics instead of taking physical education.

From the ninth through the twelfth grade, the religious studies program uses a set of texts prepared by the Ministry of Education for the boys schools and by the General Presidency for the girls schools. These texts are mandatory for all schools, whether public or private, and cover four subjects: Tawhid (Islamic monotheism), Hadith (the canonized sayings of the prophet Mohammad), Tafsir (quranic exegesis), and Fiqh (Islamic jurisprudence). In all of these texts the method of explicating scriptural texts is similar. A passage of Hadith, for example, is presented, followed by a definition of words and an explication of the passage's meaning coupled with similar or supporting passages from the Quran or Hadith. Then lessons are drawn to make the passage relevant to everyday life, or in some cases, such as a lesson on hunting while on pilgrimage, irrelevant to everyday life. The literal meaning of the Hadith passage is presented as if it were not debatable. Sometimes parts of a single Hadith are presented out of context, or the supporting passages chosen selectively to bolster the textbook author's interpretation. Sometimes the lesson incorporates an implied threat by suggesting that deviance from the prescribed path corrupts society, or worse, makes the deviant ipso facto guilty of immorality.

With the exception of the Tawhid texts, the single most prevalent theme throughout the four-year course is gender. The ninth-grade Hadith text, for example, contains a lesson based on the following words attributed to the prophet Mohammad: "A man must not be alone with a woman unless he is her mahram" (a mahram is a woman's closest male relative and her guardian, usually her father or husband, or someone to whom the woman could not be legally married). A "guide" to the Hadith explains that being alone with a woman is a cause for her falling into prostitution, and for that reason Islam forbids it. The lesson then extrapolates advice for the modern day from the Hadith: a man is not to be alone in the house with an unrelated woman; a woman must not ride in a car alone with a hired driver; a female servant must not stay in the house alone with a male member of the family. Finally, the students are warned that leniency in matters ordered by God spreads corruption in the individual and in society (Mamlakat al-'Arabiyya al-Sa'udiyya, Wizaarat al-Ma'aarif, 2000b: 94–95).

The same text has a lesson titled "Gazing at Women." The prophet Mohammad is asked about inadvertently glancing at a woman, and advises that one should look the other way. The guide to the Hadith tells the student that seeing an unrelated woman opens the door to Satan, and puts one on the path to fornication, even if seeing the woman was unintended, and whether a man sees a woman directly or in a magazine or in a film. Barricading the door against Satan, the lesson reminds students, increases the faith of the worshipper of God (Mamlakat al-'Arabiyya al-Sa'udiyya, Wizaarat al-Ma'aarif, 2000b: 96–97).

The ninth-grade text of Fiqh puts the onus on girls to protect themselves from being seen by any man except a mahram. Titled "What Is Obligatory Regarding Clothing and Adornment," the lesson teaches that Islamic clothing must cover the private parts of the body (*'awra*), which for a man is the area from the navel to the knee. For a woman, however, the *'awra* means all of her body. She is therefore entirely private and all of her body must be covered, unless she is praying, and then her face and the palms of her hands should be visible. Whenever she is in the presence of a man to whom she is not closely related, all of her body, including her face and hands, must be covered, although exceptions are allowed for medical care or betrothal. The text gives no scriptural evidence for equating the *'awra* of a woman with her whole body, though this interpretation is well established in the Hanbali school to which Najd ulama subscribe (Stowasser, 1994: 93).[2] The lesson warns students that the Muslim woman must wear the hijab for the sake of her religion and for safeguarding her reputation, and continues with a prescription for proper Islamic dress: the hijab should be made of thick cloth, not of something flimsy that would show skin; it should be wide, not narrow so as to outline the parts of her body; it should not resemble the clothing of non-Muslim women or the clothing of men. The lesson concludes with a warning never to uncover one's face or hands in front of unrelated men, for it is a great wrong and a grievous fault (Mamlakat al-'Arabiyya al-Sa'udiyya, Wizaarat al-Ma'aarif, 2000a: 62–65).

Almost every text for the four years from ninth through twelfth grade includes a lesson offering some version of Islamic scripture enlisted in the service of promoting sex segregation. A tenth-grade lesson dealing with Islamic greetings in the *Hadith and Islamic Culture* text has a subsection advising boys never to shake the hand of a nonmahram woman, although exceptions may be made if the woman is old (Mamlakat al-'Arabiyya al-Sa'udiyya, Wizaarat al-Ma'aarif, 2001: 67). The twelfth-grade Fiqh text published by the General Presidency for Girls' Education, like the Fiqh text for the same grade published for boys by the Ministry of Education, concentrates on the laws of marriage and the rights and duties of husbands and wives (Mamlaka al-'Arabiyya al-Sa'udiyya, al-Ri'aasat al-'Ama lita'lim al-Banaat, 2001). The text for girls, however, begins with legal issues relating to women's menstruation and includes a repeat lesson on Islamic requirements for women's total body covering, including the face, followed by citations from quranic suras that are supposed to stand as evidence, even though the suras cited (33:59 and 24:31) actually say nothing about covering the face (p. 17 of the

Fiqh text for the twelfth grade).³ This same text reviews the mahram rules, and applies them to women's work, listing permissible places for women to work as extensions of women's nurturing roles: girls' education and healthcare, or in vocations such as seamstress, or nursemaid for small children. Women may, however, engage in "buying and selling," so long as a mahram is present or the woman has deputized a man to act on her behalf (Mamlakat al-'Arabiyya al-Sa'udiyya, al-Ri'aasat al-'Ama lita'lim al-Banaat, 2001: 106–109). In the same textbook, girls are taught details concerning the duty of obedience that a wife owes her husband, such as pleasing a husband sexually upon request, not leaving the home without his permission, and taking care of the house and children (66–73).

While the messages about gender and the inherent limits to women's nondomestic potential couldn't be clearer, other messages embedded in the religious studies texts can be equally incapacitating. In the method of presenting the lessons of the texts, knowledge is something already known and memorized, not researched and created. Proofs are derived by weighing the veracity of one statement against another, and by compiling highly selective samples of scriptural text that all say the same thing or are interpreted to say the same thing, not by logic or deductive reasoning or linguistic analysis. Through these texts students enter a closed system based on presumed infallible truths and circular reasoning (a hallmark of religious fundamentalisms), and this closed system, however comforting in its assurance that what one already knows is right, forestalls creativity, experimentation, and logical thinking.

The Upside of Mass Education

The full effect of mass education, including religious studies, is just beginning to be realized in the Arab world, where mass education is a phenomenon of only the last half century. It is clear, however, that despite the potential liabilities of incorporating religion into a national curriculum, mass education can still contribute to a forward-looking agenda: as Dale Eickelman has observed, mass education can "reconfigure the nature of religious thought and action and encourage explicit debate over meaning" (1992: 644). What has happened in Saudi Arabia, as elsewhere, is that by teaching students to read, and by distributing scripture in written texts as opposed to using rote memorization, and by teaching students the sources and methodologies of classical interpretation, the prerogative of interpretation has been removed from the exclusive domain of male religion specialists and into the potential purview of the general public.

The transformative potential of mass education is more transparent when looking at its secular component. Over half the female population is now literate, with illiteracy concentrated in the generation over the age of thirty, for whom little opportunity for public education was available. Young women are graduating from high schools in ever increasing numbers and continuing on to study in the thirty-four public colleges and university programs for women. By the year 1994 the huge gap that had existed between the ratio of boys to girls who continued on from middle school to enroll in high schools had almost closed (Salloom, 1995: 68), and in the country's colleges and universities together, in the year 2000 the majority of students, 55 percent of the total, were women.[4] In the coming years more women will be studying in medical faculties as the state plans to construct seventeen new medical colleges by 2005, eight of them exclusively for women. Added to higher education programs for women is a private college for women, Queen Effat College, in Jeddah, and in 2002 a new women's campus is being added to King Sa'ud University. In both cases these private institutions, like public education for women, were initiated by members of the royal family.

Apart from these secular education opportunities, Saudi Arabia has seen a proliferation in private elementary and secondary schools for both boys and girls, which are expensive and therefore cater to affluent Saudis and the children of foreigners. In the private schools it is likely that the quality of teaching in secular subjects, including English, is better than what is available in the national schools. However, the national curriculum, including the religious studies program with its approved texts, is mandatory for all schools, and the Ministry of Education places a representative in all schools to ensure that the national curriculum is followed. In addition to these private schools, according to Mai Yamani, wealthy Saudis and those who are able to obtain subsidies from the government tend to send their children abroad for high school or university (2000: 54). The students who attend private schools and go abroad to study are most likely to acquire the necessary skills in English and in professions to take the lead and compete successfully in Saudi Arabia's globalized marketplace.

These colleges and university programs, along with the secular courses in secondary schools, are an inevitable counterweight to the prevailing paradigm of sex segregation that is inculcated through compulsory religious studies. Secular education inherently challenges segregation, not just by preparing women to work in specific professions, but also by raising expectations for one's own potential and giving women the intellectual tools with which to experiment. Whether providing secular or religious learning, whether the goal is to engineer the shape of change or to stop it, public education at any level alters the gender paradigm because attendance at schools, colleges, and universities means breaking boundaries and physically leaving one's home. It means girls have legitimate destinations, and these are destinations that provide an unprecedented locus for forming empowering personal connections outside the family network.

Stimulus from a Faltering Economy

The Saudi economy has emerged as the single most important stimulus for bringing women into the workforce: not the success of an oil economy that is able to fund development, but its failure to produce a nonoil private sector that can grow and succeed at job creation to meet the needs of its burgeoning population, which is growing at the rate of 3.27 percent annually (CIA, 2001). Since the oil windfall of the late 1970s, Saudi Arabia's economy has suffered a mighty fall. In 1980 the average household income reached U.S.$18,000 and every citizen was guaranteed a house, a piece of land, free medical care, free schooling, and no taxes. Today the average household income is less than a third of what it was in 1980, and with the government running a deficit each year, and U.S.$17 billion being sent abroad through remittances by foreign workers, the majority of young Saudis today cannot hope to duplicate the financial security experienced by their parents' generation.[5]

Some 150,000 graduates and dropouts enter the job market each year, 27 percent of the males among them dropouts from elementary school, to compete in a market where there is already a rate of unemployment estimated to be as high as 18 percent for males. For women graduates, the rate of unemployment is far higher, estimated in 2001 at 95 percent, which is what it was ten years earlier, according to a Ministry of Planning study done in 1990 that determined the rate of women's unemployment to be 94.7 percent (Chaudhry, 1997: 297).[6] The employment rate for women, therefore, has not increased despite the huge increase in the number of women university graduates and the actual number of women employed. The reasons are many, not the least of which is the heavy social value placed on homemaking for women, and the propensity for large families (the fertility rate is 6.25 children born per woman; CIA, 2001).

In addition, however, legal impediments that stem from religious considerations drastically hinder job opportunities for women. Saudi labor law, for example, as discussed above, prevents women from working in places where they will come in contact with men, while royal decrees impose impediments on women's transportation so that they not only can't drive themselves to work, but they are also not allowed to ride in a car with a hired driver, to take lodging where offered employment, unless a mahram accompanies the employee, or to receive a commercial license without a first hiring a male manager to obviate the need to work directly with the public or male employees. Consequently, women can only work within commuting distance of a job, and their options are concentrated in the sex-segregated education system and in hospitals, in women-only service businesses, and in professions or businesses in which they can work at home, although some do work in offices among men, but with discretion.

Heavy reliance on foreigners in the labor force is also a factor limiting employment options. Saudis constitute only about 25 percent of the kingdom's total labor force, or about 2.5 million workers, while 4.7 million workers are foreigners.[7] While 375,000 of these foreign workers are female domestic servants, and others are construction workers and menial laborers who hold jobs Saudis wouldn't want, many others are employed in office work, sales positions, and management, jobs that could easily be filled by women were it not for sex-segregation rules.[8] The Seventh Five-Year Development Plan (2000–2005), like the two earlier five-year plans that failed to reduce the number of foreign workers, has a program to lower the reliance on foreign workers by replacing almost half a million of them with Saudi nationals, and a specific commitment to allocate a portion of those positions to women.[9]

It is in the need to work, the need to help support a family, that women are finding the incentive to change the facts on the ground, and women have become a formidable—if barely visible—presence in the economy. Women are reported to own 40 percent of private wealth (which is probably a passive achievement due to inheritance laws). Women also own approximately 15,000 commercial establishments, or about 10 percent of private businesses in the kingdom.[10] Examples of the type of businesses being created by women include art galleries and retail specialty shops, a successful example being a combination retail/manufacturing business that makes and distributes traditional styles of clothing, jewelry, and artifacts that have been refashioned for modern tastes. In addition, there are for-profit training institutes for high school graduates and dropouts. Considering the potential for women to fill Saudi-ized positions identified in the Seventh Development Plan, the market is wide open, as the quality of preparation for work is so low in the public schools that expectant workers need training in English, simple math and accounting, basic computer skills, and workplace etiquette.[11] Wedding services, event facilities, and restaurants are also becoming lucrative areas of investment as society comes to accept the propriety of women entertaining outside a private home.

Women continue to petition for changes in regulations that hinder them in business. Women investors have asked, for example, for a woman's section in the Riyadh Chamber of Commerce and Industry because they have the same need to interface with state regulators that men do, but don't have direct access to state bureaucracy. In addition, Saudi businesswomen have invested in industries such as iron and steel, clothing, furniture, plastic products, and solar-cell technology. But while women can get loans from the Industrial Development Fund for up to half the cost of an investment project, most industries cannot employ female workers and cannot be managed by the women who own them. As a result, the Ministry of Industry was asked, no doubt facetiously but to make a point, that women be allocated industrial cities so that they can operate their own businesses with a female workforce.[12]

Despite these efforts at private-sector investing, the vast majority of employed women continue to be concentrated in the public sector, as teachers, lab technicians, doctors, administrators, social workers, and professors, but the definition of women's space within the public sector is expanding with women's demands for work. As of 2002, for example, plans are under way to set up a women's police academy, whose graduates would be recruited to work for women-only departments of public institutions.[13] The new library of the King Abd al-Aziz Foundation has a women's section that employs librarians to catalog materials for research on women, and historians and other regional experts to mount exhibitions related to the cultural history of Saudi Arabia.

It is among elites that the bulk of both public- and private-sector initiative is occurring, not just royal family elites but the new industrial, landed, and merchant elites with powerful ties to the bureaucracy and religious establishment created during the development boom years through state spending and commissions (Chaudhry, 1997: chap. 7 and 316–317). For women of these new elites, use of discretion as a tool of entrepreneurship and professional work cannot be emphasized strongly enough. The reality is that almost nothing can be accomplished without working in association with men. Saudi Arabia has many woman journalists, for example, who could not possibly write their stories and check their facts if they had no access to unrelated men. Every businesswoman needs to deal with her manager, who by law must be a man. Even within the segregated school system women administrators had to deal with their counterparts in the General Presidency for Girls' Education (and now with their counterparts in the Ministry of Education), just as university students have to deal with men to use the main library, which is housed on the men's campus. Every woman who goes anywhere, and doesn't have a father or brother or son to drive her, has to deal with a male driver who is an employee and not an approved male relative.

A certain hypocrisy is therefore built into the sex-segregation system. In order to function in a business or professional environment, and engage in activities outside one's home, either one pretends that interaction does not occur, as in the hospitals, which for all practical purposes are fully integrated; or one must intellectually categorize male intermediaries as gender-neuter, especially drivers, business managers, and house cleaners; or one must confine business relationships within lofty and rarefied elite circles that are above sex segregation rules among themselves. For all women, discretion in public is the sine qua non of social survival.

Conclusion: Hungry, but Not There Yet

This chapter began with a description of barefaced women wearing modern abayas in an upscale mall. At the women's division of the General Presidency for Girls' Education in downtown Riyadh is another image to ponder: the entrance is at the back of the presidency's building, the main entrance of which is for the men in charge. Two sets of glass double doors, darkened to prevent visibility to the inside, present an unwelcoming face to the visitor: on one set of doors, the outside handles have been removed, their gaping screwholes left open, and the inside handles were sealed with a chain and padlock, leaving only one set of doors for women to enter and leave. I found the air-lock foyer cluttered with coatracks and file cabinets, and inside was a rabbit warren of small offices with tables and desks and far too many people to even pretend to have something to do. My mission was to obtain a copy of the presidency's published statistics on girls' education. After being lead from office to office, and each time asked to explain what I wanted, I was finally told to write a letter to the male director of the presidency, and he would decide whether to give me the statistics. The women in this building appeared powerless next to their male employers, and as much locked in as men were locked out. In comparing the offices of the presidency to the mall, one finds that Saudi women at both ends of the spectrum and everywhere in between are conditioned by class, religious affiliation, wealth, and political connections, and most of them have been exposed to the public education curriculum, with its emphasis on religion and women's segregation.

What can be learned from this exploration into religious education, gender, and economic opportunity? Mary Ann Tétreault invites us to think about "weapons of the weak" as we consider women's approaches to getting what they want (2000b: 273–274). For Saudi Arabia, I would begin by asking in what ways women truly are weak, for among those who inaugurated girls' education, lobbied for improved economic opportunities, founded girls colleges, filled the ranks of college professors, and established social welfare programs, we find women. But these are also almost invariably elite women with *wasta,* connections in high political places, in fact the very places from which Saudi Arabia's "state feminist" agenda originated. These women may be ambitious, well educated, competent, and rich, but at the same time, being women, they could not do what they do unless in their arsenal was the ability to approach the right men.

In this sense women are weak, but men in general are also weak because in the absence of democracy and clear protections for the rights to organize, speak out, and petition the government, connections and the ability to use them well (or, put another way, the ability to manipulate connections, a classic weapon of the weak) become a substitute for power and ingenuity. Women are weaker than men because through law and custom they are not full adults, but also because, as a group, they cannot overcome the infusion of gender ideology that constructs them categorically as responsible for the moral behavior of men, and on whom the entire religious establishment hangs its hopes to preserve a past that in their own terms can be called "Islamic." For this reason we might look to Tétreault's observation that everywhere "female activism is rooted in gender-based claims of authority" (2000b: 274). We see this illustrated in Saudi Arabia, where we find that women who break through the established paradigm are also carefully dressed in full hijab, claiming fealty to Islamic values, and invoking models of liberated women from an Islamic past in order to justify asking for what they want for their future.

Are incentives in place to change the education curricula, and would changing the curricula help to change the gender paradigm? To the first question the answer is yes, because the education system has failed to properly prepare students to be productive employees and entrepreneurs, and popular discontent with the curricula is vocal and demonstrable as middle-class Saudis move their children to the private schools. In addition, international criticism of Saudi education in the wake of the events of September 11, 2001, encouraged the Ministry of Education and other agencies in the kingdom to reevaluate the national curriculum, especially its religious component. Cited in particular by critics were lessons that teach students to see themselves in opposition to those who don't subscribe to Sunni Islam, and the extensive time devoted to religious studies during the school day, which crowds out subjects that would help young people, including women, find productive work instead of frustration and unemployment.

As to the second question, the gender paradigm within the religious studies curriculum is unlikely to be changed so long as Saudi Arabia's Wahhabi ulama remain a political force that must be appeased. Compelling circumstances, however, have undercut the moral authority of these ulama and provided an opportunity for the Saudi rulers to take some risk in this regard: fourteen girls died in a fire in an overcrowded school that had inadequate exits and was patrolled by religious police, who prevented the escape of some girls because they were not wearing their abayas. In the wake of wide-spread outrage, King Fahd ordered the dismissal of the director of the General Presidency for Girls' Education and folded the agency into the Ministry of Education.[14]

What this change will mean for the content of the national curriculum is unclear. While a board of ulama will no longer act as sole arbitrator of what constitutes Islamic studies for girls, the religion curriculum prepared for boys by the Ministry of Education is nearly identical to the ulama-prepared curriculum for girls, and the minister of education, Muhammad al-Rasheed, claims that Islamic studies will continue to receive priority in both boys' and girls' education.[15] Still, the unchallenged closing of what had been for forty years an institutional power base for religious conservatives is politically very significant, and may signal a reassessment in the weight allotted by the ruling family to the demands of competing constituencies. One thing is certain: whatever changes may be contemplated in the content of the curriculum, whether in its secular or religious component, the last item on any list of priorities will be a reshaping of the gender paradigm.

Notes

1. For a discussion of the historical development of gender ideology under the Wahhabis, see Doumato, 2000.

2. The school of Shafi'i also includes a woman's face and hands as part of her *'awra*. The schools of Malik and Abu Hanifa exclude the hands and face (Stowasser, 1994: 93).

3. The interpretation of the suras that are given as evidence for total body covering, Quran 33:59 and 24:31, are discussed by Khaled M. Abou el-Fadl (2001: 289–301), who shows how this interpretation, as translated in the Saudi-financed English translation of the Quran (which is identical to the Arabic interpretation appearing in the school text cited), is derived in the absence of historical and linguistic analysis as well as consistent moral principle.

4. "'No Debate' over Saudi Women," British Broadcasting Corporation (BBC), January 25, 2001, bbc.co.uk.

5. A study based on interviews with 2,000 individuals and 1,000 Saudi businesses carried out by the Saudi Economic Studies Center in 1998 showed that half of employees earned a monthly salary less than 4,000 riyals, or U.S.$1,212 (at 3.3 SR to the dollar), and a third of employees earned between 4,000 and 8,000 riyals. "Saudi Study on Imported Labor,

Working Women," Al-Wasat in Arabic, London, February 2, 1998, pp. 38–39 (Foreign Broadcast Information Service [FBIS]–translated text).

6. Other estimates put the number of job seekers closer to 100,000 and the unemployment rate at 10–15 percent. "Saudi Arabia and the Political and Economic Reforms," Al-Quds al-Arabi in Arabic, London, August 19, 2001, p. 19 (FBIS-translated text). Another source also suggests a lower unemployment rate. A report by the Saudi American Bank (SAMBA) estimated unemployment for males at close to 14 percent in the year 2000, and about 15 percent in 2001, but the rate of female employment in the Kingdom's labor market as low as 5 percent. *Saudi Gazette* (Jeddah), September 21, 2001, p. 3 (FBIS-transcribed text).

7. Muhammad Najib Sa'ad, "4.7 Million Foreign Workers Transfer 62 Billion Riyals Annually," Al-Wasat in Arabic, London, February 2, 1998, pp. 38–39 (FBIS-translated text).

8. On female domestic servants, see ibid.

9. Muhammad Samman, "Saudi 5-Year Plan Foresees Economic Growth, Saudis Replacing Expat Workers," *Arab News* (Jeddah), August 19, 2000, pp. 1, 2 (FBIS-transcribed text).

10. On women's ownership of commercial establishments, see "'No Debate' over Saudi Women," BBC, January 25, 2001, bbc.co.uk. These Saudi-ization schemes have failed in the past because they ran afoul of the interests of powerful merchant, landholding, industrial elites who exert a defining influence on economic policy. See Chaudhry, 1997: chap. 7. On the percentage of private businesses owned by women, see Frank Gardner, "Saudi Women Defy Business Curbs," BBC, January 21, 2001, bbc.co.uk.

11. Author interviews with Saudi businesswomen, Riyadh, January 11, 12, and 17, 2002.

12. Fathimah Basmall, "Saudi Businesswomen Call for Revision of Investment Regulations," *Saudi Gazette,* October 4, 2000, p. 2 (FBIS-transcribed text).

13. "Saudi Authorities to Allow Women to Join Police Force," *Arab News,* October 7, 2000, p. 1 (FBIS-transcribed text).

14. "Cleric Sacked over Saudi Fire," *Arab News,* March 25, 2002.

15. "Mixed Schools Ruled Out," *Arab News,* April 1, 2002.

Marsha Pripstein Posusney
Eleanor Abdella Doumato

Epilogue

This book was planned and in process well before the events of September 11, 2001. Because the aftermath of those events, including the U.S. "War on Terrorism," has created economic, political, and cultural repercussions across the region, it is worthwhile to make some observations about the possible implications of these repercussions for women in globalizing Middle East economies.

As for the impact on local economies, September 11 is not likely to have a positive effect, especially in light of the subsequent Israeli invasion of the West Bank and Gaza in April 2002 and the U.S.-announced plan to attack Iraq. Foreign investors, wary of regional instability, will be hesitant to place money in privatization programs, and the tourism industry, important especially to Egypt, Jordan, and countries of North Africa, has fallen off sharply and is likely to remain depressed as long as the threat of war persists. Meanwhile, defense spending seems certain to rise in countries whose budgets are already operating at a deficit. These developments will mean slower growth overall, and the probability of cutbacks in government social spending. This will increase the daily challenges facing all women who must manage their household budgets, and for unemployed women and those seeking work outside of government, job prospects are now gloomier. One bright spot, however, is that for women employed by the public sector, the dampening of privatization programs may mean the forestalled threat of job loss, at least in the short term.

The political and cultural fallout of September 11 has two dimensions. On the one hand, the militant extremism articulated by bin Laden and his supporters provoked a regionwide attempt to reclaim Islam on the part of mainstream Muslims after a generation of silence in the face of the spreading Islamist movement. For

259

women, this new assertiveness means opening the door to religious interpretation, and more open discussion and public debate about the meaning of religious laws in society and in women's lives.

On the other hand, the aftermath of September 11 revealed that there are deep-seated resentments against the United States in the region. These exist for a number of reasons: U.S. sponsorship of the open-ended ten-year embargo against Iraq and all the suffering that this has meant for Iraqi civilians; the planting of U.S. military bases in the Gulf, especially in Saudi Arabia; and the sustained U.S. support for Israel's encroachment into Palestinian territory, with all of the civilian displacement and control tactics that this entails. In the face of all of the negative Western media attention focused on the Middle East after September 11, there emerged in the region a commonly perceived bereavement, an increased identification with Islam and with Muslim neighbors who share the same experiences and perceptions, and a renewed desire to see their own governments, as Muslim governments, stand up to the United States and defend them. These responses were only aggravated by the U.S. bombing of Afghanistan carried out in response to the attacks, and by the U.S. decision to impose "regime change" in Iraq.

In some countries, such as Egypt, Islamic movements are playing a leading role in organizing the daily demonstrations against the United States and Israel that are unfolding as we write. The prospect that the unintended consequence of U.S. policy in the wake of September 11 will be an increase, rather than a decline, in Islamic influence on government policies, cannot be discounted. But as it pertains to gender, any such development would, as we have indicated here, elicit a reaction by women that would shape the ultimate impact of any such changes on gender relations.

At the same time, this clamor for action from unresponsive governments has once again laid bare the discontent and frustration of citizens with their own governments, which are unrepresentative and perceived to be supported by the United States at the expense of the interests of their own citizens and in the face of opposition from them. The lack of democracy and accountability remains a problem in most of the region. In the Gulf, however, given the atmosphere after September 11, this exposure of the fault line between the rulers and the ruled has had a positive impact. In Saudi Arabia, for example, the press has been allowed to publish much more critically and openly, even to criticize the venerable religious establishment for its oppressive morals police and for encouraging hatred of foreigners through the schools. Vulnerable to international scrutiny because most of the September 11 hijackers came from Saudi Arabia, the Saudis took the previously unimaginable step of dismantling the ulama-controlled General Presidency for Girls' Education and shifting girls' education to the Ministry of Education. In Bahrain we've seen an expansion of avenues of political participation. In February 2002, Shaikh Hamad bin Isa Al Khalifa agreed to set up a bicameral National Assembly (only one chamber elected and the other appointed, however), with the first elections to take place in 2002 and both men and women eligible to vote and stand for office. In both countries, where political activism has been crushed in the past, demonstrations have been tolerated and political prisoners released. In Kuwait, women demanding the right to vote have demonstrated, unmolested, at registration centers as part of a campaign to change Kuwait's election law. In the Gulf, this new receptiveness to public opinion, along with open debate over religious interpretation, could auger an era of unprecedented opportunity, especially if the political issues that divide the United States and the Middle East and embroil the region in turmoil can be healed and economic progress allowed to go forward.

We thus refrain from predicting any single, regionwide outcome from these unfolding events. Indeed, in positing that gender, politics, culture, and economics all come into play as we try to understand the impact of globalization on women in the Middle East, this book has also maintained that the experience of each country in the region is unique; in each country globalization processes are refracted through different political, economic, and ideological structures. What can be claimed with certainty, however, is that everywhere, globalization produces effects that can be particular to women, and that women as actors play a role in shaping them.

References

'Abd al-Gadir, Nur al-Tayib. 1984. *El-Amila fil-Sudan* (The Working Woman in Sudan). Khartoum: Department of Labor and Social Security, Division of Research, Information, and Media.

'Abd al-Hady, Aisha. 1996. *Women and Trade Unions.* Cairo: Egyptian Trade Union Federation. In Arabic.

Abou el-Fadl, Khaled M. 2001. *Conference of the Books: The Search for Beauty in Islam.* New York: University Press of America.

Adams, Richard H., Jr. 1997. *The Status of Women in Rural Egypt: Final Report on Summary Results from 1995–1996.* Egyptian Ministry of Agriculture (PCUWA)/World Bank Survey of Rural Egypt, International Food Policy Research Institute, Washington, D.C.

Afshar, H., and C. Dennis. 1992. *Women and Adjustment Policies in the Third World.* New York: St. Martin's Press.

Agence France Press. 2000. "Kuwait Nabs Islamist Ring After Attack on Girl." April 9. Gulf 2000 archive.

Agrebi, Saida. 1992. *Les Droits de la femme rurale.* Tunis: La Presse.

Ahmed, Medani M. 1987. "The Political Economy of Development in the Sudan." African Seminar Series no. 29. Khartoum: Institute of African and Asian Studies, University of Khartoum.

Alliance for Arab Women. 1995. *Report of the Working Group for the Preparation for the Beijing Conference.* Cairo: Alliance for Arab Women. In Arabic.

Alonso-Gamo, Patricia, and Mohamed El-Erian. 1997. "Economic Reforms, Growth, Employment, and the Social Sectors in the Arab Economies." In Taher Kanaan, ed., *The Social Effects of Economic Adjustment on Arab Countries,* pp. 7–37. Washington, D.C.: International Monetary Fund.

Aly, Abdel Hamid. 1994. "The Impact of Structural Adjustment and Stabilization Policies on the Labor Market in Egypt." Paper prepared for the Third World Forum and UNICEF, June.

263

Amin, Samir. 1977. *Unequal Development*. Brighton: Harvester.

Amnesty International. 1994. *Tunisia: Rhetoric Versus Reality—The Failure of a Human Rights Bureaucracy*. New York: Amnesty International. January.

Anderson, Benedict. 1991. *Imagined Communities: Reflections on the Origin and Spread of Nationalism*. Rev. ed. London: Verso.

Anker, R., and Martha Anker. 1989. "Measuring the Female Labor Force in Egypt." *International Labor Review* 128, no. 4.

Anscombe, Frederick F. 1997. *The Ottoman Gulf: The Creation of Kuwait, Saudi Arabia, and Qatar*. New York: Columbia University Press.

Aslanbeigui, N., S. Pressman, and G. Summerfield. 1994. *Women in the Age of Economic Transformation: Gender Impact of Reforms in Post-Socialist and Developing Countries*. London: Routledge.

Assaad, Ragui. 1997a. "The Effects of Public Sector Hiring and Compensation Policies on the Egyptian Labor Market." *World Bank Economic Review,* January 11.

———. 1997b. "The Employment Crisis in Egypt: Current Trends and Future Prospects." In Karen Pfeifer, ed., *Research in Middle East Economics,* vol. 2. Greenwich, Conn.: JAI Press.

———. 2002. "The Transformation of the Egyptian Labor Market: 1988–1998." In Ragui Assaad, ed., *The Labor Market in a Reforming Economy: Egypt in the 1990s*. Cairo: American University in Cairo Press.

Badawi, Suad al-Fatih el-. 1986. "The Women Members of the Constituent Assembly." *El-Sahafa,* May 3.

Badran, Margot. 1996a. "Khartoum's Answer to Beijing." *Al-Ahram Weekly* 12 (September 5–11).

———. 1996b. "Gendering the Islamic Globalization Offensive." *People's Rights, Women's Rights: Quarterly Women's Human Rights Journal* 3.

———. 2002. "Islamic Feminism: What's in a Name?" *Al-Ahram Weekly Online* no. 569 (January 17–23), http://web7.ahram.org.eg/weekly/2002/569/cu7.htm.

Barber, Benjamin. 1996. *Jihad vs. McWorld*. New York: Ballantine Books.

Barnett, Tony. 1975. "The Gezira Scheme: Production of Cotton and the Reproduction of Underdevelopment." In I. Oxaal, T. Barnett, and D. Booth, eds., *Beyond the Sociology of Development: Economy and Society of Latin America and Africa*. London: Routledge and Kegan Paul.

———. 1988. "Introduction: The Sudanese Crisis and the Future." In Tony Barnett and Abbas Abdelkarim, eds., *Sudan: State, Capital, and Transformation,* pp. 1–17. London: Croom Helm.

Baumol, William J., and Alan S. Blinder. 1999. *Macroeconomics, Principles, and Policy*. 8th ed. New York: Dryden Press.

Becker, Gary, and Nigel Tomes. 1976. "Child Endowments and the Quantity and Quality of Children." *Journal of Political Economy* 84, no. 4 (pt. 2, August): S143–S162.

Behar, Cem. 1995. "The Fertility Transition in Turkey: Reforms, Policies, and Family Structure." In Carla Obermeyer, ed., *Family, Gender, and Population in the Middle East: Policies in Contest,* pp. 36–56. Cairo: American University in Cairo Press.

Beinin, Joel. 1999. "The Working Class and Peasantry in the Middle East: From Economic Nationalism to Neoliberalism." *Middle East Report* no. 210 (spring): 18–22.

Beneria, L., and S. Feldman, eds. 1992. *Unequal Burden: Economic Crisis, Persistent Poverty, and Women's Work.* Boulder: Westview Press.

Beneria, Lourdes, and Martha Roldan. 1987. *The Crossroads of Class and Gender: Industrial Homework, Subcontracting, and Household Dynamics in Mexico City.* Chicago: University of Chicago Press.

Bergman, Barbara R. 1995. "Occupational Segregation, Wages, and Profits When Employers Discriminate by Race or Sex." In Jane Humphries, ed., *Gender and Economics.* Gloucestershire: Edward Elgar.

Berik, G. 1987. *Women Carpet Weavers in Rural Turkey.* Geneva: International Labor Office.

Birks, J., I. Papps, and C. Sinclair, eds. N.d. *Expansion of Female Employment in the EMENA Region: Synthesis Report of Phase 1.* Durham: Birks, Sinclair, and Associates.

Bourguignon, François, and Christian Morrisson. 1989. *External Trade and Income Distribution.* Paris: Development Center of the OECD.

Bourqia, Rahma. 1995. "Women in Families: Cultural Constraints and Opportunities." In Carla Obermeyer, ed., *Family, Gender, and Population in the Middle East: Policies in Contest,* pp. 136–146. Cairo: American University in Cairo Press.

Brand, Laurie A. 1988. *Palestinians in the Arab World: Institution Building and the Search for State.* New York: Columbia University Press.

———. 1998. *Women the State and Political Liberalization: The Moroccan, Jordanian, and Tunisian Cases.* New York: Columbia University Press.

———. 1999. "The Effects of the Peace Process on Political Liberalization in Jordan." *Journal of Palestine Studies* 28 (2), no. 110 (winter): 54–67.

Brown, Clair, and Joseph A. Peckman, eds. 1987. *Gender in the Workplace.* Washington, D.C.: Brookings Institution.

Cagatay, N., and G. Berik. 1990. "Transition to Export-Led Growth in Turkey: Is There a Feminization of Employment?" *Review of Radical Political Economics* 22, no. 1: 115–134.

CAPMAS (Central Agency for Public Mobilization and Statistics, Egypt). 1991. *Women's Participation in the Labor Force.* Egypt: UNICEF, Women and Child Research Unit.

———. 1995a. *Program of Surveys for Monitoring Social Developments in Egypt, 1992–1995: The Priority Survey.* Cairo: CAPMAS.

———. 1995b. *Statistical Year Book.* Cairo: CAPMAS.

———. 1998. *Labor Market Sample Survey, 1995–1998.* Cairo: CAPMAS.

Carapico, Sheila. 2000. "NGOs, INGOs, GO-NGOs, and DO-NGOs: Making Sense of Non-Governmental Organizations." *Middle East Report* no. 214 (spring).

Charrad, Mounira. 1996. "State and Gender in the Maghrib." In Suha Sabbagh, ed., *Arab Women: Between Defiance and Restraint,* pp. 221–228. New York: Olive Branch Press.

Chaudhry, Kiren Aziz. 1997. *The Price of Wealth: Economics and Institutions in the Middle East.* Ithaca, N.Y.: Cornell University Press.

CIA (Central Intelligence Agency). 2001. *The World Factbook for 2001, Saudi Arabia.* www.cia.gov/cia/publications/factbook.

Cochrane, Susan M., Ali Khan, and Ibrahim Khodair Osheba. 1990. "Education, Income, and Desired Fertility in Egypt: A Revised Perspective." *Economic Development and Cultural Change* 38, no. 2 (January).

Collins, Carole. 1976. "Sudan: Colonialism and Class Struggle." *Middle East Research and Information Project* no. 46.

Combs-Schilling, M. E. 1989. *Sacred Performances: Islam, Sexuality, and Sacrifice.* New York: Columbia University Press.

Cooke, Miriam. 2001. *Women Claim Islam: Creating Islamic Feminism Through Literature.* New York: Routledge.

Courbage, Youssef. 1995a. "Changing Hierarchies of Gender and Generation in the Arab World." In Carla Obermeyer, ed., *Family, Gender, and Population in the Middle East: Policies in Contest,* pp. 179–198. Cairo: American University in Cairo Press.

———. 1995b. "Fertility Transition in Mashriq and the Maghrib: Education, Emigration, and the Diffusion of Ideas." In Carla Obermeyer, ed., *Family, Gender, and Population in the Middle East: Policies in Contest,* pp. 80–104. Cairo: American University in Cairo Press.

CREDIF (Center for Studies, Documentation, and Information on Women). 1995. *Femmes de Tunisie: Situation et perspectives.* Tunis: CREDIF.

Crystal, Jill. 1990. *Oil and Politics in the Gulf: Rulers and Merchants in Kuwait and Qatar.* Cambridge: Cambridge University Press.

de Montéty, Henri. 1993. "Femmes de Tunisie." *Women of Tunisia: Their Struggle and Their Gains.* Tunis: Tunisian External Communications Agency (TECA), March.

Doumato, Eleanor Abdella. 1991. "Women and Political Stability in Saudi Arabia." *Middle East Report* no. 171 (July–August): 34–37.

———. 1999. "Women and Work in Saudi Arabia: How Wide Are Islamic Margins?" *Middle East Journal* 53, no. 4 (autumn 1999): 568–583.

———. 2000. *Getting God's Ear: Women, Islam, and Healing in Saudi Arabia and the Gulf.* New York: Columbia University Press.

———. 2001. "Women in Saudi Arabia: Between Breadwinner and Domestic Icon?" In Suad Joseph and Susan Slyomovics, eds., *Women and Power in the Middle East,* pp. 166–175. Philadelphia: University of Pennsylvania Press.

Duncan, G. M., and D. E. Duncan. 1955. "A Methodological Analysis of Segregation Indices." *American Sociological Review* 20 (April): 210–217.

Durrani, Lorna Hawker. 1976. "Employment of Women and Social Change." In Russell A. Stone and John Simmons, eds., *Change in*

Tunisia: Studies in the Social Sciences. New York: State University of New York Press.

Eickelman, Dale. 1992. "Mass Higher Education and the Religious Imagination in Contemporary Arab Societies." *American Ethnologist* 19, no. 4.

El Amouri Institute. 1993. "Women's Role in the Informal Sector in Tunisia." In Joyselin Massiah, ed., *Women in Developing Economies: Making Visible the Invisible,* pp. 135–166. Paris: Berg.

Elson, Diane. 1991. *Male Bias in the Development Process.* New York: St. Martin's Press.

Erian, Mohamed el-, ed. 1996. *Growth and Stability in the Middle East and North Africa.* Washington, D.C.: International Monetary Fund.

Evans, Sara M., and Harry C. Boyte. 1992. *Free Spaces: The Sources of Democratic Change in America.* 2nd ed. Chicago: University of Chicago Press.

Fargues, Philippe. 1994. "Demographic Explosion or Social Upheaval?" In Ghassan Salame, ed., *Democracy Without Democrats,* pp. 156–182. London: Taurus.

———. 1995. "Changing Hierarchies of Gender and Generation in the Arab World." In Carla Obermeyer, ed., *Family, Gender, and Population in the Middle East: Policies in Contest,* pp. 179–198. Cairo: American University in Cairo Press.

Fergany, Nader. 1998. "Arab Economies Are Failing the Test: Poverty Is Growing." *Economic Research Forum* 5, no. 1 (May): 1–9, www.erf.org.eg/nletter/may98-01.asp.

Fischer, David Hackett. 1996. *The Great Wave: Price Revelations and the Rhythm of History.* New York: Oxford University Press.

Folbre, Nancy. 1994. *Who Pays for the Kids? Gender and the Structures of Constraint.* London: Routledge.

Friedman, Thomas. 1999. *The Lexus and the Olive Tree.* New York: Farrar, Strauss, and Giroux.

Funk, Nanette, and Magda Mueller, eds. 1993. *Gender Politics and Post-Communism.* New York: Routledge.

Galal, Salma, 1995. "Women and Development in the Maghreb Countries." In Nabil Khoury and Valentine Moghadam, eds., *Gender and Development in the Arab World: Women's Economic Participation—Patterns and Policies,* pp. 49–70. London: Zed Books.

Galaleldin, Mohamed el-Awad. 1985. *Some Aspects of Sudanese Migration to the Oil-Producing Arab Countries During the 1970's.* Khartoum: Development Studies and Research Centre, University of Khartoum.

Garrett, Geoffrey. 1998. *Partisan Politics in the Global Economy.* Cambridge: Cambridge University Press.

Ghabra, Shafiq al-. 1987. *Palestinians in Kuwait: The Family and the Politics of Survival.* Boulder: Westview Press.

———. 1991. "Voluntary Associations in Kuwait: The Foundation of a New System?" *Middle East Journal* 45, no. 2 (spring): 199–215.

———. 1997. "Kuwait and the Dynamics of Socio-Economic Change." *Middle East Journal* 51, no. 3 (summer): 367.

Ghannouchi, Rachid al-. 1988. "Deficiencies in the Islamic Movement." *Middle East Report* (July–August): 24.

———. N.d. "The Participation of Islamists in a Non-Islamic Government." Tunis. Mimeo.

Giddens, Anthony. 1990. *The Consequences of Modernity.* Stanford, Calif.: Stanford University Press.

Gilbar, Gad. 1997. *Population Dilemmas in the Middle East: Essays in Political Demography and Economy.* London: Frank Cass.

Gladwin, Christina H. 1993. "Women and Structural Adjustment in a Global Economy." In Rita Gallin and Anne Ferguson, eds., *The Women and International Development Annual,* vol. 3. Boulder: Westview Press.

Goldstone, Jack A. 1986. "The English Revolution: A Structural-Demographic Approach." In Jack A. Goldstone, ed., *Revolutions: Theoretical, Comparative, and Historical Studies,* pp. 88–104. New York: Harcourt, Brace, Jovanovich.

Government of Tunisia. 1988. *The National Pact.* November 7.

Haddad, Tahar. 1978. *Notre femme: La Législation Islamique et la société, Maison Tunisienne de l'Édition.* Tunis. First published 1930.

Haddad, L., L. Brown, A. Richter, and L. Smith. 1995. "The Gender Dimensions of Economic Adjustment Policies: Potential Interactions and Evidence to Date." *World Development* 23, no. 6: 881–896.

Hale, Sondra. 1996a. "'The New Muslim Woman': Sudan's National Islamic Front and the Invention of Identity." *Muslim World* 86, no. 2: 177–200.

———. 1996b. *Gender Politics in Sudan: Islamism, Socialism, and the State.* Boulder: Westview Press.

Hall, Marjorie, and Bakhita Amin Ismail. 1981. *Sisters Under the Sun: The Story of Sudanese Women.* London: Longman.

Handoussa, Heba, and Gillian Potter, eds. 1991. *Employment and Structural Adjustment: Egypt in the 1990s.* Cairo: American University in Cairo Press.

Handy, Howard, et al. 1998. *Egypt: Beyond Stabilization, Toward a Dynamic Market Economy.* Washington, D.C.: International Monetary Fund.

Hatem, Mervat. 1994. "Privatization and the Demise of State Feminism in Egypt." In Pamela Sparr, ed., *Mortgaging Women's Lives: Feminist Critiques of Structural Adjustment,* pp. 40–60. London: Zed Books.

———. 1996. "Economic and Political Liberalization in Egypt and the Demise of State Feminism." In Suha Sabbagh, ed., *Arab Women: Between Defiance and Restraint.* New York: Olive Branch Press.

Heiberg, Marianne, and Geir Ovensen. 1993. *Palestinian Society in Gaza, West Bank, and Arab Jerusalem: A Survey of Living Conditions.* FAFO report no. 151. Oslo: Fafo Institute for Applied Social Science.

Held, David, et al. 1999. "Globalization." *Global Governance* 5, no. 4 (October–December): 483–486.

Hijab, Nadia. 1988. *Womanpower: The Arab Debate on Women at Work.* Cambridge: Cambridge University Press.

Hoodfar, Homa. 1997. *Between Marriage and the Market: Intimate Politics and Survival in Cairo.* Berkeley: University of California Press.

Hopwood, Derek. 1992. *Bourguiba, Habib of Tunisia: The Tragedy of Longevity.* London: Macmillan.

Hudson, Aida. 1998. "Fertility and Family Planning in a West Bank Village." In Robin Barlow and Joseph W. Brown, eds., *Reproductive Health and Infectious Disease in the Middle East,* pp. 92–113. Brookfield, Vt.: Ashgate.

Hunt, Lynn. 1988. *The Family Romance of the French Revolution.* Berkeley: University of California Press.

Hunter, Shireen T. 1986. "The Gulf Economic Crisis and its Social and Political Consequences." *Middle East Journal* 40, no. 4 (winter): 592–613.

Ibrahim, Saad Eddin. 1995. "State, Women, and Civil Society: An Evaluation of Egypt's Population Policy." In Carla Obermeyer, ed., *Family, Gender, and Population in the Middle East: Policies in Contest,* pp. 57–79. Cairo: American University in Cairo Press.

IMF (International Monetary Fund). 1998. *International Financial Statistics Yearbook.* Washington, D.C.: IMF.

International Planned Parenthood Federation. 1971. *Islam and Family Planning: Proceedings of the International Islamic Conference, Rabat, Morocco.* Beirut: International Planned Parenthood Federation.

———. 1975. *Country Profile: Tunisia.* Tunis: International Planned Parenthood Federation, Arab World Regional Office, November.

———. 1995. *Country Profile: Tunisia.* Tunis: International Planned Parenthood Federation, Arab World Regional Office, November.

Jaquette, Jane, ed. 1994. *The Women's Movement in Latin America: Participation and Democracy.* 2nd ed. Boulder: Westview Press.

Joekes, Susan. 1982. *Female-Led Industrialization and Women's Jobs in Third World Export Manufacturing: The Case of Moroccan Clothing Industry.* Sussex, England: Institute for Development Studies, University of Sussex.

———. 1985. "Working for Lipstick? Male and Female Labour in the Clothing Industry in Morocco." In Haleh Afshar, ed., *Women, Work, and Ideology in the Third World,* pp. 183–212. London: Tavistock.

———. 1995. *Trade-Related Employment for Women in Industry and Services in Developing Countries.* Geneva: UNRISD.

Juergensmeyer, Mark, ed. 1992. *Violence and the Sacred in the Modern World.* London: Frank Cass.

Kandiyoti, Deniz. 1995. "Reflections on the Politics of Gender in Muslim Societies: From Nairobi to Beijing." In Mahnaz Afkhami, ed., *Faith and Freedom,* pp. 19–32. London: I. B. Tauris.

Khlat, M., M. Deeb, and Youssef Courbage. 1997. "Fertility Levels and Differentials in Beirut During Wartime: An Indirect Estimation Based on Maternity Registers." *Population Studies* no. 51: 85–92.

Khouja, M. W., and P. G. Sadler. 1979. *The Economy of Kuwait: Development and Role in International Finance*. London: Macmillan.

Khoury, Nabil, and Valentine Moghadam, eds. 1995. *Gender and Development in the Arab World: Women's Economic Participation— Patterns and Policies*. London: Zed Books.

King, Stephen J. 1999. "Structural Adjustment and Rural Poverty in Tunisia." *Middle East Report* no. 210 (spring): 41–43.

Langmuir, Gavin I. 1990. *History, Religion, and Anti-Semitism*. Berkeley: University of California Press.

Lindblom, Charles E. 1977. *Politics and Markets: The World's Political-Economic Systems*. New York: Basic Books.

Longva, Anh Nga. 1996. *Walls Built on Sand: Migration, Exclusion, and Society in Kuwait*. Boulder: Westview Press.

Maciejewski, Edouard, and Ahsan Mansur, eds. 1996. *Jordan: Strategy for Adjustment and Growth*. Occasional Paper no. 136. Washington, D.C.: International Monetary Fund.

Magnuson, Douglas K. 1991. "Islamic Reform in Contemporary Tunisia: Unity and Diversity." In I. W. Zartman, ed., *Tunisia: The Political Economy of Reform*, pp. 169–192. Boulder: Lynne Rienner.

Mahmoud, Fatima Babiker. 1984. *The Sudanese Bourgeoisie: Vanguard of Development?* London: Zed Books.

Mallakh, Ragaei el-, and Jacob K. Atta. 1981. *The Absorptive Capacity of Kuwait: Domestic and International Perspectives*. Lexington, Md.: Lexington Books.

Mamlakat al-'Arabiyya al-Sa'udiyya, al-Ri'aasat al-'Ama lita'lim al-Banaat, al- (Kingdom of Saudi Arabia, General Presidency for Girls' Education). 2001. *Al-Fiqh al-Murhala al-Thaanawiyya al-Saff al-Thaalath* (Jurisprudence for the Third Grade of the Secondary Level). Riyadh: Kingdom of Saudi Arabia, General Presidency for Girls' Education.

Mamlakat al-'Arabiyya al-Sa'udiyya, Wizaarat al-Ma'aarif, al- (Kingdom of Saudi Arabia, Ministry of Education). 1995. *Siyaasat al-Ta'lim fi al-Mamlakat al-'Arabiyya al-Sa'udiyya* (Education Policy of the Kingdom of Saudi Arabia), 1416 H. Reprinted in Riyadh: Kingdom of Saudi Arabia, Ministry of Education. First printing 1970.

———. 2000a. *Al-Fiqh l'il-Saff al-Thaalith al-Mutawassit* (Jurisprudence for the Third Grade of the Intermediate Level). Riyadh: Kingdom of Saudi Arabia, Ministry of Education.

———. 2000b. *Al-Hadith l'il-Saff al-Thaalith al-Mutawassit* (Hadith for the Third Grade of the Intermediate Level). Riyadh: Kingdom of Saudi Arabia, Ministry of Education.

———. 2001. *Al-Hadith wa al-Thaqaafa al-Islaamiyya, l'il Saff al-Thaani al-Thaanawi, Aqsaam al-'Uluum al-Idaariyya wa al-Ijtimaa'iyya wal Tabii'iyya wa Tafanniyya* (Hadith and Islamic Culture for the Second Grade of the Secondary Level). Riyadh: Kingdom of Saudi Arabia, Ministry of Education.

Marty, Martin E. 1992. "Fundamentals of Fundamentalism." In Lawrence

Kaplan, ed., *Fundamentalism in Comparative Perspective*, pp. 15–23. Amherst: University of Massachusetts Press.

Masry, S. el-. 1993. *Urban Women, Employment, and Poverty Alleviation in Egypt*. Cairo: El Mishkat with UNICEF.

McLoughlin, Peter. 1962. "Economic Development and the Heritage of Slavery in the Sudan Republic." *Africa* 23: 355–391.

Mernissi, Fatima. 1991. *Islam and Democracy: Fear of the Modern World*. Trans. Mary Jo Lakeland. Reading, Mass.: Addison Wesley.

Mikawy, Noha el-, and Marsha Pripstein Posusney. 2002. "Labor Representation in the Age of Globalization: Trends and Issues in Non-Oil-Based Arab Economies." In Zafiris Tzannatos and Heba Handoussa, eds., *Employment Creation and Social Protection in the MENA Region*, pp. 49–94. Cairo: American University in Cairo Press.

Ministère de la Femme et de la Famille (Tunisia). 1993. *Statut juridique de la femme réformes, 1993*. Tunisia: CREDIF.

Ministry of Education (Saudi Arabia). 2000. "Summary Statistics on Male Education as of Oct. 23, 2000." Riyadh: Ministry of Education, Computer Department. In Arabic and English.

Mitchell, Timothy. 1988. *Colonizing Egypt*. Cambridge: Cambridge University Press.

Moghadem, Fatemeh E. 2000. "Ideology, Economic Restructuring, and Women's Work in Iran (1976–1996)." In Wassim Shahin and Ghassan Dibeh, eds., *Earnings Inequality, Unemployment, and Poverty in the Middle East and North Africa*, pp. 205–223. Westport, Conn.: Greenwood Press.

Moghadam, Valentine, ed. 1993. *Democratic Reform and the Position of Women in Transitional Economies*. Oxford: Clarendon Press.

———. 1995a. "Economic Reforms, Women's Employment, and Social Policies." *UNU World Institute for Development Economic Research*. UNU Wider, August.

———. 1995b. *Manufacturing and Women in the Middle East and North Africa: A Case Study of the Textiles and Garments Industry*. Occasional Paper no. 49. Durham: Centre for Middle Eastern and Islamic Studies, University of Durham.

———. 1995c. "The Political Economy of Female Employment in the Arab Region." In Nabil Khoury and Valentine Moghadam, eds., *Gender and Development in the Arab World: Women's Economic Participation— Patterns and Policies*, pp. 6–34. London: Zed Books.

———, ed. 1996. *Patriarchy and Economic Development: Women's Positions at the End of the Twentieth Century*. Oxford: Clarendon Press.

———. 1998. *Women, Work, and Economic Reform in the Middle East and North Africa*. Boulder: Lynne Rienner.

Moore, Clement Henry. 1965. *Tunisia Since Independence: The Dynamics of One-Party Government*. Berkeley: University of California Press.

Mu'adh, Da'd. 1986. "Tajribat al-Ittihad al-Nisa'i (1974–1981)." *Al-Urdunn al-Jadid* no. 7 (spring).

Mughni, Haya al-. 1993. *Women in Kuwait: The Politics of Gender*. London: Saqi Books.

———. 2000. "Women's Movements and the Autonomy of Civil Society in Kuwait." In Robin L. Teske and Mary Ann Tétreault, eds., *Conscious Acts and the Politics of Social Change: Feminist Approaches to Social Movements, Community, and Power*, pp. 170–187. Columbia: University of South Carolina Press.

Munson, Henry, Jr. 1986. "Islamic Revivalism in Morocco and Tunisia." *Muslim World* 76, nos. 3–4 (July–October).

Nagar, Samia el-. 1985. "Patterns of Women Participation in the Labour Force in Khartoum." Ph.D. diss., University of Khartoum.

Najjar, Ghanim Hamad al-. 1984. "Decision-Making Process in Kuwait: The Land Acquisition Policy as a Case Study." Ph.D. diss., University of Exeter, United Kingdom.

Nassar, H. 1996a. *The Employment Profile of Women in Egypt*. Cairo: Friedrich Ebert Stiftung and Social Research Center.

———. 1996b. "Socio Economic Factors Affecting Education and Employment of Females in Egypt." In Reiner Biegel and Riad Zgha, eds., *Education et formation profesionelle des femmes dans le monde Arabe et en Europe*. Tunis: Konrad Adenauer Stiftung.

Nawar, Laila. 1995. "Overview: International and Regional Perspectives on Reproduction Choice." In Carla Obermeyer, ed., *Family, Gender, and Population in the Middle East: Policies in Contest*, pp. 16–35. Cairo: American University in Cairo Press.

Nawar, Laila, Cynthia Lloyd, and Barbara Ibrahim. 1995. "Women's Autonomy and Gender Roles in Egyptian Families." In Carla Obermeyer, ed., *Family, Gender and Development in the Middle East: Policies in Contest*, pp. 147–178. Cairo: American University in Cairo Press.

NBK (National Bank of Kuwait). 1997. *Economic and Financial Quarterly* no. 3.

Niblock, Tim. 1987. *Class and Power in Sudan: The Dynamics of Sudanese Politics, 1898–1985*. Albany: State University of New York Press.

Nitzan, Jonathan. 1998. "Differential Accumulation: Toward a New Political Economy of Capital." *Review of International Political Economy* 5, no. 2 (summer): 169–216.

Norton, Augustus Richard, ed. 1995. *Civil Society in the Middle East*, vol. 1. Leiden: E. J. Brill.

Nsouli, Saleh M., Sena Eken, Klaus Enders, Van-Can Thai, Jorg Decressin, and Filippo Cartiglia. 1995. *Resilience and Growth Through Sustained Adjustment: The Moroccan Experience*. Occasional Paper no. 117. Washington, D.C.: International Monetary Fund.

Nsouli, Saleh M., Sena Eken, Paul Duran, Gerwin Bell, and Zuhtu Yucelik. 1993. *The Path to Convertibility and Growth: The Tunisian Experience*. Occasional Paper no. 109. Washington, D.C.: International Monetary Fund.

Nyberg, Anita. 1993. "The Social Construction of Married Women's Labor

Force Participation." Paper presented at the conference "Out of the Margin: Feminist Perspectives of Economic Theory," University of Amsterdam, June.

Obermeyer, Carla, ed. 1995. *Family, Gender, and Population in the Middle East: Policies in Contest.* Cairo: American University in Cairo Press.

Olmsted, Jennifer. 1998a. "Linking Fertility, Economic Policies, and Gender: A Case Study of Fertility Patterns Among Bethlehem Area Palestinians." Working paper.

———. 1998b. "What Would Your Father Think? Family Attitudes, Gender, Education, and Employment in Bethlehem." Working paper.

———. 2001. "Men's Work/Women's Work: An Analysis of Employment, Wages, and Occupational Segregation in Bethlehem." In E. Mine Cinar, ed., *The Economics of Work in the Middle East and North Africa,* vol. 4 of *Research in Middle East Economics,* pp. 151–174. Amsterdam: Elsevier.

Omran, Abdel R., and Farzaneh Roudi. 1993. "The Middle East Population Puzzle," *Population Bulletin* 48, no. 1 (July). Washington, D.C.: Population Reference Bureau Inc.

O'Neill, Norman. 1988. "Class and Politics in the Modern History of Sudan." In Norman O'Neill and Jay O'Brien, eds., *Economy and Class in Sudan,* pp. 25–59. Avebury, London: Gower.

O'Neill, Norman, and Jay O'Brien, eds. 1988. *Economy and Class in Sudan.* Avebury, London: Gower.

Papps, Ivy. 1993. "Attitudes Towards Female Employment in Four Middle Eastern Countries." In Haleh Afshar and Mary Maynard, eds., *Women in the Middle East: Perceptions, Realities, and Struggles for Liberation,* pp. 96–116. Women's Studies at York. London: Macmillan.

Payne, Rhys. 1993. "Economic Crisis and Policy Reform in the 1980s." In I. William Zartman and William Mark Habeeb, eds., *Polity and Society in Contemporary North Africa,* pp. 139–167. Boulder: Westview Press.

Pearl, Daniel. 2001. "Kuwait Is Divided over Support of U.S." *Wall Street Journal,* October 24, p. C9.

Peter, Christine. 1995. *Frauen in der Arbeitswelt Agyptens.* Cairo: Friedrich Ebert Stiftung, 1995.

Polanyi, Karl. 1944. *The Great Transformation.* New York: Farrar and Rinehart.

Posusney, Marsha Pripstein. 1999. "Privatization in Egypt: New Challenges for the Left." *Middle East Report* no. 210 (April–May): 38–40.

———. 2001. "Labor Protection in Non-Oil Adjusting Arab Countries: Present Realities and Future Prospects." Paper presented at the Second Mediterranean Social and Political Research Meeting, European University Institute, Florence, March 21–25.

———. 2002 (forthcoming). "Egyptian Labor Struggles in the Era of Privatization: The Moral Economy Thesis Revisited." In Marsha Pripstein Posusney and Linda Cook, eds., *Privatization and Labor: Responses and Consequences in Global Perspective.* Gloucestershire, England: Edward Elgar.

Prusher, Ilene R. 2000. "Pushing the Boundaries on Islam and Women." *Christian Science Monitor,* August 11. Gulf 2000 archive.

Qudsi, Sulayman al-. 1996. "Labor Markets in the Future of Arab Economies: The Imperatives and Implications of Economic Structuring." In Ismail Sirageldin and Eqbal al-Rahmani, eds., *Population and Development Transformations in the Arab World.* Greenwich, Conn.: JAI Press.

Qudsi, Sulayman al-, Ragui Assaad, and Radwan Shaban. 1993. "Labor Markets in the Arab Countries: A Survey." Paper presented at the First Annual Conference on Development Economics, Cairo.

Radcliff, Sarah, and Sallier Westwood, eds. 1993. *Viva: Women and Popular Protest in Latin America.* New York: Routledge.

Rahmani, Eqbal al-. 1996a. "The Impact of Traditional Domestic Sexual Division of Labor on Women's Status: The Case of Kuwait." *Research in Human Capital and Development* 9: 79–101.

———. 1996b. *The Impact Revolutions and the Rhythm of History.* New York: Oxford University Press.

Rai, Shirin, Hilary Pilkington, and Annie Phizacklea, eds. 1992. *Women in the Face of Change: The Soviet Union, Eastern Europe, and China.* New York: Routledge.

Rapley, John. 2002. *Understanding Development: Theory and Practice in the Third World.* 2nd ed. Boulder: Lynne Rienner.

Reuters. 2000. "Attackers of Unveiled Kuwaiti Woman Arrested." April 9. Gulf 2000 archive.

Richards, Alan, and John Waterbury. 1996. *A Political Economy of the Middle East.* 2nd ed. Boulder: Westview Press.

Roden, David. 1974. "Regional Inequality and Rebellion in the Sudan." *Geographical Review* 64, no. 2.

Rodrik, Dani. 1997. *Has Globalization Gone Too Far?* Washington, D.C.: Institute for International Economics.

Roy, Olivier. 1994. *The Failure of Political Islam.* London: I. B. Tauris.

———. 2001. "Bin Laden et ses frère." *Politique Internationale* 93.

Rush, Alan. 1987. *Al Sabah: History and Genealogy of Kuwait's Ruling Family.* London: Ithaca Press.

Sabagh, Georges, Jodi Nachtwey, and Mark Tessler. 1998. "Gender, Islam, and the Demographic Challenge in North Africa: Evidence from Survey Research in Morocco." Working paper presented at the Middle East Studies Association meetings, Chicago, November.

Said, Mona. 1994. *Public Sector Employment and Labor Markets in Arab Countries: Recent Developments and Policy Implications.* Washington, D.C.: International Monetary Fund.

Salih, M. A. Mohamed. 1989. "'New Wine in Old Bottles': Tribal Militias and the Sudanese State." *Review of African Political Economy* nos. 45–46: 168–174.

Salloom, Hamad al-.1995. *Education in Saudi Arabia.* Beltsville: Amana.

Sanyal, B. C., L. Yaici, and I. Mallasi. 1987. *From College to Work: The*

Case of the Sudan. Paris: UNESCO, International Institute of Educational Planning.

Sayed, Hassan Mahmoud, el-, and Khaled al-Wahishi. 1995. *Report on Economic Contributions of Women: The Case of Egypt.* Cairo: Public Administration for Social Affairs, Unit for Population Researches and Studies, Arab League. In Arabic.

Sayed, Haneen, and Zafiris Tzannatos. 1999. Sex Segregation in the Labor Force. In Nelly P. Stromquist, ed., *Women in the Third World: An Encyclopedia of Contemporary Issues,* pp. 302–313. New York: Garland.

Seddon, David. 1993. "Austerity Protests in Response to Economic Liberalization in the Middle East." In Tim Niblock and Emma Murphy, eds., *Economic and Political Liberalization in the Middle East,* pp. 88–113. London: British Academic Press.

Sells, Michael. 1996. *The Bridge Betrayed: Religion and Genocide in Bosnia.* Berkeley: University of California Press.

Sen, Gita, and Caren Grown. 1988. *Development Crises and Alternative Visions.* London: Earthscan.

Shah, Nasra. 1994. "Changing Roles of Kuwaiti Women in Kuwait: Implications for Fertility. Paper presented at the First Post-Liberation Conference on Women's Role in Cultural, Social, and Economic Development, Kuwait, April 11–13.

Shaheen, Laila. 2000. "Debate Rages over Acquittal in Girl's Assault." *Gulf News,* June 15. Gulf 2000 archive.

Shi, Anqing, and Chang-po Yang. 1996. "Egypt: The Long Term Demographic Trend and Its Economic Implication." Cairo: World Bank.

Simone, Timothy Maliqalim. 1990. "Metropolitan Africans: Reading Incapacity, the Incapacity of Reading." *Cultural Anthropology* 5, no. 2.

Sirageldin, Ismail, and Eqbal al-Rahmani, eds. 1996. *Population and Development Transformations in the Arab World.* Vol. 9. Research in Human Capital and Development series. London: JAI Press.

Sparr, Pamela, ed. 1994. *Mortgaging Women's Lives: Feminist Critiques of Structural Adjustment.* London: Zed Books.

Spaulding, Jay. 1985. *The Heroic Age in Sinnar.* East Lansing: Michigan State University Press.

Standing, Guy. 1989. "Global Feminization Through Flexible Labor." *World Development* 17, no. 7: 1077–1095.

Starrett, Gregory. 1998. *Putting Islam to Work: Education, Politics, and Religious Transformation in Egypt.* Berkeley: University of California Press.

Stauffer, Thomas. 1984. "Oil and the Norwegian Economy: A Comparison with Major OPEC States." *Middle East Economic Survey,* May 21.

Stone, Russell A., and John Simmons. 1976. *Change in Tunisia: Studies in the Social Sciences.* Albany: State University of New York Press.

Stowasser, Barbara. 1994. *Women in the Qur'an, Traditions, and Interpretation.* New York: Oxford University Press.

Sudan Socialist Union. Section for Political and Organizational Affairs. 1980. *Summary of Working Plans for the Executive Office of the Union of Sudanese Women.* Khartoum: Sudan Socialist Union.

Suleiman, Michael W. 1993. "Political Orientation of Young Tunisians: The Impact of Gender." *Arab Studies Quarterly* 15, no. 1 (winter): 61–80.

Taha, Batoul Mukhtar Mohamed. 1987. "Today, No Guardian." *Sudanow* 13 (January–February).

Tall, Suhayr al-. 1985. *Muqaddimat Hawla Qadiyat al-Mar'ah w-al-Harakah al-Nisa'iyyah f-il-Urdunn.* Beirut: Al-Mu'assasah al-'Arabiyyah l-il-Dirasat w-al-Nashr.

Tanski, J. M. 1994. "The Impact of Crisis, Stabilization, and Structural Adjustment on Women in Lima, Peru." *World Development* 22, no. 11: 1627–1642.

Teske, Robin el-, and Mary Ann Tétreault, eds. *Conscious Acts and the Politics of Social Change: Feminist Approaches to Social Movements, Community and Power.* Columbia: University of South Carolina Press.

Tessler, Mark, and Ina Warriner. 1997. "Gender, Feminism, and Attitudes Toward International Conflict." *World Politics* 49 (January): 251–257.

Tétreault, Mary Ann. 1985. *Revolution in the World Petroleum Market.* Westport, Conn.: Quorum Books.

———. 1990. "Kuwait's Democratic Reform Movement." *Middle East Executive Reports* (October): 17–18.

———. 1993. "Civil Society in Kuwait: Protected Spaces and Women's Rights." *Middle East Journal* 47, no. 2 (spring): 275–291.

———. 1995. *The Kuwait Petroleum Corporation and the Economics of the New World Order.* Westport, Conn.: Quorum Books.

———. 1996. "Designer Democracy in Kuwait." *Current History* (January): 36–39.

———. 2000a. *Stories of Democracy: Politics and Society in Contemporary Kuwait.* New York: Columbia University Press.

———. 2000b. "Women, Power and Politics." In Robin el-Teske and Mary Ann Tétreault, eds. *Conscious Acts and the Politics of Social Change: Feminist Approaches to Social Movements, Community and Power,* pp. 273–284. Columbia: University of South Carolina Press.

———. 2000c. "Women's Rights in Kuwait: Bring in the Last Bedouins?" *Current History* 99 (January–December): 27–32.

Tétreault, Mary Ann, and Haya al-Mughni. 1995a. "Gender, Citizenship, and Nationalism in Kuwait." *British Journal of Middle Eastern Studies* 22, nos. 1–2: 64–80.

———. 1995b. "Modernization and Its Discontents: State and Gender in Kuwait." *Middle East Journal* 49, no. 3 (summer).

Thakeb, Fahed al-, and Joseph E. Scott. 1982. "Islamic Fundamentalism: A Profile of Its Supporters." *International Review of Modern Sociology* 12: 175–195.

Thorne, Melvyn, and Joel Montague. 1976. "Family Planning and the Problems of Development." In Russell A. Stone and John Simons, eds.,

Change in Tunisia, pp. 201–216. New York: State University of New York Press.

Toth, James. 1991. "Pride, Purdah, or Paychecks: What Maintains the Gender Division of Labor in Rural Egypt?" *International Journal of Middle East Studies* 23 (May): 213–236.

Tzannatos, Zafiris. 1990. "Employment Segregation: Can We Measure It and What Does the Measure Mean?" *British Journal of Industrial Relations* 28, no. 1: 107–111.

———. 1999. "Women and Labor Market Changes in the Global Economy: Growth Helps, Inequalities Hurt, and Public Policy Matters." *World Development* 27, no. 3: 551–569.

UN (United Nations). 1995. *The World's Women 1995: Trends and Statistics.* New York: UN.

UN Economic and Social Commission for Western Asia. 1990. "Women in Arab Society: Work Patterns and Gender Relations in Egypt, Jordan, and Sudan." New York: UN Economic and Social Commission for Western Asia.

———. 1995. "Arab Women in the Manufacturing Industries." New York: UN Economic and Social Commission for Western Asia.

UNDP (UN Development Programme). 1991a, 1995, 1996, 1998, 2000. *Human Development Report.* New York: UNDP.

———. 1991b. *World Economic Survey.* New York: UNDP.

UNDP and NIP (National Institute of Planning, Egypt). 1998. *Human Development Report in Egypt.* Cairo: UNDP and NIP.

UNIDO. 1993. *Women in Industry Country Information: Tunisia.*

U.S. Department of State, 2000. "Human Rights Report, Kuwait." Gulf 2000 archive.

Wallerstein, Immanuel. 1973. *The Modern World-System I: Capitalist Agriculture and the Origins of the European World-Economy in the Sixteenth Century.* New York: Academic Press.

———. 1986. *The Modern World-System II: Mercantilism and the Consolidation of the European World-Economy, 1600–1750.* New York: Academic Press.

Waltz, Kenneth. 1979. *Theory of International Politics.* Reading, Mass.: Addison Wesley.

Waltz, Susan. 1986. "Islamist Appeal in Tunisia" *Middle East Journal* 40, no. 4 (autumn): 651–670.

Waylen, Georgina. 1994. "Women and Democratization: Conceptualizing Gender Relations in Transition Politics." *World Politics* 46, no. 3 (April): 327–354.

Wolf, Eric R. 1982. *Europe and the People Without History.* Berkeley: University of California Press.

World Bank. 1991–1992. *World Debt Tables.* Washington, D.C.: World Bank.

———. 1993. *Developing the Occupied Territories: An Investment in Peace.* Washington, D.C.: World Bank.

———. 1995. *Claiming the Future: Choosing Prosperity in the Middle East and North Africa*. Washington, D.C.: World Bank.

———. 1997a. "Education in MENA: Benefits and Growth Pay-Offs Now and Then." Washington, D.C.: World Bank.

———. 1997b. *Democratic and Popular Republic of Algeria: Growth, Employment, and Poverty Reduction*. Washington D.C.: World Bank.

———. 1997c. *Kingdom of Morocco: Growth and Labor Markets: An Agenda for Job Creation*. Washington D.C.: World Bank, November.

———. 1997d, 1998, 1999a. *World Development Indicators*. Washington, D.C.: World Bank.

———. 1999b, 2001, 2002. *World Development Report*. New York: Oxford University Press.

———. 2000. *MENA Regional Social Protection Strategy Paper*. Washington D.C.: World Bank, Human Development Department, August.

Yamani, Mai, ed. 1996. *Feminism and Islam: Legal and Literary Perspectives*. New York: New York University Press.

———. 2000. *Changed Identities: The Challenge of the New Generation in Saudi Arabia*. London: Royal Institute for International Affairs.

Zaalouk, Malak. 1991. "Women." CAPMAS, Labor Information System Project preliminary report, December.

Zulficar, M. 1995. "Women in Development: A Legal Study." New York: UNICEF, January.

The Contributors

Ragui Assaad is associate professor at the Humphrey Institute of Public Affairs, University of Minnesota. He is the author of many articles and editor of the book *The Labor Market in a Reforming Economy: Egypt in the 1990's* (AUC Press).

Laurie A. Brand is professor of international relations, University of Southern California. She is the author of many articles on Middle Eastern politics and three books, the most recent being *Women, the State, and Political Liberalization: Middle Eastern and North African Experiences* (Columbia University Press).

Eleanor Abdella Doumato is a visiting scholar at the Watson Institute, Brown University, Providence, R.I. A past president of the Association for Middle East Women's Studies, she is the author of numerous articles on gender and the state in the Gulf region, and of the book *Getting God's Ear: Women, Islam, and Healing in Saudi Arabia and the Gulf* (Columbia University Press).

Sondra Hale is professor of anthropology and women's studies at the University of California–Los Angeles, and a past president of the Association for Middle East Women's Studies. She is the author of many articles on women, politics, and gender, and of the book *Gender Politics in Sudan: Islamism, Socialism, and the State* (Westview Press).

Iqbal Kaur is a social protection specialist in the Department of

Human Development, Middle East and North Africa (MENA) regional division of the World Bank. She has contributed extensively to the Bank's Social Protection Sector analysis on issues of education, labor markets, welfare policies, social assistance, gender, and child/labor protection in MENA countries.

Emma C. Murphy is a senior lecturer at the Institute for Middle Eastern and Islamic Studies, University of Durham (UK), and is the author of *Economic and Political Change in Tunisia: From Bourguiba to Ben Ali* (St. Martin's Press) and *Israel: Challenges to Identity, Democracy, and the State* (Routledge; coauthored with Clive Jones).

Heba Nassar is professor of economics and director of the Center for Economic and Financial Research and Studies, Faculty of Economics and Political Science, Cairo University, and research professor, Social Research Center, American University in Cairo.

Jennifer Olmsted teaches at Occidental College in California. She is a founding editor of the *Journal of Feminist Economics,* editor of the *Middle East Women's Studies Review,* and author of many articles on women and economy in the Middle East.

Karen Pfeifer is professor of economics at Smith College, Northampton, Mass. She has served several times as an editor of *Middle East Report,* and was a founding editor of the Middle East Economics Association's annual journal, *Research in Middle East Economics.* She is the author of numerous published works concerning various countries in the MENA region, on subjects including agrarian reform, Islamic economics, and most recently the economics of conflict and conflict resolution.

Marsha Pripstein Posusney is associate professor of political science at Bryant College, Smithfield, R.I., and adjunct associate professor of international relations (research) at the Watson Institute, Brown University. Her first book, *Labor and the State in Egypt: Workers, Unions, and Economic Restructuring* (Columbia University Press), won the Middle East Studies Association's 1998 Albert Hourani award. A second volume, *Privatization and Labor: Responses and Consequences in Global Perspective,* was recently published by Edward Elgar (coedited with Linda Cook). She is also the author of numerous articles on economic and political reform in the Middle East.

Mary Ann Tétreault is the Una Chapman Cox Distinguished Professor of International Affairs at Trinity University in San Antonio, Texas. She has written or edited more than a dozen books. Her most recent volume on Kuwait is *Stories of Democracy: Politics and Society in Contemporary Kuwait* (Columbia University Press).

Zafiris Tzannatos is adviser to the managing director of the World Bank, where he was formerly manager of social protection in the Middle East and North Africa region and leader of the Global Child Labor Program. Prior to joining the World Bank he held a series of senior academic appointments and advised governments and many international organizations. His more than 100 publications include eleven books on labor economics, gender, and broader social policy.

Index

gender/sex; Sudan, women in
military service
General Federation of Jordanian
Women (GFJW), 150, 152–157
General Union of Palestinian
Women, 147–148, 151
GFJW. *See* General Federation of
Jordanian Women
Ghabra, Shafiq al-, 228
Ghannouchi, Rachid, 189–190
Ghazelah, Haifa Abu, 155
Globalization, 3–8, 261; conserva-
tive reaction to Western cultural
penetration, 2–3; gender ideolo-
gies, cultural context of changing,
8–11; protests against, 4. *See also*
Economies and globalization,
Arab; Market-oriented strategies
of development; Western culture
GNP. *See* Gross national product
Goldstone, Jack, 235
Great Britain, 145, 220
Gross domestic product (GDP): clas-
sifying Arab economies, 25;
development trends in Arab
region, 37, 38; Egypt, 98; fertility, 78–80; Morocco, 41
Gross national product (GNP), 28,
30, 31
Gulf War (1980–1988), 225–226
Gulf War (1990–1991), 41

Haddad, Tahar, 171–172
Hadith, 241, 246–248
Hall, Majorie, 204
Hijab, Nadia, 83
Human development index (HDI),
59–60
Human rights, 7–8, 36, 188
Hussain, Fatima, 225
Hussein I (King), 146, 163
Hydrocarbon exports. *See* Oil issues

Ibrahim, Saad Eddin, 86
Illiteracy. *See* Literacy/illiteracy
IMF. *See* International Monetary
Fund

Import-substitution industrialization
(ISI), 34, 45
Income, per capita, 40, 78–80
India, 43
Industrialization and fertility, 75
Industry, labor market survey of
women in MENA, 64–65
Infant mortality, and fertility, 78–
79
Informal-sector employment, 66–67,
205–206
International Food Policy Research
Institute (IFPRI), 66
International Labour Organization
(ILO), 45
International Monetary Fund (IMF):
Egypt, 40; export-led growth and
role of foreign capital, 49; Jordan,
women's political struggles in,
152; Morocco, 42; privatization
and employment, 47; SAPs, 31;
Sudan, 200; Turkey, 43
Iran: agriculture, 64; economic
nationalism, 34–35; economic
reform, 50; Gulf War
(1980–1988), 225–226; social
justice, 11
Iraq: birth control, 87; embargo
against, 260; employment
issues/statistics, 81; fertility, 81,
87; Gulf War (1980–1988),
225–226; Gulf War (1990–1991),
41; land reforms, 35; state-centered economic strategies, 35;
U.S. plans to attack, 259
ISI. *See* Import-substitution industrialization
Islam: Bourguiba, 172–173; employment issues/statistics, 83; feminism, 9–10; fertility, 86–87; gender ideologies/roles, 89; Haddad,
171; Kuwait, 227–235; labor
market, 62; political movement to
control public, 9–11; Saudi
Arabia, 241–248; segregation,
gender/sex, 11; terrorist attacks of
September 11, 259–261; Tunisia,

226–235; women's organizations, 223–225
Kuwait National Petroleum Corporation (KNPC), 221
Kuwait Oil Company (KOC), 219
Kuwait University, 225, 227, 233

Labor federations, national, 36
Labor market, survey of women in MENA, 70–71; Duncan index of segregation, 68–69; formal and informal sectors, 66–67; global context, 55–61; industry, employment by, 64–65; international comparison, 67–70; level/type of employment, 65–66; participation, female labor force, 61–64; patterns of female employment, 63–67. *See also* Economic reform and structural adjustment programs; Egyptian labor market; Employment issues/statistics
Land ownership, 58–59
Land reforms, 35–36
Latin America, 143, 144
Lebanon: birth control, 87–88; borrowing, foreign, 32; domestic market size, 29; fertility, 80, 87, 88; gross domestic product, 37; laissez-faire economy, 35; literacy/illiteracy, 55, 57, 81; manufacturing and production, 65; organizational activity, women's, 7; service sector, 64
Libya: domestic market size, 30; mineral exports, 27; state-centered economic strategies, 35
Life expectancy, 55, 56, 78–79, 182
Literacy/illiteracy: ERSAPs, 104; fertility, 78–81; Saudi Arabia, 11, 242; statistics of MENA region, 55–57; Tunisia, 171, 179–181
Loans and ERSAPs, 117–118. *See also* International Monetary Fund; World Bank
Lorimer, John G., 219

Macroeconomic policies. *See* Economic reform and structural adjustment programs; Market-oriented strategies of development
Mahdi, Wisel al-, 208
Malaysia, 124
Managerial positions, 65, 104, 105
Manufacturing and production: career advancement, 112; employment, private-sector, 124; employment statistics, 125; ERSAPs, 104; labor market, 64–65; wages, 111, 112
Market-oriented strategies of development, 37–39; fertility, 77, 88–89; mineral exports to Arab economies, 26–29; oil-poor countries, privatization and employment in, 45–48; poverty, 44–45, 108, 117; social protections, 6, 77; and state-centered economic strategies, 5–6; SAPs, 31, 37; Sudan, 199–200; terrorist attacks of September 11, 259; Tunisia, 183–185; vulnerable position of women in the labor market, 119. *See also* Economic reform and structural adjustment programs; Economies and globalization, Arab; Globalization; Kuwait, politics of economic restructuring in
Marriage: family law, 10; fertility, 78–79, 82, 85; Kuwait, 82; Oman, 82; Tunisia, 179, 182
Maternal mortality, 57, 59
Maternity leave, 114
MENA (Middle East and North Africa). *See individual countries*
Mexico, 124
Middle-class: and land reforms, 35–36; Shia and politics in Kuwait, 226
Middle East and North Africa (MENA). *See individual countries*
Mineral exports, 26–29. *See also* Oil issues

and globalization, Arab; Kuwait, politics of economic restructuring in; Market-oriented strategies of development

Sudan: agriculture, 34; domestic market size, 29; economic reform, 89; employment issues/statistics, 81; fertility, 80, 81; gender ideologies, 9; politics/public policy, 89; social justice, 11

Sudan, women in military service and rise of Islamic sentiment in, 195–196, 210–211; complementarity approach to gender, 208–210; employment issues/statistics, 202–206; Greater Khartoum, 201–202; history and political economy, 197–200; informal economic sector, 205–206; market-oriented strategies of development, 199–200; National Congress, 196; National Islamic Front, 196; networks, loose urban, 202; new Muslim woman, 196, 206–210; New Sudanese Movement, 211; postindependence politics, 198–199; transformative processes taking place, 196–197; Union of Sudanese Women, 203

Syria: birth control, 87–88; domestic market size, 29; fertility, 87, 88; land reforms, 35; literacy/illiteracy, 81; state-centered economic strategies, 35; unemployment, 127

Taliban, 11
Taxes and fertility, 76
Teaching occupations and career advancement, 112
Terrorist attacks of September 11, 259–261
Tessler, Mark, 87
Thatcher, Margaret, 37
Trade unions, 36, 115–116

Training and ERSAPs, 118
Transportation and ERSAPs, 113
Tunisia: administrative positions, 65; borrowing, foreign, 32, 42–43; domestic market size, 29; economic reform, 42–43, 89; employment issues/statistics, 81; export-oriented growth, 133; fertility, 80, 81; informal-sector employment, 67; manufacturing and production, 124; Neo-Destour party, 173; politics/public policy, 89; poverty, 44–45; privatization and employment, 46–48; professional positions, 66; social protections, 44–45; state-centered economic strategies, 35

Tunisia, feminism and economic reform, 192; Ben Ali, legal status of women under, 169–170, 176–180; Ben Ali's wider reforms, impact of, 183–185; Bourguiba, rights for women under, 172–176; Center for Studies, Documentation, and Information on Women, 177, 187; Code of Nationality, 179; Code of Obligations and Contracts, 174; Code of Personal Status, 172–175; constitution and women's voting rights, 173; conventions concerning women's rights, international, 174; corporatist political system, 169–170; democratic/political pluralism, 187–192; discrimination, 182–183; Haddad, 171–172; Islam, 188–191; Law of Political Parties (1988), 177; life in the 1990s, 180–182; National Pact (1988), 177; National Solidarity Fund, 186; National Union of Tunisian Women, 173, 175, 179–180, 183; Neo-Destour party, 175, 176; political life and civil service, 181; poverty and government programs, 186–187;

activity, women's, 7; Sudan,
200
World Trade Organization (WTO), 4

Yamani, Mai, 242, 249
Yemen: agriculture, 64; birth control,
87; borrowing, foreign, 32; edu-

cation, 81; fertility, 80, 87; land
reforms, 35; literacy/illiteracy, 55,
57; mineral exports, 27; state-centered economic strategies, 35

Za'ama syndrome, 158–159
Zumaylah, Mahdiyyah, 155

About the Book

This original work assesses the impact of globalization on women in Middle Eastern societies. To explore the gendered effects of social change, the authors examine trends within, as well as among, states in the region.

Detailed case studies reveal the mixed results of global pressures. For some women, for example, globalization has meant increased access to education and employment; for others, it has resulted in heightened repression under ideologically conservative regimes. The authors' nuanced analyses document how women's responses to these changes are affecting the future of the Middle East.

Eleanor Abdella Doumato is a visiting scholar at the Watson Institute for International Studies, Brown University. She is author of *Getting God's Ear: Women, Islam, and Healing in Saudi Arabia and the Gulf.* **Marsha Pripstein Posusney** is associate professor of political science at Bryant College and adjunct associate professor of international relations at Brown University. She is author of *Labor and the State in Egypt: Workers, Unions, and Economic Restructuring.*